THE MIGHTY FRANKS

THE
MIGHTY
FRANKS

A MEMOIR

MICHAEL FRANK

4th ESTATE • *London*

4th Estate
An imprint of HarperCollins*Publishers*
1 London Bridge Street
London SE1 9GF
www.4thEstate.co.uk

First published in Great Britain in 2017 by 4th Estate
First published in the United States in 2017 by Farrar, Straus and Giroux

1

Copyright © 2017 by Michael Frank

Michael Frank asserts the moral right to be identified
as the author of this work in accordance with the
Copyright, Designs and Patents Act 1988

A catalogue record for this book is
available from the British Library

ISBN 978-0-00-821519-4 (hardback)
ISBN 978-0-00-821520-0 (trade paperback)

Grateful acknowledgment is made for permission to reprint the following material:
Excerpt from "Make Your Own Kind of Music." Words and music by Barry Mann and Cynthia Weil.
Copyright © 1968 Screen Gems–EMI Music Inc. Copyright renewed. All rights administered by Sony/
ATV Music Publishing LLC, 424 Church Street, Suite 1200, Nashville, Tennessee 37219. International
copyright secured. All rights reserved. Reprinted by permission of Hal Leonard LLC.

Excerpt from "Our House." Words and music by Graham Nash. Copyright © 1970 (renewed) Nash
Notes. All rights for Nash Notes controlled and administered by Spirit One Music (BMI). All rights
reserved. Used by permission of Alfred Music.

Epigraph to Maxine Kumin's poem "Looking Back in My Eighty-First year" by Hilma Wolitzer.
Courtesy of Hilma Wolitzer.

All rights reserved. No part of this publication may be
reproduced, stored in a retrieval system, or transmitted,
in any form or by any means, electronic, mechanical,
photocopying, recording or otherwise, without the
prior permission of the publishers.

This book is sold subject to the condition that it shall not, by
way of trade or otherwise, be lent, re-sold, hired out or otherwise
circulated without the publisher's prior consent in any form of
binding or cover other than that in which it is published and
without a similar condition including this condition being
imposed on the subsequent purchaser.

Designed by Jonathan D. Lippincott

Printed and bound in Great Britain by
Clays Ltd, St Ives plc

MIX
Paper from
responsible sources
www.fsc.org   **FSC˚ C007454**

FSC is a non-profit international organisation established to promote
the responsible management of the world's forests. Products carrying the
FSC label are independently certified to assure consumers that they come
from forests that are managed to meet the social, economic and
ecological needs of present and future generations,
and other controlled sources.

Find out more about HarperCollins and the environment at
www.harpercollins.co.uk/green

To my parents and (how not?) my aunt
and in memory of my uncle

Omnia mutantur, nihil interit.
(Everything changes, nothing is lost.)
—Ovid, *Metamorphoses*

CONTENTS

THE MIGHTY FRANKS

OVERHEARD

"My feeling for Mike is something out of the ordinary," I overhear my aunt say to my mother one day when I am eight years old. "It's stronger than I am. I cannot explain it. He's simply the most marvelous child I have ever known, and I love him beyond life itself."

Beyond life itself. At first I feel lucky to be so cherished, singled out to receive a love that is so vast . . . but then I stop to think about it. I am not sure what it means, really, to be loved *beyond life itself.*

Do I love my own mother that way? Does she me? Is such a thing even possible?

And why me and not my two younger brothers? What do I have that they do not?

"I wish he were mine," my aunt blurts after a moment.

From where I am crouching on the stairs in the entry hall, I can feel the weather in the room change. A long, tense pause opens up between the two women. I hear them breathing, back and forth, into that pause.

They are sitting at right angles to each other, I know, my aunt on the sofa, my mother in the chair next to it. This is how they always sit in our living room, not face-to-face but perpendicular, so that they don't have to make eye contact if they don't want to.

"I wish you had a child of your own," my mother says carefully. Ever the second fiddle, the third born. The diplomat.

"So do I," says my aunt in a pitched, emotional voice.

Maybe you would be a different person if you did.

My mother does not say this. She thinks it, though. Everybody in our family does. But that's not what happened.

This is.

PART I

THE APARTMENT

For a long time I used to wait in the dining room window. I waited in the afternoon, when I returned from school, and I waited on Saturday mornings. Now and then I waited at the edge of the driveway, because from there I could see farther up the hill, almost to the top. When the Buick Riviera appeared, its fender flashing a big toothy metallic grin, I felt happiness wash over me; happiness braided together with anticipation and excitement too, since it meant that within minutes my aunt would be pulling up to take me on one of our adventures.

My aunt was the one person in the world I was always most eager to see. Sometimes she came bearing gifts, special books or treasures related to the special interests she and my uncle and I shared: art and architecture, literature, and, since my aunt and uncle were screenwriters, movies (*never* "film," that was the celluloid of which movies were made). But what I loved even more than receiving tangible things was going off with her, alone, without my younger brothers or my parents; being alone with her, with the force of her attention, the contents of her mind. And her talk, which was like an unending river emptying itself into me. Our time together was *larky. You really are the best company a person could ever hope for, Mike,* she said, *bar none.* She made me feel clever merely by being with her and listening to her, learning what she had to teach, absorbing some of her spark— her sparkle.

My aunt and I went off alone together often because she and my uncle didn't have any children of their own, and they lived within minutes of our house, and because we were doubly related. There was a refrain we children learned to recite when people asked us to explain our intertwined family—

Brother and sister married sister and brother.
The older couple have no children, so the younger couple share
*   theirs.*
The two families live within three blocks of each other up in
*   Laurel Canyon—*
and the grandmothers live in an apartment together at the foot
*   of the hill.*

It wasn't very poetic, but it got the facts across and made the situation seem almost normal, as summaries sometimes do.

The situation was not remotely normal, but naturally I did not understand that at the time.

Our relationship, my aunt said, was *special*. She called our two families *the larky sevensome* or, quoting my grandmother, *the Mighty Franks. But even within the larger group, she said, you and I, Lovey, are a thing apart. What we have is nearly as unusual as what I have with Mamma. The two of us have pulled our wagons up to a secret campsite. We know how lucky we are. We're the most fortunate people in the world to have found each other, isn't it so?*

Only we hadn't found each other. We had been born to each other; to—into—the same family. Did that make a difference? Was a bond this strong meant to grow in this soil, and in this way? I was far too besotted with my aunt to ask any of these questions. My aunt was the sun and I was her planet, held in devotional orbit by forces that felt larger than I was, larger than we were. You could call it gravity. Or alchemy. Or intoxication. Or simply love. But what an unsimple love this was.

I heard the car before I saw it: the familiar motor slowing as it approached Greenvalley Road . . . the high-pitched squeak the wheels made as they widened into that precise turn that landed the Buick smack-dab in the center of our driveway . . . and then the horn, whose coloration changed depending on the driver's frame of mind. The jubilant *tap-tap* that soon ricocheted across the canyon meant *Come along quick-quick*, which was my aunt's preferred pace in all matters always.

I flew out the front door, for a moment forgetting my ever-present Académie sketch pad and pouch of pencils. Halfway down the garden path, I remembered and doubled back to retrieve them from the entry hall. Outside again, something, some sense, made me glance back at the dining room window. My two younger brothers were standing and looking for me in the same place where I had been looking for my aunt. I lingered just long enough to see the confusion in their faces. Then I headed for the car.

Once I had settled into the front seat, but before my aunt had backed us out and on our way, I glanced again at the window, where my mother had now joined my brothers. She had placed a comforting palm on each boy's shoulder. There was no confusion in *her* face. It was very clear. To me it said: Why just Mike, why yet again?

It was the cusp of the 1970s, and my mother had cut off all her hair, which until recently her hairdresser used to pile up on top of her head like an elaborate pastry. She'd stopped wearing heavy makeup too. She'd exchanged her dresses and skirts and blouses for blue jeans and T-shirts accessorized with colorful beads, and she'd begun putting strange new music on our record player, albums by Carole King and Joni Mitchell and the Mamas and the Papas, all of whom lived near where we lived in Laurel Canyon. As she cooked and cleaned and took care of my younger brothers she sang—

> *But you've got to make your own kind of music*
> *Sing your own special song*
> *Make your own kind of music*
> *Even if nobody else sings along*

Where is the wit? my aunt said when she heard these lyrics. *Where is the panache?* She and my uncle believed that Brahms was the last composer to belong in what they called the top drawer, though they did open a tiny side compartment for Irving Berlin and the Gershwins, especially when sung by Ella, whom they referred to solely by her first name.

This recent haircutting of my mother's was the first of many evolutions in her appearance over the decades—her look changed with the times, while my aunt's remained fixed in 1945, the year she met my uncle at Metro-Goldwyn-Mayer, where they were both young screenwriters.

My mother was short—*petite and mignonne, that's our Merona*, my aunt said. *Adorable*, she said, pronouncing the word *à la Française*, as if she were speaking about a little girl, or a doll. My mother's doll-like tendencies—such as they were—had been in slow retreat ever since she had had her children, but to my aunt, Merona was in many ways still the timid thirteen-year-old she first met a few months after she and my uncle had begun going out together.

There was nothing remotely doll-like about my aunt. She was a tall, big-boned, round-faced, incandescent-eyed woman—formidable, people often said of her, though never with the hint of mockery that was conveyed when the word was pronounced with a French accent and certainly never to her face. I considered her quite simply to be the most magical human being I knew. Everything she touched, everything she did, was golden, infused with a special knowledge and a teeming vitality that transformed an ordinary conversation, or meal, or room, or moment, into an enchanted one. Not just to me but to lots of other people, she was a great beauty, part Rosalind Russell, part (brunette) Lucille Ball, though she mockingly—apparently mockingly—described herself as the forever too-tall, too-ugly adolescent with the imperfect nose that her mother had had "revised" as a seventeenth-birthday present. Her hair went up—high—higher even than my mother's ever did—well before the bunning years. She fastened flowers or, memorably, leaves in these rounded towers, or wrapped them in scarves (bandannas, leopard or zebra prints, plaids), or concealed them behind berets, tams, cloches, or baseball caps she chose for their color, not because of her affinity for any particular team. She colored her eyelids blue or violet and well into the 1990s penciled a flapperish beauty mark at the top of her right cheek. She wore quantities of jewelry, and as she aged, more and more of it, often collated into thematic collections as profuse as the collections of objects in her house, ivory one day, amber the next; coral, gold, silver, crystal, malachite, lapis, pearl, or jet, depending on her mood or outfit. She treated herself, essentially, as a surface to decorate and, like the other surfaces she decorated, the finished effect asked to be noticed, always. Was noticed, always.

Her linguistic powers were inimitable. Intimidating, at times. She commanded torrents of words that merged into impeccable sentences the way raindrops collected into puddles. In story meetings she was a master of the pitch. She sat forward in her chair, elbows on her knees, a Merit smoking itself in one hand, and let fly. In fifteen, twenty minutes, to a hushed room, she would render an entire movie, from FADE IN to FADE OUT, without glancing at a single written note.

Her scent was a Caswell-Massey men's cologne she bought at I. Magnin. When I climbed into the car its spiciness came gusting up out of her collar as she lowered a rouged cheek down to my height.

I kissed her, and she eased the Buick out of the driveway. "Reach around in back, Lovey," she said.

I brought forward a wrapped package tied with a bow so crisp it might have been dipped in starch.

"What are you waiting for? Go ahead. Open it."

The present was a book titled *Famous Paintings*. I glanced inside. Each chapter was devoted to a different subject: landscape, portraits, people working, children at play.

"Thank you, Auntie Hankie," I said. "It's beautiful."

Again the cheek lowered. Again I kissed it.

"A little something to celebrate our Saturday together." She nudged me with her elbow. "I'm sure that you will be an artist one day, Mike. I'm convinced of it. Everything you do has such *style*. Really and truly. It's as if you've been immersed in aesthetics your whole entire life."

I was nine.

"*Make beauty at all times.* It's one of our family tenets, you know."

"What's a tenet?"

"A rule you live by. You build your life by."

"Make beauty. At all times."

"Yes. In what you draw or paint, in the houses you inhabit. In the way you speak too. And write. And of course be fast about it. Quick-quick. You've heard me say that before."

I nodded.

"There's plenty of time to sleep in the grave."

I must have seemed puzzled, because she added, "It means no stopping, no roadblocks allowed. No naps."

My mother took one every day.

"You must make every moment count," she went on. "And you must never be afraid to dare. Imagine if Huffy had not dared— imagine if after ten long, horrible years of the Depression in Portland she had not seized the opportunity when Mayer granted her an interview. She piled your father and me and Pups Frank into the Nash and drove straight to Los Angeles, and she knocked the socks off old L.B.M. Everything changed after that. Everything, all of it, everything that makes us the Mighty Franks, comes from that moment, from Huffy, because of her boldness and her courage. Do you understand?"

I shook my head.

"Well, you will. One day. I'll make sure of that."

We had glided down out of the canyon. As she turned right onto Laurel Canyon Boulevard, she continued, "Follow your heart wher- ever it takes you. And always give away whatever possession is most precious to you."

I looked down at the pages of my new book.

"You mean I have to give this to Danny or Steve one day?"

She cocked her head. "I would say not in this particular case, Lovey. Your brothers' interests are so markedly different from yours, wouldn't you agree? Danny—now he is a budding scientist. A logistician. It's written all over him. He's going to be a man of facts. I'm as sure of it as I am of my own breath. As for the little one . . . I see athletics in his future. He's very *skilled* physically, just like my brother. Maybe like him he'll develop a gift for business. Yes, I'm sure he will. We need that in the family, do we not? As a kind of ballast. It's only practical. Literature, though? Art, architecture? The creative in any and all forms of expression? That's your purview."

Purview was like *tenet*, but I didn't have to ask. "It means area of expertise. Strength." She gestured at the book. "No, this one is ear-marked for you. As is so much more."

So much more what? I wondered. As if she could read my mind, my aunt added, "A collector does not spend a lifetime assembling beautiful things merely to have them scattered after she's gone."

She turned her face toward me. In her eyes there was that familiar sparkle. It blazed for a moment as she smiled at me, then drove on.

At Hollywood Boulevard we veered left onto a stretch of road that was wholly residential and lined, on the uphill side, with a series of houses that my aunt had previously taught me to identify. Moorish. Tudor. Spanish. Craftsman. Every time I watched these houses flash by the car window I wondered how they could be so different, one from the other, and yet stand next to one another all in an obedient row. Entire streets, entire neighborhoods, were like that in L.A.: mismatched and fantastical, dreamed-up houses for a dreamscape of a city.

At Ogden Drive we turned right, as we always did, and my aunt pulled up in front of number 1648. The Apartment. That is simply how it was known to us: The Apartment. We're stopping by The Apartment. They need us at The Apartment. Your birthday this year will be at The Apartment. There has been some very bad news at The Apartment.

She never taught me to identify the style of The Apartment, but that was probably because it didn't have one, particularly. A stucco building from the 1930s, it wrapped around an interior courtyard that was lushly planted with camellias and gardenias and birds-of-paradise, but what mattered most about The Apartment was that, for many years, since well before I was born, my two grandmothers had lived there—together.

"Quick-quick," my aunt said as she turned off the ignition. "We're nearly ten minutes late for Morning Time. Huffy will be worried to death."

Huffy—the older of my two grandmothers, the mother of my aunt and my father—was sitting up in bed, reading calmly, when we hurried into her room. She was in the bed closest to the door. The two beds were a matched pair whose head- and footboards were capped with gold-painted, flame-shaped finials. She looked like she was riding in a boat, a gilded boat that was bobbing in a sea of embossed pink and white urns and wreaths that were papered onto the walls.

"I'm sorry we're late, Mamma," my aunt said. "Mike and I were engaged in rapt conversation, and I lost track of the time."

My grandmother's hair had come loose in the night, and she wasn't wearing any makeup, but with her erect posture and her dark focused eyes she still, somehow, seemed alert and all-seeing. "It's Saturday," she said as she removed her reading glasses. "Today is the one day you are *meant* to slow down, my darling. I've told you that before."

"There's plenty of time to slow down in——" my aunt started to say. "Anyway we're here now."

"Is the boy going to noodle around with us this morning?" my grandmother asked.

My aunt smiled at me. "We need his eye, don't we?"

"He does have a good one," said my grandmother.

"Of course he does. I trained him myself."

Morning Time was the sacred hour or so during which my aunt brushed her mother's hair, wound it into a perfect bun, and pinned it to the top of her head before helping her put on her makeup and her clothes. Afterward she made my grandmother breakfast and sat nearby while my grandmother ate, so that they could visit before my aunt drove back up the hill and (on weekdays) sat down with my uncle to write.

This ritual went back to before I was conscious. It began when my grandmother had The Operation—never further detailed or explained—after which, for a while, she needed help dressing and doing up her hair. It had long since evolved into the routine with which the two women began their days, seven days a week without exception.

During the first part of Morning Time, the grooming and dressing part, I was always sent to wait in the living room. Often, as on this morning, I waited until my aunt had closed the door behind me, then I slipped down the hall to Sylvia's room. Sylvia was my "other" grandmother, Merona and Irving's mother.

Her door was closed, as usual. I pressed my ear to it, then knocked. "Michaelah?"

I opened the door just wide enough to fit myself through, then I closed it again. "I wasn't even sure you were here," I said.

"I don't like to be in Hankie's way when she's making breakfast."

"What about yours?" I asked.

"Later," she said with a shrug.

She was sitting on the corner of her bed, fully dressed, a folded newspaper in her lap. Her room was half the size of Huffy's, and had no grand headboard with leaping gold flames. The bed was the only place in the room to sit other than a low, hard cedar hope chest.

Besides the hope chest, there was a high dresser on top of which stood several photographs of Sylvia's husband, my striking-looking rabbi grandfather who died before I was born; these pictures were the only thing in the entire room—the entire apartment—that was personal to Sylvia, other than the radio by the bed, which was tuned to a near whisper and always to the local classical station.

"Are you coming out with us this morning?" I asked.

Sylvia's head fell to an angle. It was as though my grandmother— my second grandmother, as I thought of her—was always assessing, or taking careful measure, before she spoke or acted.

"I think not—today."

Physically Sylvia was smaller and shorter than Huffy, as my mother was smaller and shorter than my aunt; even her nose and eyes were smaller, more delicate and tentative. Dimmer too, you might say, except that they missed very little.

These small noting eyes of hers peered down the hall, or where the hall would have been visible if the door had been open.

"Maybe next week," she added.

I knew she was lying. She knew I knew she was lying. We'd had a version of this conversation many Saturdays before.

"Monday I'm on the hill," she said, meaning at our house on Greenvalley Road, where she could cook in our kitchen and eat kumquats off the tree and read in the garden under the Japanese elm in the backyard and let the vigilance drain out of those small eyes. "I'll make tapioca."

"Oh, yes, please," I said. "And a sponge cake?"

"If you like."

I nodded.

"Michaelah," she said.

"Yes, Grandma Sylvia?"

"They'll be impatient if you're gone too long."

"It's only been a few minutes."

She glanced at the door again. "Best to close the door when you go back out."

The door to Huffy's room was still closed. I found my sketch pad and stretched out on the braided rug in the living room.

As I tried to decide what to draw, my eye landed first, as it often did, on the painting that hung just above and to the right of the wing chair where Huffy preferred to sit during family gatherings. If there had been a fireplace, the painting would have hung over the mantelpiece, but there wasn't, and this picture didn't need that extra emphasis. It was already italicized—underlined. The painting was a portrait of my aunt, the epicenter of the room as she was of our family.

Harriet—Harriet Frank, Jr.—was her public name, her professional name. At home she was known as Hank or Hankie, therefore Auntie Hankie, or sometimes Harriatsky or, later, Tantie.

There was quite a confusion around the nomenclature of these women. Huffy had been born Edith Frances Bergman in Helena, Montana. She discarded the Edith early on because she disliked it. She went by Frances as a girl in Spokane and a young married woman in Portland. She remained Frances Goldstein—her married name—until in the mid-1930s she hosted a local radio program, which she called *Frances Frank, Frankly Speaking*; soon afterward she became reborn as Frances Frank, changing her last name and persuading her husband to change his and the children's too. Several years later, in 1939, when she remade her life again, moving from Portland to Los Angeles, she appropriated her daughter's name, a new name for a new life. She became Harriet senior, and my aunt, therefore undergoing a name change of her own, became Harriet junior.

No one thought this was strange: a mother taking her daughter's name so that they could become a matched set.

"Harriet is an interesting name," my grandmother declared. "Harriet is a writer's name."

Harriet junior became a writer—a screenwriter. No one thought this was strange either.

Or this: "Huffy and I know each other's most intimate secrets. There's nothing really that we don't know about each other. Not one stitch of a thing."

Or: "We've never had a cross word in our lives. Not a single one."

Or: "Hankie and I are not merely mother and daughter. We're best friends. We're *beyond* best friends."

They loved their pronouncements, my grandmother and my aunt, almost as much as they loved their nicknames. My uncle was Dover (his middle name bumped forward), Puddy, Corky. Another aunt was Frankie or Baby. My father was Martoon, Magoofus, Magoof.

I was Lovey or Mike.

Harriet senior was Huffy (as in: HF + y), always. Sylvia, my other grandmother, never had a nickname. Sometimes she might be shortened to Syl, but that was all. My mother, Merona, sometimes became Meron. But never anything more affectionate than that.

It was California. Blazing, sun-bleached Southern California: most any other nine-year-old boy would have spent his time outdoors playing under all that sun and sky. I spent mine lying on the braided rug, looking up at the painting of my aunt—my sun, my sky.

The portrait had been painted by a Russian cousin of my grandmother's called Mara, who during the war had been banished to Siberia, where she was sent to a gulag and forced to paint pictures of Stalin for the government. "Your aunt and I went to Yurp together in 1964," Huffy told me—Yurp being, like Puddy or Hankie or Magoof, a nickname, though for an entire continent instead of a person. "It was a dream of ours forever. Mara's sister, Senta, who survived by hiding in an attic, had spent nearly twenty years trying to get her out of the Soviet Union. We found them living together in an apartment in Brussels. Every morning after breakfast your aunt and I went to their house and sat for her until dinner. We made up for a lot of lost time on that visit. And while I sat there, can you guess what I thought about?"

I shook my head.

"How grateful I was to my parents for deciding to come to America when they did. Do you know what I mean by that?"

I shook my head again.

"I mean that otherwise I might well have perished, like so many people in our family."

My grandmother focused her dark eyes on me. "That's what would have happened to me for no reason other than I had been born a Jew," she said. "And if I had been murdered, that means your father would not be here, which means you would not be here."

"Not Auntie Hankie either?" No Auntie Hankie was almost more difficult to conceive of than no me.

"No, not even our darling Hankie would be here . . ."

Her dark eyes shone. She was quiet for a moment. "That is very difficult to imagine, is it not?"

"It's impossible," I said.

My grandmother smiled enigmatically. "Yes, impossible. I quite agree."

My aunt and my grandmother each had the other's portrait hanging in her house. The portrait of my aunt was the larger of the two and darker, both in its palette and in the way it hinted at my aunt's lurking black moods. How this distant cousin—a painter of Stalin—got at this in my aunt, and after knowing her for only a week, was a mystery.

Then there were her eyes. It was the kind of thing people made jokes about in portraits, but my aunt's eyes truly did seem to follow me wherever I went. This may have had to do with the fact that her eyes weren't merely in the painting but reflected in several other places in the room at the same time: in the reverse paintings on mirrored glass of Chinese ladies that hung over the bookshelves and, more prominently, on the wall opposite the portrait, where there was a mirror, very old, as in seventeenth-century old, Flemish, with a thick Old Master frame made out of alternating strips of ebon-ized and gilded wood. Its dim spotted glass showed my aunt back to herself, so that when I came between the painting and the mirror, I felt my aunt was looking at me from two directions, or else that I was interrupting a secret conversation, self unto self unto self, into infinity.

The mirror also made it possible for my grandmother, from her customary place in the wing chair, to look across the room at the mirror image of the painting of her daughter, who was therefore never out of her sight.

I decided that for my drawing I would try to capture the mirror capturing the picture of my aunt. Clever! I started with the frame, and then I moved toward the shape of Auntie Hankie's head. It wasn't easy to get right; not easy at all.

After half an hour the door swung open, and in an explosion of sound and shifting currents of air my aunt came barreling toward the kitchen like a fighter stepping into the ring. She busied herself there for sev-eral minutes, then just as the smell of toasting bread began to reach the living room, she poked her head in to check on me. With a rapid glance at my sketchbook she said, "But, Lovey, is doodling the absolute best use of your time when right over your shoulder a whole library is just *waiting* for you to explore?"

I looked down at my drawing. A doodle? I felt my cheeks burn with shame for being such a failure. How was I ever going to be an artist if I couldn't draw one of the subjects I knew best in the world? I quietly folded the drawing in two and closed my sketch pad.

My aunt approached the bookshelves and bent down. She ran her fingers along the spines of novels by Dickens . . . then Thackeray . . . then Trollope. She stopped at *How Green Was My Valley.* "This was an absolute favorite of mine when *I* was a girl," she said, before moving on to two other books, which she lifted down from the shelf and handed to me. "Take my word for it, Lovey, between *Of Human Bondage* and *Sons and Lovers* you'll learn everything you need to know about what it feels like to be a certain kind of young person. *Your* kind, if I may say."

I let the books fall open in my lap and peered dubiously at the river of dense print. My aunt said, "But you have a sharp mind, Mike, do you not? Of course you do. It's time to get started, quick-quick, on reading grown-up novels . . ."

When I didn't say anything, she added, "You don't want to be average, do you? To fit in? Fitting in is death. Remember that. You want to stand apart from your peers. Always."

Thanks to my aunt—my aunt and uncle—I was as far from fitting in with my peers as it was possible for a nine-year-old to be. I didn't even know what fitting in felt like. And I was proud of that. Ridiculously proud, at times.

——— ———

Nearly as sacrosanct as Morning Time were my aunt and grand-mother's Saturday antiquing excursions. These were *mental health* days, but they also had a clear purpose, since *a static room is a dead room, and living in a dead room wreaks havoc on the spirit* (—Harriet junior).

Senior and junior both approached shopping, this kind of shopping, with a connoisseurial rigor. Setting off with them on a Saturday was similar, I imagined, to what it must have felt like to travel with them to Yurp, which was in a way what these excursions of theirs were like, mini voyages across time, history, and culture, to distant worlds—worlds reconstituted by the past as contained in things.

Only they weren't merely looking for a pair of candlesticks or a charger or another piece of Chinese lacquer; they were also training "the boy" in what was *authentic* or a *repro*, *g.* or *n.g.*, *period* or—heaven forbid—*mo-derne*, a word whose second syllable was drawn out and pronounced with an exaggerated sneer.

I found these Saturdays to be alternately thrilling and unnerving. Heaven help me if I picked up something, even merely to investigate, and heard that piercing sotto voce *n.g.*—for "not good." It was the equivalent of being told that *I* was *n.g.*, or that I was an idiot. Of course I was an idiot. What could a kid know about Lewey Schmooey (as he, or it?, was described in a lighter spirit); how could he tell vermeil from ormolu, Palladio from Piranesi? It was as hard (almost as hard) as being read a paragraph of Dickens and another of Austen and being asked to say which was which. A boy who wanted to remain in this school (this family) made it a point to learn. The names and dates, the facts and figures, the periods, the styles (in prose, the voices; in movies, the look). The techniques: dovetailing over mitering, chamfering and pegging, feather- versus sponge-painting . . . before long it would be showing versus telling, the active versus the passive voice, plain transparent Tolstoyan prose versus Faulknerian flourishes versus Proustian discursions . . .

My aunt had several places she liked to *noodle around*—in Pasadena and out along Main Street in Venice and, when she was feeling particularly ambitious (or flush), in Montecito or down near San Juan Capistrano, where some of the more *top drawer* dealers did business. Today we were staying local, though—our destination was a cluster of shops way down on Sunset Boulevard near Western Avenue.

In the first shop we came to I picked up a lacquer tray that had two Chinese figures on it. This looked like it would fit into my grandmother's apartment, and so it felt like a safe choice. No sooner had I reached for it than my aunt's hand shot out. "No, not that, Mike. It's repro. N.g."

It was all in the tone, an icy dismissal that made an already small me feel like an even smaller me. And yet I kept trying, I kept yearning to be one of them, to know what they knew, to see what, and how, they saw; to win, and keep, their approval, their acceptance, their love.

Again and again my aunt's head shook dismissively. Again and again I would try.

"That's better. There you go."

And again.

"Better still."

But why? The why always came from my grandmother. Why is this good, why do we care? "Discernment is about judgment. It's about knowledge. This is a good desk because it has good lines. Because no one has put garbage on it to make it look new, or fake. Because it makes you imagine."

"Imagine what?"

We were standing in front of a tall piece of furniture. A secretary. I knew that much at least. It had a drop front, behind which there were many secret compartments. Some of them with tiny keyholes so that they could be locked.

"The man—no, the woman—who sat here, and wrote letters. Secret letters. Or in her diary. Imagine writing it two hundred years ago." My grandmother opened one of the compartments. "And keeping it here."

"And this ink stain," said my aunt, joining in. "It's from when she was disturbed at her work."

"Disturbed?" I asked, confused.

"By her husband," said my aunt. "Think of the painting by Vermeer. The woman writing a letter? It's in your book. She looks up with a start, just like in the painting. She knocks over the bottle. The ink, just a few drops, sinks into the wood as a human fate is being decided, and quickly . . ."

My aunt and my grandmother exchanged one of those glances— I knew them well—that suggested they had sidestepped into their own private communication, the equivalent of a compartment in the desk I did not have access to.

"She doesn't want him to know what she's writing," said my grandmother. "She has to choose between protecting her diary and protecting the table. She chooses the diary, of course. Because of her secret life. Do you understand?"

I nodded, because that was what was expected. But I had no idea what they were talking about. None at all.

Better had turned out to be a pencil box; even though it was Victorian (which like *mo-derne* usually received a crisp, definitive *n.g.*), it had two figures painted on its lid—in the Chinese manner, of course— and was useful what's more. "You can keep the tools of your trade in it," my aunt said jovially. "We can do away with that ordinary little pouch of yours. What do you think, Lovey? Would you allow me to make you a present of it?"

The suspensefully anticipated question. It came along at one point, sometimes at several points, on each antiquing excursion.

"Oh, yes, Auntie Hankie."

"And what about these bookends?" she said, taking down from a shelf two bronze bookends in the shape of small Greek temples. "They would help organize your library at home."

"They're beautiful, Auntie Hankie."

"We don't mind if there's a small scratch on one of them, do we?"

I shook my head. "It's a sign of age," I said.

"A sign of age!" said my grandmother, delighted. "The boy truly is a quick study."

———— ————

A very special treat after one of these Saturdays was being invited to spend the night on Ogden Drive. The invitation would emit from the wing chair, which was hard not to think of as my grandmother's throne. (Sylvia's chair, which stood across from it, was smaller, its seat closer to the ground.) If my mother had not been alerted ahead of time and had not prepared a suitable bag, there would be a flurry of discussion: What will the boy sleep in? ("His underpants?"—the very word, spoken by my grandmothers, caused my cheeks to leap into flame.) How will he wash his teeth? (With toothpaste spread on a cloth wrapped around an index finger.) What will he read? (The big Doré edition of the English Bible? Surely not yet the leather-bound Balzac that had belonged to Huffy's mother, Rosa . . .) Who would return me to the canyon was never a concern, since everyone knew the answer to that: aunt would drive nephew back up the hill following Morning Time the next day.

The invitation came soon after we had returned from our antiquing excursion that afternoon, when Huffy realized that Sylvia was out for the evening, at one of her concerts downtown. "We'll keep each other company tonight," she said to me. Auntie Hankie made sure that there was enough food in the house for dinner and then headed home.

After she left, Huffy said, "How about if we just have two large bowls of ice cream and then get into bed and read?"

"Is there chocolate sauce?"

She laughed. "There can be."

When we finished our "dinner," Huffy said, "I have something for you. I bought it for you last week."

She went into her room and then returned with a small package in a brown paper bag. Inside there was a blank book bound in orange leather. Its paper was ruled, and it closed with a tiny brass lock and key. On the cover, embossed in gold, was a single word: *Diary*.

"I keep one," she said. "I have since I was a young woman in Portland. When you're older you'll read it. You and your brothers. You'll be able to know me in a way that you cannot possibly now." She looked at me. "That doesn't make much sense to you, does it?"

I shook my head.

"You're old enough to begin writing about your own life."

"Write?" I asked, confused. "What kinds of things?"

"You can write about the world you've been born into. It's always interesting, no matter when you are born into it. And you can put down a record of who you are to yourself."

Who. You. Are. To. Yourself. These words meant nothing to me.

"And what the people around you are like."

This I understood better. Or was beginning to understand better.

Grandma Huffy often gave me guidance like this. They weren't rules *exactly*; they were more like principles to live by, sized down and age-appropriate—most of the time.

During the long, tedious, full-out Haggadah Seder at our cousins' house in the deep Valley, for instance, after every few prayers she would whisper, "Spirituality has nothing to do with this excruciating tedium, remember that."

If we were in a shop and she picked up an object and saw the words *Made in Germany* stamped on the bottom, she would set it down with a decisive thud and declare, "Never as long as I live—or you do either."

"You must always be a Democrat," she said to me one day. "In this family that is what we are."

In this case there was no explanation—only the edict.

She told me stories too, some of which I could not stop replaying over and over in my head, like the one about the painting or Aunt Baby.

We were driving in her blue Oldsmobile one afternoon when I had asked her where Aunt Baby got her nickname. "It's very simple. She's the baby of the family."

"But she's not *your* baby"—even I grasped that much already.

"No, she's not. But that doesn't make any difference to me. To me she is another of my children. Would you like to hear how she came to live with us?"

I nodded.

"Her mother died when she was a small girl. Her father was a friend of your grandfather Sam's from Portland," she began, saying the name of her dead husband, my grandfather, for the first and, I believe, only time in the whole ten years I knew her. (There were no photographs of *him* standing on the top of her dresser, no sign of his existence anywhere at all in The Apartment.) "He was a decent man, but he was an alcoholic. An alcoholic is someone who cannot stop himself from drinking, and when he drinks is not, shall we say, at his most worthy. A father who drinks like that is not a good father. He cannot be. It is not possible. I saw this, and it disturbed me. Deeply. So one summer I invited Baby to come stay with us. She was thirteen, and she had a wonderful time. Your aunt was like a sister to her, your father a brother."

She paused. "At the end of the summer I took her for a walk. Just the two of us alone. And I said to her, 'Baby, I would like to make you an offer. But I want you to know first that my feelings will not be hurt if you say no to me. Do you understand?' And she let me know she understood that, which was important. Then I said, 'I would like to invite you to come live with us here in Los Angeles. To make your home with us for good. I want you to think it over, and let me know when you have.'"

"And what did she say?"

"She said she did not need to think it over for even one minute. She wanted to stay with us forever. Which, until she was married, she did."

Looking through the windshield, she said, "It's important to be able to decide matters for yourself sometimes. Even when you are still a child."

She saw that as the point of the story. I saw something else: a child entrusted to parents who were not her own, as I was so often entrusted to my uncle and my aunt.

Precisely an hour after we climbed into our beds with our books, my grandmother announced that it was time for us to sleep. She turned off her light, and I obediently turned off mine. Then she arranged her pillows, centering herself between the bedposts with the leaping flames, and within minutes was definitively, snufflingly, out. I, instead, took what felt like hours to find a way to put myself to sleep. Everything in The Apartment was just so humming and unfamiliar and alive, from the bursts of traffic up on Hollywood Boulevard to the sound of Sylvia, who had returned from her concert, puttering busily (once Huffy's light went off, she began walking from room to room), to the rumblings that originated from deep in my grandmother's chest and didn't seem able to decide whether they should come out through her mouth or nose. Every now and then there would be a raspy explosion, half snore and half shout, that would send me flying down under the blankets; I came up again afterward even more awake, with nothing to keep me company other than the wallpaper, whose embossed wreaths and urns I traced with my finger over and over and over. When that didn't help I returned to Doré's terrifying renditions of Adam, Moses, Jonah, et al., which were even more alarming when examined, squinting, in the dark of the night, or else I studied the bust of Madame de Sévigné that stood up on an onyx column and had been chosen, my aunt said, because she adored her daughter and wrote some of the most memorable letters in all of literature. In front of the bust a small, armless rocking chair moved back and forth on its own, very slightly, as if it were being rocked by a ghost.

And then suddenly, somehow, it was morning, a day awash with eyeball-stinging Southern California sunlight, and Sylvia was bringing me a glass of hand-squeezed orange juice strained of its pulp, which, wasting nothing, she herself ate with a teaspoon. "Drink, Michaelah," she said. "Good health is built on vitamin C. Every day a dose."

Huffy was already up and dressed, a rarity and something that happened only on the days I slept over, since normally she waited in bed, reading, until my aunt came for Morning Time.

After I finished the orange juice, Sylvia asked if I'd like to help make the bed. "I can show you how to miter the corners the way they do in a hospital," she said.

A bed with hospital corners? It sounded exciting, a nifty trick, something to be good at. I loved tricks and I loved learning. I got up eagerly.

First we angled the mattress frame slightly away from the wall. Then we pulled up the crisp white sheet and the blanket. She lifted up the mattress, folded one sandwich of sheet and blanket underneath, held it there firmly, then reached around for the other flap.

"It's like wrapping a package," I said.

"Yes, exactly," she said with a smile.

Suddenly from the doorway a sharp voice: "But whatever are you doing?"

Sylvia stiffened. "Teaching him how to make a bed with hospital corners," she explained.

"Oh, please, the boy is never going to need to know how to do anything remotely like that."

Sylvia, her shoulders deflating, abandoned the bed-making where it was and hurried off to the kitchen.

I was still holding the edge of the blanket. I watched her go, paralyzed. Even though Sylvia was walking away from me, I could feel the upset pouring out of her whole body. I turned to look at Huffy's face to see if there was any clue there, any hint that she knew what she had done. There was nothing.

"Leave that nonsense and go get dressed now," Huffy commanded. "It's time for breakfast."

In the bathroom the washcloth was already prepared with toothpaste, the face soap smelled of gardenias, and there was a thick, soft towel to dry myself with afterward. I put on the clothes I had worn the day before, and then I opened the door and stopped to listen. I often stopped to listen before I left one room and walked into another.

I could hear the sounds of utensils touching metal, then glass. I approached the kitchen door. My grandmothers were not speaking to each other, but they were cooking. They were standing at the same stove, working over separate burners. In silence each was preparing her own version of the same dish for me to eat, a thin crepe-like pancake. Sylvia was making hers, ostensibly, as the wrappers for the cheese blintzes that were one of her specialties: light, fluffy rolls of sweetened hoop cheese wrapped in these nearly translucent covers. Her pancake barely rubbed up against the pan; she siphoned one off for me and served it with strawberry jam and a dollop of sour cream. Huffy's was browned and glistening from its immersion in a puddle of butter and offered with a tiny pitcher of golden maple syrup.

Two plates, two pancakes, two women waiting expectantly for my verdict: What was a child to do with all this—choose? Declare one tastier than the other, one woman more capable, more lovable, more *loved*? All I could think to do was eat both, completely, alternating bite by bite between the two versions.

"Are you still hungry?" Huffy asked slyly when I finished.

How did I know not to give myself to the trap? From looking at Sylvia's face, with its well-proportioned nose, small and round and with a spiderweb of wrinkles in-filling around it; and its too-perfect front teeth, which were dropped into a glass of blue effervescence at night, leaving behind a silent, sunk-in mouth; and its faded watchful eyes, which so vividly showed a registry of pain.

"I'm done," I said. "But thank you. They were both delicious."

———   ———

Before she dropped me at home after Morning Time, my aunt pulled over to the side of Lookout Mountain Avenue.

"There's something I wish to say to you, Mike," she declared ominously, or in a way that sounded ominous to me.

I thought I had done something wrong during my stay at The Apartment, something worse than drawing ineptly or being receptive to the idea of Sylvia teaching me how to make hospital corners.

She removed her dark glasses. "I just want to thank you for being such a good friend to Mamma." She took my hand and squeezed it forcefully.

"Your visits lift her spirits in countless ways," she continued. "You know what I wish? I wish it could just be the three of us forever, living far away, on an island somewhere, or in Yurp . . ."

The three of us? On an island? In Europe? I wasn't quite sure what my aunt was saying, but just as confusing, even more so, was the way she was saying it, with an odd lilting voice and a far-off look in her eyes.

"You mean . . . without my parents and Danny and Steve? Without Uncle Irving or Grandma Sylvia?"

"The four of us, I should have said. Puddy and I are symbiotic. I've told you that before." She paused. "Sylvia," she said her name, only her name. It was followed by a dismissive shrug. A whole human being dispatched, just like that.

She did not say anything about my brothers or my parents. The air in the car suddenly felt humid, the Caswell-Massey suffocatingly sweet.

"I don't know if you realize what a remarkable woman Grandma Huffy is. She's the most *independent* woman I have ever known. A freethinker. It's her religion, really, the only one she believes in. Free, bold thinking—it's at the very core of what it means to be a Mighty Frank. Mamma is its perfect embodiment. She thought for herself, she lived on her brains, she followed her heart wherever it took her, even when it took her to unconventional places."

Unconventional places? My face must have asked the question I would not have dared to put into words.

"It's never too soon to learn about the ways of the heart. Your grandmother," she said, turning to face me, "married young and, you might as well know, for the wrong reasons. She was one person at twenty, another at thirty. Portland, Oregon? For Harriet Frank senior? She had been to Reed, to Berkeley. She had brains, and pluck. And ambition, that most of all. But ambition did not get you very far in the Depression, did it? There was nowhere to *go*. She outgrew that dreary city, she outgrew the shabby little house we lived in, she outgrew your grandfather. He was a decent man, hardworking, moral, I might as well say, blah and blah. He was not in her league, not intellectually, not emotionally. And so she took it upon herself to find love elsewhere . . ."

Again she glanced at my face. "Don't be so conventional, Mike." Her eyes began to glitter. "I was not much older than you are when I guessed. He was the rabbi at our temple. It started there, the opening up of her life. With Henry. Why, I was half, more than half, in love with him myself, in the way you can be when you are twelve and a charismatic man comes along who is everything that your father is not . . ."

I tried to picture my grandmother with a man other than my grandfather. And a rabbi. The rabbi at their temple. There seemed to be rabbis everywhere in this family, yet we rarely went to synagogue. But a rabbi with whom my grandmother found love *elsewhere*? What did that mean, exactly?

I did not, at that point, know the specifics of what it was that a man and a woman did with each other, aside from raise children. Or yearn for the children they did not have.

My aunt emitted a long sigh, then started the car again. "These talks of ours make me feel so much better. You help me in countless ways, Lovey. I wonder if you realize that?"

She adjusted her head scarf, then leaned over. "Of course what we say to each other stays between thee and me, understood?"

When I didn't immediately answer she said, "Mike?"

I nodded. She nodded back at me conspiratorially. Then she pulled the Riviera away from the curb.

At Greenvalley Road she lowered her cheek for me to kiss good-bye. I collected my treasures and waited until she backed out of our driveway. Then I made my way along the curved walkway that led to our front door.

That spring my mother had planted white daisies on the uphill side of this path, and they had grown into thick bushes that gave off a strong spicy scent when I brushed by them. The daisies were notable because they were lush and perfumed but also because they were one of the few independent domestic gestures my mother had made in her own house and garden, the decoration and landscaping having been other-wise commandeered by my grandmother and my aunt.

The style of our house—a white clapboard Cape Cod—my parents had chosen jointly. My father contracted and supervised the construction of the house himself while my mother was pregnant with my next-youngest brother, Danny, but that seemed to have been the last independent decision my parents made with regard to their own surroundings.

Very American, my aunt said in that assessing voice of hers. *At least it's not* mo-derne. *Traditional we can work with*.

"We," naturally, were the two Harriets, who had submitted our garden to a rigorous Gallic symmetry: two pairs of ball-shaped topiary trees flanked the two front windows and were separated by a low boxwood hedge that was kept crisply clipped on my aunt's instructions to the gardener shared by both families. The front door was framed by stone urns, and the central flowerbed was anchored with a matching gray stone cherub *because every garden needs a classic figure to set the atmosphere just so*. Most of the flowers, those daisies included, were white.

Inside the house almost all the furniture and pictures had been chosen by my grandmother and my aunt, who had sent over containers from Yurp or otherwise outfitted the rooms with discoveries made during their Saturday excursions or castoffs from their own homes. The furniture was arranged in the rigid, formal groupings my aunt favored. She and my grandmother would often come over at the end of their Saturdays, and even, maybe especially, if my mother wasn't home they would introduce a new table or print or vase, readjust or rearrange several other pieces, and sometimes rehang the pictures, with the result that our house looked like a somewhat sparser cross between my grandmother's apartment and my aunt's house.

My mother, while raising three young boys and at the same time helping to take care of her mother, did not have so much time for interior decoration. In these early years she appeared to tolerate these *ferpitz*ings of her in-laws. Sometimes she would walk in and say, opaquely, "Ah, I see they've been here again"; sometimes she was so busy that it took her a day or two to notice that there had been a change. I was not like her. I noticed the most minute shift in any interior anywhere.

Upstairs alone in the quiet of my room I took special pleasure in unwrapping my new treasures. It was like receiving them all over again. Methodically I laid out on my desk my new art book, my pencil box and bookends, the copy of *How Green Was My Valley* that my aunt decided, after all, might be a better choice for me to borrow from my grandmother's library, and the set of colored pencils that she stopped to buy me at an art supply store on our way up the hill that morning, since mine, she had noted critically, were used practically down to the nub.

I put the diary that Grandma Huffy gave me in the drawer of the table by my bed and soon became so absorbed in *Famous Paintings*, which was my favorite of all the gifts my aunt gave me that weekend, that I was unaware of the door to my room cracking open to allow eyes, two sets of them—my brothers' two sets—to observe me.

The door cracked, then creaked. I looked up. It opened wider, and first Danny, then Steve, stepped in.

The three of us were graduated in size. I was the tallest and, in these years before adolescence hit, had thick, silky hair that I had recently begun wearing longer over my ears. I had a version of my aunt's botched nose, though I had been born with mine, which angled off slightly to the left; my eyes were green and often, even then, set within dark black circles that my mother said I had inherited from her father, my rabbi grandfather, but my aunt said were a sign of having such an active, curious mind that was difficult to slow down even in sleep. Danny came next in line. His hair, also longer now, had a reddish tinge, and his face looked as if someone had taken an enormous pepper shaker and sprinkled freckles across it. *His* eyes were not circled in black; instead they went in and out of focus, as if he were intermittently listening to some piece of private music or following a conversation that he had no intention of sharing with anyone, ever. Steve was the "little one"; compact, wiry, athletic (as my aunt often said), he had a sly sense of humor and agate-like gray-green eyes that, even from the doorway, took rapid inventory of the new things on my desk.

"What're you doing, Mike?" asked Danny.

"Reading," I said.

"Is that book new?"

I nodded. "It's a book about art."

He approached my desk. Steve followed.

"You went to a bookstore without me?" Danny loved bookstores. The books he loved were simply different from the ones I loved. The ones my aunt and uncle and I loved.

I shook my head. "It's something Auntie Hankie bought for me."

He shrugged, too casually. "What's that one?"

"I'm borrowing it from Grandma's house. It's a novel. Auntie Hankie read it when she was about my age. It's for grown-up kids," I added.

"You're a grown-up kid?"

When I didn't answer, Danny moved closer.

"I read novels too, you know."

"You read science fiction. That's different."

"It's still made-up. It's still a story," Danny said.

He picked up the pencil box and asked what it was for. I explained its purpose. I used the words *artist, tool of an artist. Patina. Fragile.* I said it wasn't anything he would be interested in. He was the scientist in the family, I reminded him.

The phrase was so expertly parroted I didn't realize I hadn't thought it up by myself.

Steve reached over and picked up the box Danny had put down.

"Be careful," I told him as he opened and closed the lid. "It's old. It's not a toy."

The hinges on the pencil box were fragile. The lid snapped off.

"Sorry," Steve said. "I didn't mean to."

"Sure you didn't," I said impatiently.

"I just wanted to see what was inside."

"I'll fix it," I said, grabbing it away from him.

There was another set of eyes at the door now. My mother's. She took in the scene as much through her pores as through her eyes.

She came in and made her own inventory. Then she looked out the window at the fold of canyon that enclosed our house in a green and brown ravine. The sky overhead was bright and nearly leached of all its color.

"Boys," she said to my brothers more than to me, "I've told you before, I know I have, that things aren't always equal, with siblings. They can't be."

She might not have always looked so carefully at the rest of our house, but in my room just then she was tracking sharply.

"Sometimes it might feel like it's more unequal than others, but . . ."

The books, the bookends. The now-damaged pencil box. The pencils. The paper wrapping and bags left from the day's loot in a hillock on the floor.

"But it all evens out in the end," she said without much conviction. Without, from what I could tell, much accuracy either.

I found her later in the kitchen before dinner. She was pricking potatoes before putting them into the oven to bake—stabbing them was more accurate.

At dusk, when the lights were on in our kitchen, the window over the sink turned into a mirror. Our eyes met there.

"It's not my fault if Auntie Hankie likes to buy me things," I said.

My mother did not turn around to face me. She spoke to the window instead. "I know that," she said.

She put the potatoes in the oven.

"Or tells me things . . ."

She closed the oven door. She turned to face me. "What kinds of things?"

I felt my skin redden. But I had started, so I had to finish. Or try to finish. So I repeated to her, as best I could, as best I understood, what my aunt had told me about my grandparents and their marriage.

I felt so . . . weighted down after that moment in the car. Telling my mother was like taking a huge rock out of my pocket.

My mother's eyebrows drew close together. "Your aunt is a screenwriter. A dramatist. She is always making up things, making them *more*—"

"But is it true, what she said?"

With some difficulty my mother regained control of her face. "Not everyone—not every marriage—is like every other," she said cautiously.

"So it is true, then."

Her intake of breath made a wheezing sound. "Yes," she said. "Your grandparents were not—happy together. But there's no reason for a child to know anything about all that. I don't know what your aunt was thinking. Really it's best put out of your mind, Mike. It's a story for later on."

My father was a large man, and as different from my uncle as my mother was from my aunt. He had a version of his mother's forceful, emphatic features, though he was darker and physically more powerful. A former high school football player, he skied and played tennis. He did everything hard. He worked hard at his own medical equipment business. He played sports hard. He chewed his food hard. He trod the stairs with a hard, loud step. When he became ill, which was rare, he became ill hard, spiking outrageous fevers or coming down with stomach bugs that would have landed other men in the hospital. He pruned trees and painted the house hard; he even washed cars hard.

My uncle was softer in every sense. He was brainy, bookish, and gentle. Curious, endlessly curious, about us children. He spoke quietly and with dry humor. He never raised his voice, at least to us, which distinguished him dramatically from my father, who had a terrific, terrifying temper. The Bergman Temper, my mother called it. In our family my father's temper was assumed to be as elemental, and as unpredictable, as a winter storm. And as natural: he inherited it from his mother; he shared it with his sister and older brother. His rages came on suddenly and were loud and fierce; when he got going there was no reaching him, not ever. "It's in his genes," my mother said, trying to explain away what she was powerless to change.

Many different things could set my father off. A dropped egg in the kitchen while he was cooking. An unruly child and (later) an adolescent who gave lip. Traffic. A traffic ticket. Republicans. Criminals. A scratch on the car. A minor loss at gin.

His wife, naturally. My mother. Who now and then, even in these early days, when she was still the good girl, would introduce a dissenting point of view, a request. That morning, a concern.

"It's breaking my heart, Marty, to see them treated so differently . . ."

These weren't the words that started their argument. They came along somewhere in the middle, after my brothers and I were already listening in.

It started when my father returned from his Sunday tennis game. He was in the kitchen, preparing breakfast. Nothing unusual there. My mother joined him. Not so unusual either. She was always going back downstairs for more coffee. More and more coffee.

What was unusual were the voices, raised so suddenly and to such a decibel that they came up through the floorboards. I was poring over *Famous Paintings* in my room, my hard-won room of my own, which about a year earlier I had convinced my parents to let me have, arguing that with my reading and drawing and my *interest in the visual*, and being after all the eldest, it only made sense.

My brothers were in their shared room next door. We came to our respective doorways at the same moment. We looked at one another and then together, in silent agreement, we slipped down the stairs, which were open to the entry hall, which was open to the dining room, which led to the kitchen . . .

"She's *your* sister. You need to speak to her."

"He's *your* brother. Why don't you speak to him? Go ahead, damn it."

"She's the one driving. You know that. She's the one taking him out nearly every week now, buying him things, never thinking of the other boys. It's as though they don't exist. You should have seen their faces. It doesn't matter *what* she buys him—the mere fact of it, week after week. It's breaking my heart, Marty."

"There is no reaching Hank. You know that."

There was a pause.

"She told him about your mother and her . . . exploits. He's nine years old, for God's sake. Nine!"

My father was silent.

"You have nothing to say to that?"

"There's no reaching Hank," he repeated.

"You don't try hard enough!"

"I do try! I have tried!"

"Not forcefully enough."

"I can't *make* her do anything. You know her as well as I do. You can't *make* that woman——"

"I think you're afraid to stand up to her. I think you're afraid, period, of your own sis——"

Loud at his end. High-pitched at hers. I did not need to see my father to know that his nostrils were flaring, his head shaking, as from a tremor.

Our parents had fought before, but not like this. Usually it was in their bedroom, with music on—and turned high. That was our mother's trick. Crank up the Mamas and the Papas, the children won't hear. Or they won't understand if they do.

The children heard. They understood. Their voices, the content. Next: objects. A spatula—a spoon? Had he thrown something? At her? We heard it clattering to the ground.

"I cannot *live* with this kind of frustration——"

Then we heard a fist, our father's fist, coming down. Hard. On what? We could not see. Not our mother. Something solid. It sounded like wood.

This sound was followed by another sound: something breaking, then falling to the ground.

There was a pause. A silence. As if even he was surprised at what he had done.

He had banged his fist on the kitchen table. Being an antique— with patina, a story, a treasure brought over from Yurp, all that—it had split in two (we saw the disjointed pieces later, lying there on the floor), scarring the wall as it went down.

"Marty, my *God*——"

"Don't you dare——"

"Don't you say 'Don't you dare'——"

My brothers looked at me, the oldest, to do something.

"I'm scared," whispered Steve.

"So am I," whispered Danny.

"Get your shoes," I whispered back. "Come on."

•

I could leave a house as stealthily as I could enter it, even with my little brothers following—tiptoeing—down the stairs and out through the glass door in the guest room, then around through the backyard, down the ivy slope, and onto the street.

On the street I noticed that Steve's shoe was not properly tied. I bent down and knotted it. Double knotted it.

"Is Dad going to hurt Mom?" he asked.

He never had before. He tended to hurt objects, feelings, souls— not people.

"I don't think so," I said. "I can't be sure."

"Where are we going?" Steve asked.

Geographically, Wonderland Park Avenue was a continuation of Greenvalley Road, the reverse side of a loop that wound around the hill the way a string did on its spool; only where Greenvalley was open and sunbaked, Wonderland Park was shady, hidden, mysterious, and at one particular address simply magical. Halfway down the block on the right and bordered by a long row of cypress trees, number 8930 was a formal, symmetrically planned, pale gray stucco house that stood high above its garden (also formal of course, with clipped topiaries and white flowers exclusively) and was so markedly different from all its neighbors that it looked like it had been picked up in Paris and dropped down in Laurel Canyon.

Everything about the house evoked another place, another time, a special sensibility; my aunt's special sensibility. The curtains in the windows, edged in a brown-and-white Greek meander trim and tied back just so . . . the crystal chandeliers that even by day winked through the glass and were reflected in tall gilded mirrors . . . the iron urns out of which English ivy spilled elegantly downward . . . the eight semicircular steps that drew you up, up, up to the front doors. The doors themselves: tall and made to look like French *boiserie*, they were punctuated with two brass knobs the size of grapefruit that were so bright and gleaming they seemed to be lit from within.

I led my brothers up the steps and to these doors. Even the doors had their own distinct fragrance, as if they had absorbed and mingled years' worth of potpourri, bayberry candles, and butcher's wax and emitted this brew as a kind of prologue to the rooms inside.

I rang the bell. We waited and waited. When I heard the gradually thickening sound of footsteps crossing the long hall (black-and-white checkerboard marble set, always, on the diagonal), I began to feel uneasy for having brought my brothers here, at this time of all times. But where else were we to go?

There was a pause as whoever it was stopped to look, I imagined, through the peephole. Then the left-hand door opened. My aunt, seeing us there, at first lit up. "My darlings, what a surprise."

It took her a moment to realize that Steve was still in his pajamas. Then she looked, really looked, at our faces. "But what's wrong?"

"Mom and Dad are having a fight, a terrible, terrible fight," Danny said, his lower lip turning to Jell-O.

She called back over her shoulder, "Irving—come, come quick."

Then she knelt down and drew my younger brothers into her arms. "Not to worry, darlings. Everything will be all right."

Those eyes of hers. Two lanterns, set on those high cheekbones. Wicks untrimmed and flaming.

Auntie Hankie sat us down in the kitchen and insisted on making us hot chocolate, even though it was already pushing eighty degrees. She found cookies in a tin too, and brought in from the living room our beloved jar of foil-covered chocolate Easter eggs, which she kept there to entice us all year long.

She brought us a deck of cards, a jar of coins from her recent European travels. My uncle rustled up some pencils and some shirt cardboards to draw on.

Then she sat down with us. "Now tell me. Tell us both."

My brothers looked at each other, then at me.

"Mom and Dad were fighting," I said.

"Yes, you said. But what about?"

My brothers looked at each other, then into their laps.

I felt my face burning. "I don't know. We were upstairs. It was loud."

"Very loud," Danny said.

"So loud," she asked, "that you couldn't hear what they were talking about?"

My brothers shook their heads. My aunt looked at me, but I didn't say anything.

"I know this may be hard for you to understand," she said, "but everyone fights sometimes—even mothers and fathers."

"Your aunt and I fight, sometimes," said my uncle.

"Puddy, we do not. We've never had a cross word in our lives."

"Well, not this week," my uncle said drily.

"Not any week that I know of," she said tartly.

My uncle emitted one of his trademark six-step sighs, a cascade of diminishing breaths that generally alerted us to his not-quite-silent dissent.

"It'll blow over, children," he said. "These things always do."

Steve said, "Dad has the Bergman Temper."

My aunt stiffened as she said, "The Bergman Temper? Now what would that be, exactly?"

The sharpness in her voice caused Steve's eyes to return to his lap.

"Do you even know who the Bergmans are—were?"

"Grandma is a Bergman," he said. "And Dad. You are and I am too." He looked up. "It's my middle name," he added.

"Yes, that's right, partially right," she said. "The Bergmans were Huffy's people," she added. And then she waited.

When none of us said anything further, she continued, "Well, your father is passionate about things, the way I am. And Mamma too. If it's passion you mean, I'll concede that, yes, it runs in *our* side of the family. It always has." She paused. "I'm just curious. That term, the 'Bergman Temper.' Who came up with it?"

Both my brothers looked at me. My stomach tightened.

"Was it your mother, by chance?"

"No," I lied. My skin, giving away my lie, began to burn red.

My aunt nodded, not to us, or to herself, so much as to some invisible off-screen observer or camera. She often did that: she pretended, or maybe assumed, that there was an audience following her—tracking her—at all times. She did not say, *I know perfectly well that it was*

*your mother. I do honestly believe that woman sometimes hates us, me
and Mamma both.* She did not need to say this, at least to me. I knew
what she was thinking, and because I knew, or believed I knew, I began to feel uneasy all over again for having brought my brothers here.
But I was scared. My father had never smashed a piece of furniture in
anger before.

"We should probably call over there," said my uncle. "They'll be
concerned."

"Oh, I'll take care of that," my aunt said to my uncle. The lift in
her voice told me that the prospect of making that call did not displease her.

My uncle emitted another one of his sighs. He said, "Maybe it
would be a better idea if I—"

But she was already on her feet. "I'll just be a minute," she said,
heading into the study so that we couldn't hear.

Ten minutes later, the doorbell rang. Its sound was amplified by all
that marble.

My aunt hurried off to answer the door. We could hear murmuring from the hall—hers and his, sister's and brother's, back and forth.
Then quiet. Then footsteps. Loud footsteps, familiar footsteps. My
father's loud, familiar footsteps.

He was still in his tennis clothes. His shirt was damp with sweat.
With anger. One of his shoelaces had come untied, like Steve's had
earlier.

"Let's go, boys," he said.

Our father was no longer angry. He was steely and quiet. This was
new. New to me, anyway. And almost worse.

He asked Danny and Steve to go into the house ahead of me. We
sat in the car in the garage: his space with his vehicles, his tools and
tool bench, his disorder. His scent: no bayberry or potpourri here; instead grease, car oil, rubbing compound, sweat. It stank.

He sat for a minute, several minutes, in silence, with the motor
turned off and the keys dangling in the ignition. The car engine produced sigh-like, crackling sounds as it cooled down.

I thought my heart would punch a hole in my chest.

"Never do that again, Mike," he said finally. "Not ever."

His voice was firm, deep, forceful. Steady.

"I—I was scared," I said, scared all over again. "So were they. Danny and Steve."

"I have the Bergman Temper. You know that. I inherited it from my mother. But it blows over, and when it blows over, it's over."

"You broke something."

"The kitchen table," he said. "I'll glue it back."

There was no apology. Only facts.

We thought you might hurt Mom, I did not say. I did not say, We're all scared of you. We hate your temper. It makes us hate you, sometimes. It makes us feel unsafe and it makes us—me—want to be with Auntie Hankie and Uncle Irving.

"You're old enough to know better, Mike. You're old enough to know what stays in this family, our family. Our part of the rest of the family."

He looked at me. His voice may have been level, but his eyes expressed something unnerving: his temper under control.

"You understand, don't you, that it was wrong—very wrong—to take this to your aunt and uncle's?"

I nodded.

"Very, very wrong," he said. "You must promise me that you will never do anything like that ever again."

When I didn't say anything, he repeated, "You must promise. Out loud. Go ahead, say it."

"I promise," I said.

"Even if your mother and I fight."

"Even if you and Mom fight."

"Even if I break something."

"Even if you break something," I said.

"Or several things."

"Or several things."

He paused. "You may go inside," he said.

As I got out of the car I said, "Aren't you coming?"

"In a bit," he said. His eyes were focused on the windshield. They were still there when I left the garage.

On my way to the front door I passed the dining room window. My brothers were standing there waiting for me. My mother was standing behind them. Her eyes were red. I looked at Danny, then at Steve, then I went upstairs to my room. I closed the door, climbed into bed, and burst into tears.

TWO

OGDEN, CONTINUED

The rhythms on Ogden Drive began to change. I still accompanied my aunt to Morning Time, but often—as often—we went to The Apartment together as a family, the five of us, my parents, my brothers, and me. We went on Sunday mornings after my father's tennis game, and we went on Friday nights after dinner. "Let's pop down to The Apartment for a few minutes," my father would say. He was not a great instigator of plans; that job tended to fall to my mother or my aunt and uncle. It seemed to mean something, something significant, that he started directing us to The Apartment in this way.

Always, almost always, we found Huffy in bed, those gold flames leaping on the bedposts, books in tall uneven stacks on the table nearby. We would all pile into the second bed or sprawl on the floor or sit in the self-rocking rocking chair and tell her about our day or our week.

I found myself waiting for an invitation to sleep over, and when it didn't come I finally took my mother aside one evening and asked her if it would be all right if I spent the night. She thought for a moment, then answered, "You'll have to ask your grandmother."

Her answer puzzled me. It was backward. Usually my grandmother asked me to stay, and then I had to ask my mother for permission.

When I approached Huffy's bed, for no reason I could then explain, my face began to burn with embarrassment, and after I got the words out—with a stutter accompanying my hot red face—Huffy said, "Darling, perhaps not tonight. I think I may be too tired. But another time, certainly."

I saw my parents exchange a look, and I saw my mother glance at her mother, who had come to join us but kept her distance, standing in the doorway as she often did, a dish towel in hand. Something was going on, but I had no idea what.

In the car as we drove back up into the canyon we were all quiet. Sad is what I was—sad and confused about why I appeared to have been cast out from the special protected garden that was Ogden Drive.

When my mother tucked me into bed that night, there seemed to be a glistening in her eyes, the very beginning of tears, as she said, "Huffy really was very sorry that she couldn't have you stay. You understand that, don't you?"

I nodded, but I didn't understand at all.

I didn't understand, but I did go on noting the things that I did not know how to put together. They were like scenes from a movie that had not yet been edited, or from a grown-up or foreign movie of the kind that my aunt and uncle preferred, only without the subtitles to help decipher their meaning.

I noted that on Saturdays now Sylvia began spending more time up in the canyon with us. This Sylvia was a different person from the Sylvia of The Apartment. She moved through our kitchen unmonitored, unjudged, unwatched, without competition and therefore at ease.

I noted that there was a change, too, in my grandmother's—both my grandmothers'—midweek habits.

One of the few things that these two such disparate women had in common was that they had both begun working when they were very young and continued to work until they were very old. Twice a week, Sylvia took two long bus rides, first down Fairfax Avenue, then west along Pico, to a synagogue on the west side of the city, where she gave Hebrew lessons to bar and bat mitzvah students, thereby winding up in life as she had set out, as a teacher of her native tongue.

Most every weekday afternoon Huffy would drive herself to my father's medical equipment business on South La Cienega Boulevard. She had a desk there and a job that my father had made—made up—

for her in the early fifties after Louis B. Mayer had been fired as the production chief of MGM and was replaced by Dore Schary, who had a different approach that did not include giving story editors like Harriet senior so much power over the kind of material that was adapted into movies. My grandmother went from helping Katharine Hepburn try to persuade Mayer to let her appear opposite Garbo in *Mourning Becomes Electra* to keeping my father's books, paying his bills, and answering his phone. This was quite a dramatic change of professional milieu and stature, but the point was to allow Huffy to maintain her financial independence and, perhaps more important, to keep her occupied.

Now when we went to visit my father at work, however, my grandmother was more and more often missing from her desk, until eventually her desk stopped being her desk and became a catchall for the flood of paperwork that came in and out of 1920 South La Cienega Boulevard. The only remaining trace of her in this workplace was the pencil cup I had made for her as an art project in school, its pens and pencils disappearing week by week as they were appropriated by other, more present employees.

Back on Ogden Drive I noticed that for the first time Huffy began to defer to Sylvia in the kitchen, handing over the responsibility for whole meals that, formerly, she would supervise down to the last thickened drop of gravy. Meanwhile she left her bed less and less. She spent much of her day reading, though her reading changed from the big classic novels that lined the shelves in her living room to paperback mysteries that it fell to my uncle Peter, my father and aunt's older brother, who also read them, to bring her, a dozen at a time.

One book appeared by Huffy's bed and never left: Adelle Davis's *Let's Eat Right to Keep Fit*, which had scraps of paper poking out of its pages, marking important passages that contributed to the change in my grandmother's diet. Now for breakfast in place of her own German pancakes (or Sylvia's paler version) or scrambled eggs with bacon and toast, she ate wheat germ and yogurt. Or pungent cereals made of bran, lots of fruit, and weak tea. Lunches were simplified to clear broths. Dinners became lighter and packed with vegetables as she ate less and less meat, less and less period.

Instead of antiquing with my aunt, Huffy began shopping in her own house, as she put it, by rummaging around in cupboards and closets to introduce an object that had long been out of view. One day, more curiously still, I arrived at The Apartment and saw at once that all kinds of things were missing, a pair of lamps, two jade birds, even the Chinese ladies painted on mirrored glass. My grandmother noticed me noticing. "I've sent some things up the hill with your aunt," she explained. "I don't need them here anymore."

"But when you sit in your chair, you won't be able to see the portrait of Auntie Hankie reflected in the mirror behind the Chinese ladies," I said, confused and also, for no reason I understood, unsettled by these changes.

·   "Ah, but I know so well what your aunt looks like all I have to do is close my eyes, and there she is."

She demonstrated. Then smiled—half smiled.

Even Morning Time underwent a change. I was no longer banished while my aunt brushed and pinned my grandmother's hair. Was it because I was a year older? Or because she was taking less care with the job now that my grandmother wasn't going out as much as she had been before?

On these mornings I often sat on the floor, bent over my ever-present Académie sketch pad, the one with the brown cover on which there was the depiction of a hand holding a pencil (a right hand; I was a leftie), poised and ready, as I was, to draw. On one particular morning I decided to capture the scene playing out in front of me: my grandmother sitting up in bed over her breakfast tray, my aunt seated across from her in the self-rocking rocking chair, with her back to me. As I drew, the atmosphere in the room changed: the two hot-tempered Bergman women, despite never having a cross word between them, were exchanging many.

The subject was one of my aunt and uncle's screenplays, which my grandmother had read and, evidently deploying some of her well-honed story editor's skills, had found wanting. She was not hesitant to express her opinion, and my aunt, her voice rising higher and higher, was similarly unafraid to express hers in powerful contradiction.

"But you're not following. If you cut all that backstory, you'll never believe his behavior in the third act," Hankie said in a voice whose firmness I had never before heard her use in conversation with her mother.

This voice was accompanied by a fist, raised and punching the air.

"There is too much static material in the story already," my grandmother said. "Too much confusion. It's confusing and slow. Your audience is sharp. You have to move them *forward*."

"You haven't read the original material. The suggestion is too radical."

"It's my take. A reasonable take, I would argue."

They moved on conversationally, but the room still felt sharpened, anxious.

In my drawing I depicted my aunt's right arm and clenched fist at four different heights, to indicate that it was gesticulating. A cloud of spark-like pencil strokes near her mouth suggested her raised voice. I thought the effect was very clever, and when it was finished I carefully tore the page out of the sketchbook and stood up to show it to her.

She looked at it for a moment. "It's clear that your skills as an artist are continuing to develop, Mike," she said flatly. "I'll give you that."

My grandmother asked to see the drawing. I took it from my aunt and presented it to her. She held it between both her hands and looked at it, then at me, then at my aunt. "This is a very accurate piece of work indeed," she said. "The boy is so very perceptive, don't you think?"

"Of course," my aunt replied.

Later, when she went to clear away the tray, I saw that she had crumpled up the page and added it to the leavings of my grandmother's breakfast. By accident, I told myself.

———— ————

Around this time there was also a shift in daily life in the canyon. It started up so gradually that I could not say exactly when it happened that my uncle Irving began coming to our house to speak to my mother every single weekday afternoon at exactly four o'clock.

I would be sitting at my desk in my bedroom, well into my homework, when the scent of freshly brewed coffee floated up the stairs.

Five or ten minutes later there would be the sound of a car parking out front, and just after that the front door would swing open as my uncle stepped into the house.

At first my brothers and I bounded down the stairs or in from the yard to see him. Irving was one of our favorite people, and it always felt like an event when he paid a visit. Not because, like my aunt, he came bearing presents or treats or had big plans but because of his attention and his spirit, the lightness of his spirit. Our uncle was avidly interested in whatever we boys had to say. From the moment he stepped out of his shoes (a lifelong habit of his whenever he walked through the front door—*I am convinced your unc was Japanese in a former life!*), he peppered us with questions about our day, our games, our friends, and later our reading and our schoolwork; he didn't ask in order to evaluate or criticize or advise, as my aunt so often did, but simply because he was curious about us and entertained by us. And he loved us. The power of his attention was like a portable sunbeam, our own source of avuncular light.

But on these new afternoon visits Irving had not come to see us; or not to see only us. At the end of his time with my mother we would be invited to join them, but at the beginning he and my mother gave us strict orders to make ourselves scarce. They had grown-up matters to discuss, they said. Boring matters, they always added, that were not of any interest to children.

Danny and Steve obeyed agreeably—innocently, you might say—disappearing back into their schoolwork or their games. I was not so compliant. I was becoming experienced enough to understand that when grown-up matters were described as not being of interest to children, they were most probably the exact opposite. Also, for me, observing was beginning to evolve into something more active, more like eavesdropping, if not (yet) deliberate spying, though that would come with time.

The design of our house, with the staircase halfway open to the entry hall and the living room beyond, was a great help to me. I had heard interesting things from the stairs before. I always waited until I detected the murmuring coming up through the floorboards, his-hers, hers-his, back and forth in somber, subdued tones, before I slipped out into our carpeted upstairs hall, first along the landing, then slowly, very slowly, down the first step . . . then the second . . . then the third. I had learned early on that when you inched along you were less likely to cause the stairs to produce a revealing creak.

The murmuring clarified into recognizable words, then phrases.

I don't know how much more of this she can take. I don't know how much more of it I *can take—*

Dr. Irvine says there is a connection between the tension and the pressure in his eyes. He says Marty has to watch the glaucoma extra closely right now. I worry he's going to go blind—

I'm concerned she's going to have a heart attack. Or a car accident. She hasn't slept through the night in more than six months. She screams whenever a spatula drops to the floor. Sometimes she wails in her sleep—

He doesn't wail. He roars, like when he's angry, but—

A creaking stair or a sound from the garden produced a sharp *Red nisht, di kinder darfn nisht hern.* But it was no good resorting to Yiddish, not *that* Yiddish, since I knew it meant they suspected someone— a *kind*—was there and were alerting each other to stop talking.

That's when we would be invited to join them. I always waited a few minutes before hurrying, pretending, that is, to hurry down the stairs. When I skidded to a stop near my uncle's chair he would look over at me with raised eyebrows that said, *I know what you've been up to, Mike.* But did he, really?

——— ———

One evening in the middle of July 1969, all nine of us assembled at The Apartment. The living room had been transformed into a little theater: Huffy's wing chair had been turned around to face the Zenith, and so had Sylvia's low-slung Victorian chair. The dining room chairs had been brought in and lined up in rows for my parents and aunt and uncle. Open space was left for us children on the braided rug.

This, all this, created a sense of suspense. A Major World Event, my uncle called it; but he might as easily have said A Major Family Event, since it was the first time in a long time we had all gathered together in The Apartment.

We watched with the rest of America, the rest of the world. We watched and we waited. The screen was gray and granular, alternately dancing with lines and spotted, or pulsing. "It's like when you have motes in your eyes," my mother said. Time seemed to move very slowly as we listened to Walter Cronkite and waited patiently, then less patiently, for the hatch of the *Eagle* module to swing open. It seemed to take forever, yet no one got up for a drink of water or to stretch. We sat where we were, transfixed.

And then, finally, just like that, it happened. The hatch opened, and Neil Armstrong backed down the ladder and set his foot right there, on the white surface of the moon. We all watched in silence for several minutes. Everyone, and everything, grew even more still. It was as though all the eyes in the room were watching with us—the eyes in the portraits and in the Flemish mirror, the eyes of all the Chinese figures in the lacquer and on the porcelain . . .

Afterward Huffy angled around to face us children, and with a strong but also strangely glazed light in her eyes she said, "When I was born, boys, we still traveled by horse and buggy. Ice was delivered by a man in a cart. Radios and telephones were still newfangled inventions. Televisions—no one had even *imagined* them. Women couldn't even *vote*—we couldn't—" She made a small sweeping gesture in the air with her right hand. "I wonder if you can understand what it feels like for me to have lived long enough to see an astronaut walk on the moon."

She turned her perfectly combed and pinned silver head back to the television screen. "The *moon* . . ."

——— ———

At three o'clock in the afternoon on the first Friday in October the school bus dropped us as usual at the bottom of our hill, and as my brothers and I walked up to our house I saw that cars were parked in our driveway and all along the street nearby. It was the weekend our new dog was supposed to come live with us in the canyon. Something must have happened to the dog, I remember thinking. Something bad.

It's a wonder how quickly the human mind—a child's mind— can conjure a plausible story out of implausible facts, how the waking mind can think as magically as the dreaming mind; or—more simply—what a thick ten-year-old I was.

As we made our way along the path to the front door I saw Sylvia standing in the guest room window, peering around the curtain.

I saw my mother come out the front door and down the steps.

Behind her I saw a room full of people. Some I recognized as members of our extended family.

My mother led us to the backyard, where my father was standing next to our yellow kitchen chairs, which in my mind had jumped all by themselves from the kitchen to the garden, where they had arranged themselves in a semicircle on the lawn. This itself was dreamlike, or like something on a movie set. But no one was dreaming, or filming, or writing, now. My father was holding on to the back of one of the chairs; gripping it, as though the chair were keeping him upright.

"Boys," he said, his voice breaking. "I have something to tell you."

He paused to steady himself because his legs were shaking under his strong torso. My brothers had already dropped down into the yellow chairs, which had been placed there for this very purpose.

"Your grandmother—my mother—Huffy—"

That was as far as he got before his face liquefied.

For some time it was difficult to breathe. I was being held so tightly by my aunt and I was being rocked by her so vigorously, back and forth on the sofa in the guest room, that I had to steal gulps of air whenever I could. She was rocking herself, and me with her, and she was emitting wild howls, animal howls, that came up from somewhere so deep in her, so bottomless and broken, that I was afraid she was going to choke. She kept howling and sobbing and saying, "Huffy wouldn't want us to cry, she would want us to be brave. That's what she would want . . ."

I did not know what to feel, what I felt. It was impossible to find my own sensations in the face of all this raging grief of my aunt's. Instead I became all eye, one big Cyclopsian eye; a dry eye, because how could any tears I might produce approach Hankie's, how could they come anywhere near the sight of my father, the man who never cried, dissolving in the garden, becoming an un-father, a non-father, a creature I had never seen before?

Locked in my aunt's embrace, I became aware of my mother standing in the doorway. On her face there was a look of alarm tinged with dismay. She was there, and then she disappeared.

Soon afterward my uncle came and detached me from my aunt's grip.

My dry unblinking eye was free now to prowl over all the surfaces on Greenvalley Road, registering every detail that underlined the inside-outness of the day. It had started with the cars, and Sylvia in the window, and the yellow chairs in the garden; now it moved on to the chicken roasting in a stew of carrots and onions and beef consommé, a familiar scent that, at three o'clock in the afternoon, was as wrong as the dining room table covered in a good linen cloth and piled with pink bakery boxes from Benês's. It was as wrong as the platter of deli meats nearby mummified under layers of plastic; as wrong as the vases of flowers jammed into water unarranged and still wrapped in their cellophane cones; as wrong as Aunt Baby and Aunt Trudy, Uncle Peter's wife, sitting together on the sofa and holding hands, their legs crossed in opposite directions, their shoes shed onto the carpet beneath them; as wrong as our dark stairwell, which I climbed alone, leaving behind the living room full of people whispering and murmuring and crying; as wrong as my parents' room, where even though it was still light out the door was closed (as wrong as that too) and where, when I cracked it ever so slightly open (wrong), I saw a body lying (*wrong*) in my parents' bed, not on the left, which was my father's side, or the right, which was my mother's, but precisely in the center, a body, covered in a blanket and seen, as I was seeing it, severely foreshortened, like the Andrea Mantegna Christ in *Famous Paintings*, so that it was all chin and nose and nostril, to me a familiar chin and nose and nostril, my *grandmother's* chin and nose and nostril, I would know them anywhere, at any time and from any angle; but why, why would they bring her body *here*, to this house, this room, this bed—

The nose exhaled, the chin ever so minutely quivered. *Wrong!*

I thought my chest would crack open and my heart bounce onto the floor. I scrambled down the stairs three at a time to find my mother and, choking on the words, asked her what—who—that was lying in her bed.

It took her a moment to absorb what I had said. Then she explained that it was my uncle Peter.

My uncle Peter, who shared some of his mother's physiognomy. Her nose, her chin.

"He was up so early," she added. "He went to deal with—matters."

"Which matters?"

If my mother found it difficult to have a child who asked questions like this, she did not give any indication. Not usually; not then.

"With Huffy's body," she answered simply.

"What did he do with it? *To* it?"

"He arranged for it to be taken away and . . ."

"And?"

"My father did not believe it was what Jews should do. He believed their bodies should be buried."

"I don't understand."

She put her hand on mine. "He arranged for your grandmother to be cremated."

I looked at her, confused.

"That means incinerated. Burned instead of buried."

I shuddered. "All of her?"

"All of her."

"Has it happened—already?"

"I don't know the answer to that. He took care of it. The logistics. That's all I know."

It was a lot to take in, a lot to put together. "When is the funeral?" I asked.

"Your grandmother didn't want a funeral. Your aunt doesn't want one either. And what your aunt wants . . ." She paused. "Huffy wished to be cremated, and then—then I don't know what. It's like she's still here. I have a feeling it will be like that for a long time."

If I was so very perceptive, how did I miss so much, how did I miss the central thing?

Was it because I was still just a child? Was it that? Or was it because the central thing had been hidden—purposefully, and with great care—from Huffy herself?

The central thing: this, too, was shared by my two grandmothers.

I had seen Sylvia's chest deflate—her bra that is, under her dress. And I had seen her reach in to inflate it again, meaning arrange the pad bulked up with crumpled tissues that stood in for her flesh. And I had seen her bra on the hope chest, folded over on itself, its aggregation of padding and tissues peeking out from behind the skin-colored fabric.

No one had ever explained who had taken away a part (two parts) of her body, or why.

What with all that dressing and undressing happening behind closed doors, I had not seen anything equivalent to Sylvia's deflating chest in Huffy, and nor had I put together all the signs of her changing habits and diminishing energies. What I learned I learned later. The Operation—the mysterious operation that established the ritual of Morning Time—turned out to be a double mastectomy that Huffy had had in October 1965. In 1968 she had a recurrence of the cancer and another surgery, after which the doctor came out from the operating room and told my father, my aunt, and my uncle Peter that he had been unable to remove it all; the disease had spread too far into her body.

"He shook his head," my mother told me, shaking her own head as she conveyed this scene to me long after the fact. "With that one sentence everything was different . . . forever different . . ."

Improbable though it seems now, absurd, really, in view of who this woman was and what her mind and character were like, her children, working in collaboration with the surgeon and our family doctor, agreed—plotted—that very afternoon not to tell my grandmother the truth about herself, about her body, about her body's fate. Instead they invented a diagnosis, rheumatoid arthritis, that would serve to explain her intermittent pain and weakening and require her to stay in bed for long stretches at a time, like one of her favorite writers, Colette.

For a brief time a stack of Colette's novels appeared by my grandmother's bed, in beautiful patterned-paper dust jackets, and my aunt talked about *dear, darling Sido*—Colette's mother—and how she and Colette, like Madame de Sévigné and Françoise, were connected in the way that the two Harriets were, *beyond mother and daughter, best friends; best friends for all time.*

Yet there was something even stranger than this fabrication, this pretend diagnosis that my aunt and my uncle and my father and the doctors devised, and that was the fact that my grandmother went along with it, acting as though she weren't dying so that her children could act as though she weren't dying, even though she told a friend of hers, who later told my mother—who was like a great fishing net collecting all the stray, and many of the essential, pieces of information that helped convey the truth of these lives, or a far truer truth than the rest of these people lived by—that Huffy knew perfectly well that the cancer had metastasized and that she was mortally ill.

Everyone was acting, everyone was pretending; too many books had been read, too many movies seen (or conceived, or made). A family that had quite literally written, or story-analyzed, itself into a better, sunnier life, a life where everyone went by new names (and nicknames) and lived in a new or newly done, or redone, house in a new neighborhood in a new city, was unable to write itself out of death. No, not even the Mighty Franks could manage that.

The house filled up with more people.

I went upstairs and changed into a black turtleneck sweater, an article of clothing I wore only when we went skiing. Being unable to cry, I felt I had to find some way to participate, to show people, my aunt above all, that I, too, was upset. When I came downstairs again my mother took one look at me and said, "We don't dress in black just because someone has died. That's not who we are or what we do in this family."

I was ashamed to have been seen through so clearly. I returned to my room and changed back into my school clothes.

I was coming down the stairs again when the doorbell rang. It was Barrie and Wendy, the girls who lived across the street and were our oldest and closest friends. They had come to see if my brothers and I were all right. Their eyes were red and swollen. They called Grandma

Huffy "Grandma Huffy" too. But then we were *practically related*—that's how we explained it when people asked what we were to each other, since we were so obviously something.

Barrie and Wendy nestled between my brothers and me chronologically, boy-girl-boy-girl-boy, oldest to youngest, tallest to shortest. We sometimes broke down into different pairs and configurations; sometimes we fought with one another, but mostly we adored each other. After school and during the summer, we were often inseparable, playing games and doing art projects and putting on shows together or playing handball or building forts up on the hill—my time with them constituted altogether the most, virtually the only, "normal" time in my childhood.

What practically related us was marriage. Trudy, their aunt, was married to Peter, my father and aunt's brother and our "outlying" uncle (Herbert was the outlying uncle on my uncle and mother's side but brought no parallel interlacing into our world); this meant that we had first cousins in common. It was a very Mighty Franks sort of situation and had not come about by accident, either. Trudy had worked as Huffy's secretary for a time at MGM and had made a good enough impression on my grandmother that when Huffy finally became exasperated by Peter's taste in women, who inevitably fell short, way short, of The Standard, she invited Trudy to dinner one Sunday and seated her next to her firstborn son. By dessert she had already nicknamed her Beaky, on account of her being tiny, birdlike, and apparently unthreatening, and declared her to be full of clever insights and perceptive conversation. And voilà: this, one of the earliest of my grandmother's many stabs at matchmaking, became also the most easily realized.

Beaky, it turned out, had a younger brother, Norm, whom Huffy looked up when she traveled to New York on one of her scouting trips for the studio; finding Norm bright and congenial, she convinced him to move to Los Angeles after he finished high school, and she absorbed him, too, into the family, moving him into a spare bedroom for a while until she got him enrolled at UCLA and on his feet. Norm and my father became great friends; after my father moved to Greenvalley Road, he convinced Norm and Linda, his new wife, to move across the street;

as before with Aunt Baby, my grandmother's conjuring yet again expanded and tightened the family weave. And the girls and their parents would have been fully absorbed into our extended family except for one thing: for reasons we never understood, my aunt developed a seething dislike of Norm, Linda, and—especially—the girls. Even on this day of all days, all she had to do for her face to turn black with disapproval was take one look at Barrie and Wendy as they stepped tentatively into the living room to pay a sympathy call.

As the oldest of the five of us kids, I felt very protective of the girls, but there was no way I could shield them from my aunt's dark look other than trying, and failing, to stand where I could block her view of them and theirs of her.

The girls seemed uncertain whether they should approach Hank or not. They went for not and received an embrace from Trudy, *their* aunt, instead.

Hank had moved into an armchair. She was no longer rocking back and forth, but then she didn't have anyone to rock with her. She was still a magnet for everyone's attention—she had no need for a black turtleneck, or a black anything else. The grief was just pouring off her, like rain. Was grief always like this? My aunt was undergoing a very private experience in a very public setting. Everyone was keeping an eye on her, wondering when she would again erupt. The room was taut with anticipation.

In the armchair she was sitting upright, talking to our family doctor. Her eyes had vanished behind her largest pair of sunglasses. My uncle was standing behind her with one steadying hand resting on her shoulder.

Dr. Derwin said, "I have never had a patient, or known a woman, quite like Senior. It's hard to think of your family without her . . ."

From behind my aunt's sunglasses tears began to shower across her cheeks as a sound formed itself deep in her chest. A moan came up out of her, and another, and soon she was howling again and trembling so violently that she slipped out of the chair. My uncle and the doctor drew in to catch her before she hit the floor.

Barrie came over to me and whispered, "I think we should go now."

"Maybe you should," I whispered back.

I walked them out. When I returned, my aunt was back in the chair, but she was still shaking.

In the kitchen my mother was on the phone speaking to Dr. Coleman, our pediatrician. "I don't think it's *healthy* for the children to witness such extreme grief," she was saying into her hand, which was cupped around the mouthpiece.

Later that night, on Dr. Coleman's advice, she would dispatch me for several days to the deep Valley, to my cousins. My brothers would be sent elsewhere, to similarly far-removed relatives.

"If you want me out of the house, why can't I just stay at Barrie and Wendy's?" I asked when she told me where I was to go.

"It's not far enough away," my mother said firmly.

I would never forgive my parents for that, for cutting me off from my own private source of oxygen, which was knowing. Knowing and noting.

My father had not yet come inside. I saw him through the large windows, standing at the edge of the lawn, looking out over the canyon, where daylight was slowly leaking from the sky.

I found Sylvia in the guest room. She was sitting patiently on the sofa, as if she had been waiting for me all this time. I sat down next to her, and she gathered me up in her arms. In her arms I could breathe.

"Are *you* going to die soon, Grandma?" I asked.

She gave me one of those knowing smiles of hers. "Not soon, my darling," she said. "No, I'm not."

"You promise?"

"Yes," she said, "I promise."

THREE

ON GREENVALLEY ROAD

"Hey, you wanna see what Suzie has in her backpack today?"

The backpack is sent flying and soon disgorges, and bruises, the cherished Académie sketch pad. Pencils bounce and scatter. Jane (as in Austen, yes) skitters across the asphalt.

"Suzie's reading a *girl's* book," observes Alfred, the ringleader. "What a faggot."

"Suzie *is* a girl," says Jared, his sidekick. "*Are* you a girl, Suzie?"

"Can you guys just leave me alone," I say firmly. My version of firmly. But my voice—I can't help it—goes up at the end of the sentence.

"Can us guys just leave you alone?" Alfred echoes. "Sure we can, sweetie. But there's something we need to check out first."

Lunch hour at Wonderland Avenue Elementary School, fall semester, fourth grade. Jared wraps his ample arms around me and drags me behind the ball shed—a dreaded, even more unsupervised corner of the school yard. Before I know it I'm flat on the ground, looking up at the giant eucalyptus trees that tower over parts of the canyon and perfume it with their spicy, pungent scent. I will loathe that scent for years—forever.

Jared is a large, heavyset specimen with oily skin. His bottom smashes onto my face; he plants his feet on my hands. Alfred sits on my legs.

"If Suzie is a girl, why is she wearing boys' clothes?" Alfred muses. "Hey, Suze, why are you wearing those boys' clothes?"

Before I can answer, think how to answer, he adds, "Why don't we see what she's got down there?"

I try to kick them off me, but they settle in like two boulders.

"I'm not touching her down there. No way."

"You could do it with your foot," says Alfred. "Your shoe."

"You can't be sure what you're feeling with your shoe," says Jared.

"We could use a stick," says Alfred.

"Same problem," says Jared.

They ponder for a moment while I try to breathe.

"I'll just do it. I'll hold my breath or something," says Alfred. "Here. Take her feet."

The two of them change places. If I'd had a chance to eat any lunch, it would have come up out of me. Instead a foul taste fills my mouth, and it goes dry.

Alfred reaches for my belt buckle and yanks it open. His eyes glitter (why do they glitter?) as his hand shoots in . . . and down. And grips. Hard. The pain is sudden and deep, as if there were a live wire running between my groin and my stomach.

Only later does it occur to me to think, If *I* am the faggot, why is Alfred going beyond grip to exploration?

"She's got one all right," Alfred informs Jared. "A small one."

He makes a show of wiping his hand off on his jeans.

"Maybe she's a hermaphrodite," Jared says.

"What's that?"

"A boy with titties. Or a girl with a dick. I saw it in a book. There's a sculpture, some ancient Roman thing, of a he-she." He turns to Alfred. "Should I look?"

Alfred nods. Jared reaches for my shirt.

"No titties." He kicks me in the chest. "But maybe this'll make a nice little bump."

"A dick and barely any titties. What is she, then?" wonders Alfred.

"Hell if I know," says Jared.

——— ——

Suzie. Sissy. Faggot. Latent homosexual (that one I had to look up). Was I what they said, what they called me? What was I? All I knew was that I wasn't a boy the way they were boys. I certainly wasn't a girl. And I didn't feel an attraction to anyone at that age. I had only one matter on my mind, one goal: to make it through the school day without these thugs or their minions (and they had them, many of them) going after me.

I honed my approach over the years. After the incident behind the ball shed, I kept myself covered up. I buckled my belt so tightly that the clasp (brass, two-pronged) bit into my flesh, leaving indentations that were visible in a certain light for days afterward. I wore layers of T-shirts, short sleeve over long sleeve, though sometimes the other way around, to help insulate my body, even on seventy-, eighty-degree days. Of course I kept my distance, sitting off in a corner of the school yard bent over my reading or my sketching, as inward-turning and balled-up as it was possible for a tall, gangly, vigilant boy to be.

My technique didn't always work. Well into middle school there was scarcely a season, outside of summer, when my body was without bruises in different evolving shades: blue-black, purple-blue, greenish-yellow, yellowish-beige.

My self—my inner self—was a different matter. From Alfred, my experience of Alfred, I trained myself to go dead. I went through a kind of ritual every morning as soon as I stepped out our front door. It lasted for the amount of time it took me to walk from our house to the bus stop. I began with my feet and worked my way up my entire body, stiffening and hardening it from within. Going dead inside in this way, deep inside, made me strong, impermeable. A warrior. That was how I thought of it: I was a warrior who every day went to do battle at Wonderland Avenue Elementary and later Bancroft Junior High. To be a target while other people did battle, though, was more accurate.

You don't want to be ordinary, do you, Lovey? To fit in? Fitting in is a form of living death. You want to stand apart from your peers. Always.

I always did.

Alfred was a dead ringer for Alfred E. Neuman, the *Mad* magazine mascot that was Danny's preferred reading material in these years. He even had his freckles, a version of his unorthodontured teeth, and a similar if slightly less exaggerated dead, mal-shaped left eye.

His modus operandi was to lie in wait, coiled and cobra-like, in all the interstitial spaces in the day where bullies tend to thrive. At the bus stop in the morning and again in the afternoon. On the playground at recess. Or at lunch hour, where he was often assisted in his machinations by his greasy, rotund sidekick, Jared.

But Alfred's deepest, strangest power was his Janus-like changeability. At school he was a combination of demon and ringmaster. On the bus ride he liked to finish off the day's work by digging his nails into the backs of my hands, gouging out tiny crescent-shaped bits of flesh into which a few drops of blood would rise up afterward. Yet as soon as the bus pulled away and the other neighborhood kids scattered, often, as often as not, he would turn to me and say, "So do you want to come over and play?" Or trade baseball cards (an early shared interest)? Or stamps (a later one)?

Absurdly to me now, I would answer, "Sure." I would go home and change out of my school clothes, pick up my handball or my trading cards or my stamp collection, and I would cross the street to his house, or else he would cross the street with his things and come to mine. We played for hours together, in relative peace. I suppose I thought, or hoped, that these companionable afternoons of ours would work like goodwill in a savings account that I could draw on when we were back at school, but that turned out to be a particularly naive form of wishful thinking. The next day Alfred would greet me at the bus stop and look me over with those hard eyes of his: "Good morning, Suzie." Then *clack!* Toe of shoe—penny loafer, cheap hard leather—striking shin or knee. I hoped for shin, since it was hard to hold yourself rigidly dead with a swollen knee.

——— ———

When I cast the eye of memory over these scenes, inevitably I wonder, Where were the teachers, the principal? Did the bus driver never glance in the rearview mirror? Was the yard supervisor, under whose watch (whose lack of watch) so many excruciating moments played out, oblivious?

Where were my parents, my aunt and uncle?

My aunt and uncle are simpler to explain. For them, school was where I, all three of us boys, disappeared while they were writing. Once we stepped off the stage of the theater that was their lives, we were offstage in the most absolute sense, non-players, non-characters, simply *non*.

My parents are trickier. I did everything in my power to make sure they didn't know what was happening to me at school. If they didn't know, then at home I didn't have to acknowledge how grueling and miserable my days were. School was a dream or (more accurately) a nightmare and therefore not real, not happening, not a place of affliction, embarrassment, and shame; or, alternatively, *if* it was happening, it was happening to a dead person, and therefore had no lasting effect. Home was different. The bookend to going dead at the beginning of the day, after all, was coming back to life at the end of it. When I climbed the hill from the bus stop to our house, I could feel the stiffness thawing and melting away from me as I resumed my more natural self, my regular shape. Home—Greenvalley Road—was my refuge, my retreat, and I did everything I could to keep it that way.

But even the best-maintained refuges can sometimes be breached.

My parents' attention was often elsewhere in these years. My father was expanding his business and responsible for his brother, for whom he'd created a job in that growing business; his mother, until her death; and afterward his mother-in-law. There were days, many days, when he came home late from work and fell asleep early after dinner; weekends he disappeared into sports and card games. His idea of parenting, for the most part, consisted of providing for us, disciplining us (typically by erupting at us), and trying to engage us in his passion for cars, tennis, and skiing; if we weren't as captivated by these things as he was, we did not see much of him.

My mother was far more present, but as we grew older and her attention was loosened from having to juggle the logistics of our lives, it began to turn inward, and soon she started to undergo a change of her own, which accelerated in late 1972 and early 1973, around the time *Ms.* magazine published an article on the subject of consciousness-raising groups. This article lit a fire under a handful of Laurel Canyon mothers, who began meeting in one another's living rooms on Tuesday evenings at six o'clock to talk about their lives and what they wanted to alter about them and how best to go about it. The husbands were asked—in some houses, instructed—to take the children out to dinner as the wives uncorked bottles of Chablis and opened up runny wedges of Brie that were paired with bunches of green grapes (unless there was a Cesar Chavez–led protest in progress) and plates of Triscuit crackers fanned out just so.

Whenever I saw my mother assemble this array of food and arrange a circle of chairs in our living room, I immediately felt a sense of agitation that I in no way understood. On these and most Tuesday evenings I peppered her with questions: Did she talk about us boys? Dad? Grandma? Auntie Hankie and Uncle Irving? I worried about them—about Auntie Hankie—most of all. "One of the rules of the CR group," my mother answered, "is that we keep everything private. It's the only way to sustain one another and ourselves. We have to be supportive, non-judging, and discreet. So I'm afraid I can't answer these questions, dear. Any questions, really."

My mother said these words lightly, but they did not sound like her—was that because they were lifted from the magazine? A dog-eared copy of the March 1973 issue appeared alongside the Brie and Chablis in the first months the group met; after that, apparently, the women knew what they were doing without such tangible editorial guidance.

What *were* they doing? It took me a while—months—before a Tuesday rolled around on which my mother was hosting and my father was kept late at work. When she received this news by telephone, my mother very solemnly gathered us boys together and, as she assembled a tray of sandwiches for us to take upstairs, explained that we were *in no uncertain terms* to think of leaving our rooms until she called up to us to say that the group had disbanded and the coast was clear.

Even as she was laying out the rules of the evening, I was already planning how to break them. Since the time of my uncle's daily visits during Huffy's illness, I had further honed my eavesdropping skills. I had learned that it was never wise to start listening at the beginning of a conversation, because that was when people (= my mother) were most suspicious. I had learned that a good time to slip down a few stairs was when someone had gotten up to, say, pour wine or go to the bathroom, since one bit of unusual noise easily masked another. And I had learned to be patient, endlessly patient, since much of what I overheard was dull and some of it wasn't even comprehensible to me; sometimes all that patience led nowhere, yet sometimes . . .

"So, Merona, last week you were talking about how you don't always feel at home in your own house. I've been thinking a lot about what you said."

"Really? What have you been thinking?"

"Well," this speaker continued, "it occurred to me that our homes are a kind of metaphor for where many of us find ourselves as women. We've arranged them for everybody but ourselves. For our husbands, our parents, our social circle. In your case, your in-laws."

"Except in my case I didn't even do the arranging."

"More of a metaphor—more of a *problem*. It's all part of the same issue. People dictating *to* us what we should be deciding *for* ourselves. The covering on a sofa can be just as important, in this sense, as the clothes we wear, the books we read, our ideas. When are we going to say what we *really* mean, wear—whatever we like? Throw out the old—the old—"

"Bronzes. Miniature Greco-Roman statues that have nothing to do with me. Views of French châteaus—when I've never even been to France."

I did not have to peer into the living room to know what the scene looked like. There were eight women sitting in a circle around our coffee table. I knew about half of them. My mother was likely sitting on a low stool, since it was a house rule, or until recently it had been a house rule, that the more comfortable seats went to guests. Across from her and doing much of the talking was Linda Berg, the most outspoken of these women and, as it happened, the mother of Barrie and Wendy, our almost cousins. Linda had recently cut off all her hair and had traded her skirts and sweaters for jeans and T-shirts—she was the first mother in the canyon to alter her appearance almost overnight. My mother's change had been more gradual. While it had been some time since she had relaxed the shellacked towers of hair she wore when I was a young child, she recently had begun going down to the Hair Palace on Beverly Boulevard where Bobby (whose tight low-riding jeans and flouncy scarf marked him as an antecedent to Warren Beatty in *Shampoo*) gave her a regular perm that produced a cascade of tightly whorled ringlets. This, together with the lightening up of her makeup, and the jeans and chambray shirts she had begun wearing, distanced her ever further from my aunt, whose bunned hair, bright lipstick, emphatic beauty mark, and proliferation of jewelry remained as entrenched as ever.

But now the changes in my mother appeared to be about more than her appearance.

"What's to stop you from getting rid of it all—just clearing out the place in one fell swoop?"

I recognized the voice that asked this question as belonging to Bea Zeiger. Bea and her husband, Irv, lived over the hill from us and had children who were older than we were by half a generation; the kids in that family had helped to radicalize the parents—at least as far as they could be radicalized from the comfort of their rambling midcentury ranch house, which stood up on a flag lot that was unusually large and sunny for the canyon. The Zeigers hosted fundraisers for Daniel Ellsberg and Angela Davis; George McGovern, of course; and Tom Hayden, whose then wife, Jane Fonda, I went to hear speak at their house later on when I was old enough to be invited to such evenings. Bea and Irv had a touch of the wattage of my aunt and uncle, though theirs was of a much more political cast.

A sound of sipping followed as the women waited for my mother to answer. "Honestly, I cannot say," she said finally. "Habit. Fear of rocking the boat. It's a very tricky boat we have here . . ."

"Some women are burning their bras," said a voice I did not recognize. "You might burn the bric-a-brac. Think how liberating it would feel."

There was a silence.

"Merona?"

"I was just trying to picture the consequences. None of you can understand what it's like in this family."

"Why not try us?" Bea said.

My toes dug into the carpet. My mother, the rabbi's daughter, had always been so private and discreet, a secret-keeper par excellence, especially when the secrets—or merely the information—concerned the people my aunt referred to as the *inner sanctum* or *the larky sevensome.*

"Do you really want to hear all this?"

Please, somebody, say no.

This was my first impulse. But then my curiosity began to kick in. Because if, after all, my mother was going to say these things, I certainly wanted to hear—to overhear—them.

"Of course we do," Bea said. "Every one of our individual stories has something to teach the rest of us."

"I don't know where to begin even."

"At the beginning, where else?"

"The beginning . . ." The ping of a bottle against glass, the gurgle of Chablis flowing from one to the other. "I suppose that was when I was thirteen. Yes." She paused. "I was the first girl in Southern California to be bat mitzvahed—that's what my father always said, anyway. Shalom was leading the service, naturally. We were in the sanctuary at his synagogue, Temple Sinai in Long Beach, the first Saturday in November, 1945. The place was packed. I hated having all that attention on me. I was so nervous my hands were drenched. Father kept his eye on the back door. The waiting was just *awful.* We were waiting for my brother Irving, who was late. When he finally walked in, he had a woman on his arm who looked like no one else in that room, no one else I had ever *seen*—except maybe in the movies. She was dressed from head to toe in emerald green, and her hair was piled up on top of her head, and she had stuck leaves in it. Leaves . . ."

The woman was my aunt—I had heard this story before. Several times. But I had never heard it offered up like this as a piece of early evidence in support of all that was wrong in my mother's life.

Hank, sweeping leafily into the room that November, was an expression of nature—a force of nature. Beautiful, exotic, in carriage and appearance so unfamiliar to the people in the sanctuary that the question *Shiksa?* flew through the audience.

Was she foreign? European? Maybe that explained it. Perhaps she was a refugee from overseas, but obviously not one of the struggling ones who appeared at Friday-night services out of nowhere and stood out with their gaunt faces and deep-set haunted eyes. She was other, that much was agreed on, and widely.

"Friends," Shalom said. "Come now. Have we never seen a gorgeous woman on my son's arm?"

"Actually, Rabbi, we haven't," someone called out, and there was laughter.

"Father, sorry," Irving mouthed as he and his date sat down. Shalom gestured at his son: no matter. And the service began.

Afterward the tall beauty joined the line of people congratulating the bat mitzvah girl, my mother, whose legs went weak in the presence of such an impossibly glamorous woman.

"I'm Harriet, though my friends call me Hank. Which is of course what you are going to call me, since we are going to be the best of friends, you and I."

We are going to be the best of friends, you and I.

"I was simply mesmerized," Merona told the group of women in our living room. "It started that day and deepened the next time I saw her, which was after she and Irving had become engaged and my parents and I drove up to Brentwood to have dinner with her family. The whole evening was like a story—a movie, really. My parents stopped at Bullocks Wilshire to buy an engagement gift for Hank, an ivory peignoir and nightgown that were on display behind a glass case in the ladies' intimates department—a place I never knew existed, and at a price, *one hundred dollars*, I'd never seen my father pay for *any*thing."

She paused—to boost all this talk with still more wine? To find the courage to dig deeper? The fact that she didn't seem to have to dig so very far was almost as disconcerting as hearing her tell these stories to strangers; it was as if she had been waiting years—decades—to speak to the right audience. "From there we drove up to Tigertail Road. My mother kept looking at a map and checking, and double-checking, the slip of paper she held in her hand. We could scarcely believe how these people lived, up high in the Brentwood hills, in a house that had three chimneys and half a dozen dormer windows and space in the garage for five cars. Five! The house impressed us even more in person than in the descriptions we'd had from my brother Herbert, who was at UCLA at the time and had been invited to several Sunday dinners. He would come home to Long Beach and tell my parents how, when they sat down at the table, Huffy would ring a bell for the maid or one of the houseboys—plural—to bring in or clear away the dishes. Herb had met a countess there, from Budapest, who also worked at MGM—and a Russian painter, and actors, and movie directors—and he said everyone always dressed up for dinner like something out of an Edwardian novel. And sure enough, when we rang the doorbell, the door opened and there was Peter, the older brother, in a tie and jacket with a pipe in his hand, and in this deep grand voice he said, 'Welcome to Tigertail.' *Welcome to Tigertail!* I will never forget that. Then I looked over his shoulder and I thought I would *die*: there was Hank gliding down a spiraling staircase followed by Trudy, who would marry Pete, and there was Baby, whom they introduced as their foster sister, and they were all wearing long hostess gowns, the same as Huffy . . ."

I knew the rest by heart; I could have told it in my mother's place: how young Marty—my future father—was just twenty and back from the war, a demining mission in the Pacific that kept the whole family scared for months and months. He was six feet tall and bronzed and had big, wide shoulders and gleaming teeth. He came bounding, not gliding, down the stairs and, landing in a skid, grinned at the group and said, "So these are the new in-laws, eh, sis?" Then, zeroing in on Merona, he said, "What's happening, tootz?" And she turned crimson and stuttered, "I'm—I'm pleased to meet you." " 'Pleased to meet you'! A regular lady." He pinched her—pinched her—and said, "How old are you anyway, you cute little thing?" "Thirteen and a half." "As much as that?"

For years Merona did not see Marty except in passing at family affairs, where he was typically accompanied by a different girl every time. She did see a lot of Hank, though: Hank and Irving. She started coming to Los Angeles on her own, riding the Red Car line up from Long Beach and then taking a bus to their apartment so that she could spend the weekend with her new "sister," as Hank insisted on

being called. "I would go anywhere with her. Even buying milk was
an adventure. She and Irving took me to the movies and gave me
books to read, ideas to think about. Hank changed the way I dressed,
the way I wore my hair and makeup. The way I *spoke*. She had such
high energy and so much assurance and style and . . . and verve. Yes,
that's probably the best word. She had verve, and she was enchanting,
or I was enchanted with her. I suppose it was a combination of the
two . . ."

One of the women I did not know said, "You were young. It sounds
like you were infatuated."

"My heart used to race when I saw her," Merona said in a quiet
voice. Then: "That kind of infatuation—it blinds you. To a lot of
things, and for a long time."

Another of the women asked the inevitable question: How was it
that she went from being *tootz* to being married to her brother's
brother-in-law?

· This, too, was a story I knew, because pretty much since the day I
understood that these two sets of siblings had married each other,
I had been asking how that had happened—everyone who met our
family wondered the same thing. Sometimes my mother made it
sound like a comedy ("There was no one else, and I was an old maid
of twenty-three"). But sometimes she told the story as though she were
looking at it herself . . . not for the first time, exactly, but with a kind
of first-time curiosity or bewilderment, as if even she, after all these
years, had not quite understood how it came about.

In the serious versions she began with her mother's illness. After
Sylvia was diagnosed with breast cancer, Shalom asked Merona to come
home from school to help out. Merona took a leave from UCLA and
returned to Long Beach. It was not an easy time for her. She had left
behind her studies, her independent life. Now she was back in the world
of her parents, the congregation, the temple. Huffy, watching all this
from a distance, and acting as a conjurer once again, came up with
the idea that Marty and his best friend, Murray, should invite her
out, just to distract her for an evening or two, to let a little air into
her life. And so on two successive weekends Merona rode up to Hank
and Irv's apartment and went out first with Murray, then with

Marty. She was eighteen; Marty was twenty-five. "He was charismatic and intelligent and more grown up than any of the other boys I'd gone out with, and once I worked up the courage to ask him to stop calling me *tootz*, we actually started to talk to each other and, what with all the people we already had in common, we found we had things to say to each other and, well, it was a *long* time ago now, dear . . ."

That was how she had put it to me. To the women in our living room she said, "I was attracted to Marty—very. I was also asleep. Weren't we all? I suppose part of me thought that it worked for my brother with his sister. My mother's illness scared me . . . and my father liked and trusted Marty, which was important to me . . . and it's not as if we hurried to get married. We got to know each other over time, several years actually, and we kept on going together even after our siblings made their disapproval known. They were so worried. 'What if something goes wrong? How will that affect *us?*' Irving said. 'Have you thought about *that?*' But I think there was more to it than their selfishness. I think Hank felt I somehow wasn't enough for Marty, smart enough or pretty enough or powerful enough to become one of the Mighty Franks, or maybe it was just simply that I wasn't Hank-like, or Huff-like, enough. Yes, it was probably that most of all . . ."

She paused. "The secret conversations—you would not believe how many there were. I would go up to Marty's house on Lookout, and by the chair in the living room there would be an ashtray full of cigarette butts with lipstick on them. I recognized the color. Salmon Ice. Hank's color. She had been there, talking and smoking and trying to convince him that it was a terrible mistake—that *I* was a mistake. It was one thing for me to be her husband's kid sister but something else entirely for me to be her brother's wife."

From her audience, murmuring, digesting.

"It's no wonder that we could only become engaged when they were away in Europe," my mother continued. "I'll never forget the letter she wrote to me from France: 'Sister-in-law twice over, hurrah!' it began. 'I think this has to be one of the happiest moments in my life.'"

The room was silent for a moment . . . then another . . .

"From the woman with the ashtray full of cigarette butts?"

"The very same," said my mother. "Welcome to my world."

Greenvalley Road: From the beginning of my consciousness it was as alive to me as certain people. I knew the house, our house, better than I knew most human beings. I knew its scents, its sounds. I knew when the light or the changing currents of air suggested dramas about to build, moods about to shift. My father's temper—I could feel it gathering steam five rooms away. I could feel it leveling off afterward too. I knew where everyone was by the way sounds carried. I knew who was awake and who was asleep. I knew from the depressions in the seat cushions which chairs or sofas had been recently vacated, and I knew who had eaten what, and often when, from the trace scents that lingered in the kitchen and elsewhere. I knew what each room looked like from the outside, the downstairs rooms anyway, because ever since I had been a child I loved to slip away, especially at night when the lights were on, and peer in through each of the windows. It was an old, old game: I would pretend that I did not live on Greenvalley, that I had happened upon it the way you happened upon an unknown house, and I would try to figure out who these people were and what their lives were like.

Even when I was inside I tried to find ways to alter my perspective. I used to play a different game when I was a very small child. I would lie on the floor on Greenvalley, in the living room or the dining room or my bedroom or even at the top of the stairs, and I would imagine the house turned upside down, and I would imagine myself walking on the ceiling-turned-floor, with its soffits and beams and thresholds underfoot altering the familiar configuration of the spaces I had known forever.

That was what listening to my mother tell her stories to the women in her consciousness-raising group was like. It was as if the house I knew and loved so well had changed shape before my very eyes, not turned upside down so much as inside out.

Where would all this storytelling lead? Nowhere simple—that one thing seemed pretty clear.

•

After the women took a break to go to the bathroom and replenish the Triscuits, they sat down again, and instead of moving on, as I prayed they would, one of them asked my mother the other inevitable question that came up when people got to know our family. Not Linda, who must have known, but one of the others wondered how it was that these two such different mothers, these grandmothers, ended up living together.

This story, too, I never before heard laid out the way my mother put it that night. She described the suddenness of her father's death—at fifty-seven, of a heart attack, just a year after he'd been "invited" to retire from the congregation that he and her mother had spent twenty years of their lives building. Sylvia and Shalom had so recently moved out to Tujunga to be near one of Sylvia's sisters that they had not yet unpacked his books. They had no life out in the deep Valley and no friends other than Sylvia's one sister—my grandmother barely knew where to buy a decent loaf of bread. Shalom, my mother told the women, had died "most inconveniently for my brother and sister-in-law"—just two weeks before Hank and Irving were due to go on location with a movie. Without consulting Merona, who had adored her father and was utterly unprepared for his death and was so grief-stricken, as she described it, that she had scarcely gotten out of bed for ten days, her brother and sister-in-law took it upon themselves to rent Sylvia a smaller place to live in Tujunga, a "little doll's house" of an apartment that Hank and Huff dived into and did up, lickety-split, down to the last curtain ruffle. They stocked Sylvia's pantry, set two pots of African violets in the windowsill, and left.

Sylvia called up my mother that very night. "I don't think I can do this," she said. "I'm sorry." "Of course you can't; it's too soon," Merona said. "I don't know what any of us were thinking—we weren't thinking. You'll come to us." "Your father and I promised each other we would never live with the children, we would never be a burden." "Consider it a visit, then," Merona said. "Open-ended, until we figure out what to do next."

Before Merona even knew what was happening she was summoned to an all-family meeting on Wonderland Park Avenue: Hank and

Irving, she and Marty, and the two mothers. My aunt and uncle, sitting in a pair of stiff French chairs, faced the rest of them over a pitcher of (untouched) pink lemonade and presented a proposal. In private, and only to the people in that room, Irving confided that he had loaned a not-insubstantial sum of money to Marty and Hank's brother, Pete, who was struggling between jobs. Huffy had offered to repay this debt, he said, by inviting Sylvia to live with her. The two women would move in together in an apartment at the foot of the hill, where they would be close to the children. They would share expenses, and they would provide company for each other. Huffy could continue with her writing, which she had returned to in her post-MGM years, and Sylvia with her teaching. "The whole family could have Sunday dinners together and when grandchildren came along we would not have to divide their time between one grandmother and another. Everything would be convenient, connected, interwoven—*more* interwoven . . ."

"Merona, what's wrong?"

Was my mother crying? I dared not look. There had been a catch in her voice. That much I detected. When she spoke again, she said emotionally, "I don't think one single person in that room asked my mother what she thought, me included. It was like we were in the hands of a puppeteer—an unnamed puppeteer."

"Your brother and sister-in-law. Your mother-in-law."

"Of course it seemed all tidy to *them*. And what did I know? I was young and newly married, I'd just lost my father, the person I loved most in the world, and I was working full-time. I went along—I was the good girl, always the good girl."

"And now?"

"Now it's all so—so complicated. It doesn't matter where I turn. My husband—my brother—my mother—my children. No conversation, no disagreement, can happen between just two people in this group. There's my brother, who is also the husband of my husband's sister. There's my husband, who is a grown man in his forties but still his sister's baby brother. There's my oldest son—"

My feet went cold. I wrapped my arms around my knees.

"My oldest son, who sometimes . . . and it's hard to say this . . . he doesn't feel like my child, like he's mine anymore. Hank has filled his head with ideas and interests that make him . . . different. She never for a moment thinks about any of this. She is just so . . . overpowering. So domineering. So—so desperate to have a child of her own." A pause. "Well, Linda, you know her."

"I do. And I don't mind saying I don't like her much."

I dug my toes into the carpet.

"That's awfully judging of you, Linda," said one of those voices I did not recognize.

"You're right. It was. And it wasn't very helpful. What I mean to say is, I understand why the situation is so difficult."

"I do too"—from more than one of the others. A sympathetic chorus followed by another long silence.

"Maybe it would help to picture that boat of yours, the one you're afraid to rock, and imagine yourself stepping out of it."

Even from upstairs I could hear my mother suck in a breath of air. "You mean *leave*? Leave this family—my family? My marriage?"

My heart was racing now, pounding.

"Leave figuratively is what I meant. Leave certain things behind. Stop being the good girl. Stop playing by the rules. Throw out the rules. Or change them."

Liquid being poured. A bottle pinging against a glass.

"That's like asking someone to imagine an earthquake. A seven- or eight-something on the Richter scale kind of earthquake."

"Well, that would be one way to redecorate," said Bea.

There was a beat . . . and then a cascade of laughter.

——— ———

Over the next few months, when I came home from school I began to find that the furniture in our house had jumped around or disappeared, as if in a dream. Piece by piece, picture by picture, my mother began reinventing Greenvalley Road. In an echo of my aunt and my grandmother's onetime sacrosanct Saturdays together, my mother went out with Aunt Baby, who had always been a particular friend to her in the family, but pointedly on a different day of the week: Thursday. They came home with roughed-up or painted tables, patchwork quilts and flowery cushions, Mexican tin candlesticks, and Sister Corita lithographs with their splashes of bright color and literary citations. Suddenly, in place of prints by Piranesi, our walls sang out with perplexing quotes like "By the street of by-and-by one arrives at the house of never" (Cervantes) and, from the in-those-days ubiquitous E. E. Cummings, "Damn everything but the circus"—whatever that meant. Merona and Baby hauled my aunt- and grandmother-sanctioned furniture up to the attic—right there, damning quite a lot of everything in our world—and then they poured themselves large glasses of Chablis, the same Wente Brothers brand that helped facilitate the consciousness-raising group. They cranked up the Crosby, Stills & Nash—

> Our house is a very, very, very fine house with two cats in the
>   yard,
> Life used to be so hard—

and, wielding a hammer and nails and pliers and wire, they spun through the shaken-up rooms as if they'd been set free from a kind of fairy-tale spell, which in a way they had.

Giddy in her gauzy blouse and curling hair, my mother gestured at our almost entirely remade living room after one of these redecorating sprees and said to me, "What do you think, darling? Do you like it?" There was so much light in her eyes and color in her face—color like there was color now in our house—that I could only say I thought it looked nice, when in fact I didn't know what I thought, really, except that it was light and different and when my aunt next came over there was bound to be an uncomfortable moment, or worse.

The day came soon enough. Actually it was an evening: a Sunday dinner on Greenvalley Road. I was upstairs when the Riviera pulled into the driveway and announced itself with a loud series of Buick honks. Instead of flying down to meet my aunt and uncle as I usually did, I hid at my listening-in spot about halfway down the stairs, from which I saw my aunt march through the front door with that high energy of hers. She was carrying flowers and a box of pastries from

Benês's and striding—always striding—forward and hurrying, always hurrying, at least until she peered into the living room, at which point she came to an abrupt standstill. She tilted her face, which sent her dark glasses sliding down her nose, and took in the whole scene in astonished silence as my uncle looked on with a wrinkled forehead.

After a moment she said icily, "Baby mentioned that you two had been out together without me."

"Yes, we have. Several times."

"She said it was quite larky."

My mother smiled. "We've had fun."

There was a long strained silence as my aunt continued taking inventory. "Well, Merona," she said finally, "it's all very cheerful and, I suppose, *au courant*. You've been working hard, I must say."

My mother's reaction to this non-compliment was a neutral nod.

"I will just say," my aunt continued, "that if you are truly done with the valuable pieces that Mother and I have bestowed upon you over the years, it would not displease me to take them back."

"You're welcome to any of them you like, Hankie," Merona said.

"When?"

"You can have them now," my mother said, gesturing at the attic. Was she calling her bluff? Was it a bluff? My stomach tightened. I waited. The women waited . . .

"Why don't we have dinner first?" my uncle said. "Something smells delicious."

My aunt, her nose back in the air, sniffed theatrically. "Roast chicken again, I suspect," she said. And that was that—for the moment.

The next time I went out with my aunt, the Riviera had barely glided down Greenvalley when she said, "I have to tell you, Mike, it hurts my feelings that your mother has discarded all my work, Mamma's and my work. It makes Mamma feel awfully *gone* now, I must say, to see her creativity—her generosity—so coldly undone in this way."

She daubed at her eyes, then added, "They are just things, though. We have to remember that, don't we? Just material things. Lovely ones, lovingly given, but still . . ."

She drove out of the canyon in rare silence. Once we had joined the busyness of city traffic, she said, "I am just curious. If you had to choose, among formal, country, and *mo-derne*, where would you stand?"

When I didn't answer right away, she added, "If you were living in a house of your own, I mean. Not now. Later on."

The air in the car suddenly felt very thin.

"Mike?"

The feeling—the *non*-feeling—began to come over me before I knew quite what it was. It happened on its own, inadvertently, but I recognized it as the same technique I deliberately used in the school yard or on the bus with Alfred and Jared. "I would probably choose formal," I said evenly.

It was as if someone had thrown on the light switch in a darkened room. Her entire face changed, and with a wide smile she said, "I *knew* that was how you were going to answer, Lovey. I just knew it! We really are made of the same stuff, thee and me." Then she reached over and set her hand on my thigh. But I didn't feel her touch. I'd gone dead.

FOUR

SAFE HOUSE

The week after my aunt saw my mother's newly remade Greenvalley living room, she hired a truck and two movers to accompany her to Ogden Drive. Up until that moment The Apartment had been left intact for Sylvia, who, after Huffy's death, had decided to continue living there on her own. Now, in a flurry of activity, my aunt picked through the furniture and bric-a-brac that had belonged to her mother. She siphoned; she rejiggered; she emptied cupboards; she took pictures off the wall, leaving ghostly shadows behind. Then she had all the best pieces moved up the hill, saying to anyone who asked, and everyone who didn't, "Sylvia is not such a house person, as we know. Mamma would have wanted me to have what I liked. It's a great comfort to me to live with objects Huffy loved. Part of a person always lives on in her things."

This represented a curious about-face for my aunt, who up to that day had had a very different policy with regard to The Apartment.

On the very first Sunday following Huffy's death she had asked me to accompany her when she drove down the hill to pick Sylvia up for dinner. She parked the Riviera across the street from The Apartment and stared out the windshield for a very long time, almost as if she was waiting for me to ask why she was being so still and so silent. When I failed to say anything, she took a long, deep breath. "Would you be a love," she said, "and go tell Sylvia that I'm outside waiting for her?"

As she said this her eyes remained focused on the windshield and, beyond it, on a tree. On the high branch of a tree.

"You want me to go tell her that you are waiting for her here, in the car?" I asked, confused.

"Yes, that's right."

"You want me to go by myself?"

"Yes."

"You're not going to come with me?"

"No, Lovey, I'm not."

I looked at my aunt carefully. She had put herself together the way she always had—her long hair piled on top of her head and tied there with a scarf; her eyelids powdered blue; the same beauty mark drawn, movie-actress-like, into the upper quadrant of her right cheek—but her eyes were not the same and her voice was not the same and her stillness, for this woman who was always in motion, was most certainly not the same.

"You and I don't have secrets between us, do we?" she added after a moment.

I shook my head no.

"So I might as well tell you," she said, turning to face me finally and pausing in that dramatic way she had. "I've decided I'm never going to set foot in The Apartment again."

"You're not going to see Grandma Sylvia again?" I asked, perplexed, since we were there to bring her up the hill.

"I didn't say that. I said I'm not going to see The Apartment again."

"But what about when there's a family dinner—or a birthday party? Or—or another moon landing?"

"Another moon landing? How about solving some of the problems we have right here on planet Earth first?" she said tartly. "And anyway, there will not be any more family dinners," she added. "Or parties. Not here." She shook her head gravely. "It's just too hard. The Apartment was my mother. She is gone, and so is The Apartment as far as I am concerned."

When it was there where it had always been.

"What about Grandma Sylvia?"

"She is not gone," my aunt said opaquely.

What did I understand of how Auntie Hankie worked, what made her work? A lot and a little at the same time. I understood that she was made very sad by her mother's death. *Altered* might be a more accurate word, but it's a word to apply from a later perspective. She had not been able to write. She had not been reading. She had not even gone out antiquing. On a certain shelf in her library she had cleared away all the books and set out nearly a dozen framed photographs of Huffy, along with a small silver vase. Every day she went into the garden to cut a new flower, an offering, to put in that vase.

My mother, observing this ritual, said that it seemed like something Catholics might do, or pagans. Not Jews. When my aunt and uncle went away to Palm Springs for the weekend, my aunt gave me the keys to her house and asked me to change the flower for her. My mother disapproved, strongly, but I changed it anyway.

———— ————

When my aunt withdrew from Ogden Drive, a different sort of life, a different world, blossomed there.

My mother dropped me off many Fridays after school, and Sylvia and I had dinner together at the white pickled table in the dining room and afterward we walked in the neighborhood or watched television in the living room, or else, especially in winter, we climbed into our beds with our books, each of us grateful, for different reasons, for all that beautiful quiet and space.

Reading in bed meant reading in the beds with the flaming bedposts, since Sylvia had moved into the larger of the two bedrooms. Symbolically and in actuality The Apartment was now entirely hers, even if the rooms had an unsettled, improvisatory quality, especially after my aunt made that thinning-out visit. But there was something beyond the physical that had changed. The atmosphere was lighter, airier. Less tense. Less *in*tense.

One thing that my aunt had left behind, curiously, was her portrait, which hung where it always had, though with the mirrored Chinese pictures gone, and now the Flemish mirror too, it had stopped showing up everywhere in the room. Sometimes Sylvia would find me standing in front of it and staring, trying to decipher the answer to a question I had not yet even fully formed. "She keeps me com-

pany when I'm up at night," she said. "She's a very good listener. So
patient."

When I failed to laugh, or even smile, she added, "Michaelah,
that was a joke."

On Saturday mornings Sylvia and I walked to the bus stop—always
by the safe route, down Ogden to Sunset, where there was a traffic signal, then on to Fairfax. We waited for the bus to take us to the Farmers Market at the corner of Fairfax and Third, where my grandmother
helped herself to one of the market's bright green or yellow slatted
wooden carts and went from vendor to vendor to do her shopping. I
remember how surprised I was when many of them greeted her by
name—it was as though I'd discovered she had a secret life. And she
had very particular shopping habits that never had managed to an-
nounce themselves quite so clearly before. She filled her basket with
persimmons, figs, tomatoes, feta, nuts, and greens. Suddenly Sylvia's
Mediterranean origins were written all over the food she bought and
prepared for us to eat.

She had friends too. When Huffy was alive, the only neighbor on
Ogden anyone spoke to was a woman called Lillian ("Lil") Lesser, who
lived in the corner unit opposite The Apartment. She was *a lady with
brains* and therefore suitable acquaintance material for my grandmother. Sylvia, on her own, gaily greeted many of her neighbors in
the building and even accepted invitations to tea from the sisters who
lived in the mirror-image apartment across the courtyard, two very
genteel white-haired widows who baked cookies that shed a dusting
of powdered sugar when you bit into them; the decoration of their
apartment had previously been pronounced *n.g.* by Huffy and my aunt,
and somehow by implication the women became *n.g.* too—but no more.

It was as though Sylvia had changed virtually overnight from
someone confined to her tiny back bedroom with its whispering radio
to a person who spread her wings, roamed free, and spoke up; spoke
up most of all.

For the first time she told me stories about her childhood in Safed,
in what was then Palestine, where in the middle of the nineteenth
century her devout grandparents had immigrated from Galicia and

where she had been born. Almost always her stories concerned her family's terrible poverty: "You cannot imagine." Only I could imagine, because she helped me to. She told me about her sister Leah (fifth in line), who had contracted polio when she was a girl, which I knew because in the few photographs of her that I had ever seen, her left leg, on which she had to wear a cumbersome metal brace, was torn out, by Leah herself. One day when they were small, Sylvia told me, Malka, my great-grandmother, took Leah to the doctor, who advised her to fatten up the stricken child by giving her butter. Butter? They had no money for butter. For seven girls? The very idea of it was unspeakable, and no one spoke of it again. Except that Malka, unable to let the suggestion go, came up with a wily solution. She would buy just enough butter for Leah—she could afford that much—and she would spread it on one side of a slice of bread: the underside. She instructed Leah to eat it discreetly, with the buttered side facing away from the others. And Leah did . . . until it happened that one of her sisters jostled her and the slice of bread flipped over onto her plate, and a great raucous, jealous, unhappy pandemonium erupted from all the girls except Sylvia. "I was the only one who realized what my mother was doing," she said. "I alone understood."

A year or so after the incident with the butter Sylvia came home from school one day to find Moses Shapiro, her rabbi father, waiting for her in their two-room stone house. Because of the war, he told her, the help that their community of Hasidic Jews had been receiving from Europe was soon to dry up. Rifka, her older sister, had just been married, but that still left a household full, too full, of hungry girls. The only possible solution he had found was to take the next two in line, meaning Sylvia and Edith, across the ocean to Canada, where a man he knew had arranged for them to work as teachers of Hebrew to well-to-do children in Montreal; how lucky it was, he added, that they had learned both French and Hebrew in school. "You see, Schifra," he said, opening the envelope to show the tickets for their passage that he had already booked, "you can save us. You and Edith are the future, our future."

In September 1914, Sylvia and Edith, ages sixteen and fourteen, respectively, left their home, their mother, their sisters, their school, and their friends, and they traveled with their father, who after a journey of ten days delivered them to a grim boardinghouse in Montreal. They went to work the next day; he left the following week.

To me all this might as well have taken place in the Middle Ages. "You were sixteen? It's not possible."

"I may have been even younger. I've told you, no one wrote down when a girl was born. Girls couldn't study Torah, so no one cared about girls."

"Edith was *fourteen*!"

"Give or take. About a year older than you are now, anyway."

A year older than me, living on her own in a boardinghouse with her older sister in a strange city, with no parents, and working at a *job*. The only paid work I had done at that point in my life was watering my aunt and uncle's plants when they were out of town.

"You do what you have to do, Michaelah," she said.

Along with the stories came the revelation of secrets—secret information.

"You have seen—that part of me, the flat part, yes?" she said to me one day. "I know you have."

I had seen it, yes. A chest as flat as a man's—flatter. Plainer too, since there were no nipples. Although there were scars, marks. Not knowing what to do with this image, I had pushed it out of my mind until that very moment, when I nodded.

She said, "I am okay. It's important for you to know that I am okay—now."

"But what did they do to you—to those pieces of you?"

"They removed them."

"Why?"

She considered for a moment. "They were diseased. And the disease would have continued to grow if they had left my breasts there."

"Did it hurt?"

She shook her head. "When you have surgery, you go to sleep, and you don't feel a thing."

"And afterward?"

"Afterward you . . . you get used to it. Anyway, it made it possible for me to live."

She told me about Merona and Irving's in-between brother, Herbert. We had come across a box of framed photographs that had belonged to her when she and my grandfather lived in Long Beach; I offered to hang them up for her on one of the walls my aunt had emptied. Among them was a photograph of Herbert standing under a huppah with a thin, bright-eyed woman who did not look remotely like his wife.

"Not that one," Sylvia said, flushing.

"Why not that one?" I asked.

She looked at me assessingly. "I suppose you're old enough to know." She placed her palm against her cheek, a familiar gesture. "Herbert was married before. To a friend of your mother's. She was not . . . right for him."

"Not right?"

"It was not easy for him—for any of us," she said obliquely. "Your cousins have not been told. This is only for you, Michaelah. *Farshteyst?*"

"*Farshtey.*" After what my aunt had told me about her parents' marriage, I understood, or was beginning to, more than Sylvia could know.

I cannot say how exactly or to what extent, but Sylvia recognized that my days at school were not easy. When she asked about the bruises on my leg one afternoon, I told her I had been hit with a handball on the playground.

"In two places?" she asked dubiously.

I nodded.

"I see," she said, though the way she said it, while looking at my legs, and then at my face, told me she knew I was lying. But she did not ask anything more. Instead she wrapped ice cubes in a dish towel and daubed them against my legs.

The ice was comforting, but Sylvia's deeper balm was the way she embraced me so completely and unquestioningly. It helped that her home, being removed from our neighborhood, was so far beyond the reach of Alfred and his gang that it might as well have belonged to a different city entirely. I didn't know any kids; I wasn't marked. I was free to be myself, much as, in the aftermath of Huffy's death, Sylvia was free to be herself.

In this safe house I was free to be myself in the company of a woman who asked nothing in return but my company. She had no agenda, no ideas to impose, no particular philosophy to advance, no competition to win, no stories to control, nothing on offer really but love.

———— ————

Huffy's death shifted life in The Apartment; it also shifted something in my aunt that became apparent only with time.

This change began slowly and organically, like a seasonal development in the garden, the way a tuber or rhizome at first sends up a few bright, gentle shoots and then before you know it is a big complex tendrilled plant that begins to dominate everything else growing nearby, blocking all the light, sucking up the water, the nutrients and minerals, until you find yourself thinking that the way this plant is behaving is the only way for a plant to be a plant and still go by that name.

There was a brilliance to the way my aunt's mind worked. Often we would be out in the car when she began her circlings. (What is it about cars and children? Cars are hermetically enclosed; you don't have to make eye contact; you're in motion, but you're trapped in your own private theater; and as a passenger you're completely and utterly powerless.)

Darling, she would begin, *there's something I've been wanting to talk to you about. You're old enough now to understand how important it is for there to be someone in your life with whom you can have a regular honest-to-goodness heart-to-heart. Someone you tell* everything *to, the very last drop of your innermost self. I had Huffy—she was that to me. Now I'm not saying that someone has to be me, for you, but I want you to know that no matter what, you can say anything you want to me, at any old time, and I will always hold it close.*

Then, leaning in—

And you know, just between us, you might well be that someone to me.

Actually, not might. *You* are. *Next to Puddy I feel I can be my truest self with you, truer than I can be with anyone else on this planet.*

Another time—

Your grandfather Shalom—now there *was a human being. Every room just felt electrified when he walked into it. He was a reader, a thinker, he had compassion, he had humor, he had a big, deep soul. You didn't have to believe in God to admire the way that man thought and spoke, I tell you. The thing is, though, I often had the feeling that if he had waited in life to marry, he might have chosen differently. He and Sylvia met so young. And women were drawn to him, oh boy were they. You have to wonder about the alternate path that magnificent man might have taken. Instead he settled. You should let that be an example to you. To settle is to limit yourself. It's to live your life in a shadow. Never* settle. *Do you hear me? Never.*

On another drive—

Darling, you do know there's nothing wrong with not liking your parent or grandparent . . . your father or [pregnant pause] *. . . your mother or* [longer pause] *. . . your grandmother perhaps? I don't mind confiding to you that I for example hated my father, every last cell of me hated that man. I could count my memories of him on one hand. That's the plain truth of it. And my Goldstein grandmother—Sam's mother— I've told you before, she was a complete and utter horror. You have to know that it would be perfectly all right if you told me what you felt deep down about your father or* [another pause] *. . . anyone else. Syl for example . . . or your mother. You know I would always understand.*

Listening to this talk was one thing, one hard thing; another was having to endure the waiting that followed, the big gap of silence that she allowed to open up between us, so that I might fill it with some kind of response. But what was I to say? I love my grandmother, I'm sorry you don't? You're right: in fact my father, your brother, with his rage and his temper and his distance, is a problem for me? My mother, *deep down*—what? Every possible answer I could think of filled me with dread.

I let the silence sit. It opened up between us like an enormous chasm that I was terrified I might fall into. Waiting with that big, dark silence between us was excruciating, but I faced it down, deliberately this time, by going dead. I went deader even than I did when Alfred and his sidekicks started in on their taunts. Deader even than when I was kicked or groped by those cretins. I went dead, but I was a special kind of dead. Dead and waiting. Dead and watching. Dead yet blisteringly awake.

On still another drive, as we were heading down the hill to pick Sylvia up for dinner one evening—

A good writer doesn't just tell, Mike. Surely we've talked about this before? A good writer shows—in stories, in a novel. The thing you have to remember about movies is that the image will always prevail over the words. Sometimes a simple action is just so much stronger than any line of dialogue your unc or I could possibly dream up together—and we dream up some pretty good ones.

My aunt pulled over, and I was sent, as usual, to collect my grandmother. It took us several minutes to return to the street because Sylvia had to finish packing up a sponge cake she had baked. She had to look for her handbag, then her glasses and her keys. And then she had to lock the door, and double-check that it was locked . . .

We returned to the street to find my aunt impatiently tapping her fingers against the steering wheel.

Once Sylvia was in the car, Hank sent her dark glasses sliding down to the tip of her nose and examined Sylvia's face.

"Really, sweetheart? Don't you think, just for the children's sake, that you should make the least little bit of effort?"

I believed I saw confusion, or maybe something stronger, something closer to dismay, flicker across my grandmother's face; but she was also strategic, always strategic, so that when my aunt said, "Sit back," she sat back.

"Now tilt your head."

She did that too.

My aunt withdrew from her compendious handbag a large transparent plastic pouch. Out came rouge, pancake, an eyebrow pencil, lipstick. She placed her hand under my grandmother's chin and tilted her graceful head back so that it was easier to apply a lathering of cosmetics. She worked with concentration over several very long, to me very disagreeable, minutes. At one point, biting her lip, she leaned back, and I saw that she had the same assessing look on her face that she did when she was redecorating a room.

When she finished, Sylvia looked like she had been frosted, like a cake. She was wearing a mask. A clown's mask, with round apple-red cheeks and her pale silver eyebrows inked over and exaggerated. They could have been drawn by a child—a naughty child.

"Much better," my aunt said, leaning back. She flipped down the visor on the passenger's side of the car, which was fitted with a mirror. Sylvia examined her new face. She said nothing.

"Irving and Merona need to know that you are well. They have so much on their plates, don't you agree?"

Sylvia nodded silently.

I tried to make contact with my grandmother in the mirror, but she didn't meet my eyes. She simply raised the visor and waited for my aunt to start the car; but once we were off, Sylvia looked over her shoulder and that red, overly red, mouth flashed me a thin knowing smile that made me feel like I had just been kneed in the stomach.

I had no idea how, but my aunt uncannily sensed, or guessed, whenever I had a plan to spend time on Ogden Drive. She would phone me up on a Friday and ask if I was free to spend Saturday with her. If I hesitated, her tone would shift, and in a voice that was half reasonable and half aggrieved she would say, "Yes is yes, no is no, and nobody's feelings were ever hurt by a plain clean no. It's just that I'm blue and it would be so larky if we could go out tomorrow and noodle around. Shall I pick you up at nine, Lovey?"

Other times, more overtly and when she was in a darker mood, I'd hear: "Saturday your mother says you are at your grandmother's. Again."

Again. How could one simple word cut with such a sharp blade?

"Can you rearrange? I thought we might go out to Pasadena for the day. I'm sure Syl won't mind—is it even *healthy* for a boy to spend so much time in the company of an old lady?"

If I did screw up my courage to say that I truly wasn't available, I would hear an icy "Well, suit yourself, then."

The phone would go dead before I had a chance to say goodbye. And it might not ring again for days afterward. Longer, sometimes.

When I next visited her house she would show me the treasures she had found on the day she had gone out without me. "Do you see all the fun you missed out on? Maybe next time you'll reconsider. Assuming there is a next time."

I tried my best to be a good boy, a good nephew. To be a good boy, a good nephew, meant being available whenever my aunt needed or wanted me; it meant enduring her subtle and not-so-subtle diminishments of my grandmother and my mother and my father in silence and apparent agreement; it meant being asked questions I was uncomfortable being asked and even more uncomfortable answering; and it meant buoying her increasingly unpredictable moods while sidestepping her flashes of vitriol and rage.

It meant having not just moments of a knotted stomach but weeks, then months. For nearly a year, more days than not I came home from school and went to bed with an electric heating pad or a scalding hot-water bottle that my mother would prepare for me; afterward she would sit by my bed and read or hold my hand until the pains passed, her face tight with distress. These episodes had no identifiable pattern. They were only occasionally related to a specific event. They would come on before I ate, after I ate. In the morning, at night. In the middle of the night. There was no habit of mine I found a way to change, even with my parents' help, that made me feel better.

They began taking me to doctors. Our pediatrician, then our family doctor, several specialists who sent me for tests: blood tests, X-rays. For one of them I was required to drink a quart of repulsive white liquid that was supposed to render my insides visible under a certain kind of X-ray. I took one sip and then threw the glass across the floor with a vehemence that left my mother alternately mopping up (with paper towels) and apologizing and finally breaking down in tears.

My stomach did not want to be seen into. I did not want my stomach to be seen into. My stomach or any other part of me.

I heard my father on the phone to Dr. Derwin, our family doctor, in a voice more worried than I had ever heard him use before: "The boy is not a complainer. He does not make up illness. That's not who he is. There must be *something* wrong. *Something* you can do . . ."

——— ——

In the end my aunt prevailed. Not because she compelled me to relinquish or betray my love for my grandmother, but because she had an ally, unchosen by her, that was an even greater threat than she could ever be to the special safe world that Sylvia and I came to share on Ogden Drive, and that was time. Nasty, unfeeling (feeling-less) time that slapped my grandmother around as it slaps everyone around eventually. Time gave her a curving, hurting back, diminishing energies, reduced hearing, a mushy heart. *Mushy* was Dr. Derwin's word, and it did not bode well; as with my mysterious stomach ailments, there was not much he could do about *mushy*, not much at all.

Time gave her glassy eyes too. I remember them particularly. The roundness and dampness of them, the redness at their rims, as though they had been outlined with a demon's felt-tip pen—here was a makeup artist far crueler than my aunt. I saw these red-rimmed eyes reflected with a special clarity in the dining room mirror on a Friday night in late March 1973, when I realized for the first time (but how only for the first time?) that with my long, bony body and frizzled mop of hair I had come to tower over my ever-shrinking grandmother. I'd taken her into my arms, briefly, to say goodbye—just for that one evening, or so I thought.

There had been a lot of debate: Should I stay over, as we had planned, or should I go to the movies with my aunt and uncle, as they wanted me to? I could not make up my mind.

Sylvia said, "Go to the movies. You can come by tomorrow for breakfast."

As usual I hesitated, I vacillated. I hesitated some more.

"It's up to you, Michael," my mother said impatiently. "But you need to make up your mind. I need to get the boys up the hill and start dinner . . ."

"We'll have another night," said my grandmother, flashing me one of her toothy smiles.

There was such a strange feeling in the air. My feet seemed to have sent roots down into the cracks between the floorboards. My stomach felt even more active than usual, gurgling and constricting as I stood there trying to make up my mind. Reluctantly I agreed to go.

"Michaelah," she said.

"Yes, Grandma?"

"Be sure to enjoy."

In our family all the truly bad things happened in the middle of the night and remained hidden from the children until after the sun rose.

That Saturday morning I woke up to find the door to my parents' room wide open at seven o'clock. This in itself was unprecedented, since as soon as we boys had been able to look after ourselves in the morning, my mother had reverted to being the late sleeper she'd always been.

My mother was sitting up in bed wearing dark glasses and sipping coffee or, rather, holding a coffee mug, which was sending up little plumes of steam that dissolved somewhere near the region of her eyes or where her eyes would have been if they weren't covered up by her dark glasses, though not even these could conceal the tears that were spilling out of them, out and down her cheeks and onto the sheets and the blanket below.

I knew what she was going to say even before she said it. I had known it in the mirror the night before, I had known it in my rooted feet, my indecisiveness, my grandmother's red-rimmed eyes, my stomach; I had known, or I had sensed, rather, that something wasn't right, or as it had been, and wasn't going to go on being as it had been, and what it had been was good, precious really, these last years with Sylvia on Ogden Drive. They had come to an end at three o'clock that morning, when the phone rang and Zora Bishop, the woman who had just recently been engaged to stay at night with my grandmother on account of that mushy heart, called to say that there was a liquidy, choking sound coming from deep inside my grandmother's chest, and would my mother and my father come as fast as possible, as fast as the ambulance she had summoned, fast, fast, fast. Which they did, though it was not fast enough to matter.

Later that same morning, my mother padded down the hall to tell me that my aunt was on the telephone.

"I'm so sorry about Sylvia," she said when I picked up. "I know how much you loved her—we all did."

My throat tightened. It tightened so much it nearly closed. Did my aunt truly love Sylvia, as she said, and had I misread her in these past months and years? Were my perceptions so off? Was it possible?

"I wonder if you might be free to spend some time with me this morning, Lovey."

I wasn't sure, I told her. I told her I would have to see what my mother had to say and would call her back when I did.

My mother was going back to sleep. She said it was fine for me to go out with my aunt, as long as I was back after lunch. People would be starting to come over then, she said. To see her, she said. To see all of us. As they had after Huffy died. "To sit shiva," she said, "even though that's not really what we do anymore, not the way we used to. Your grandfather Shalom, when his father died, surely I must have told you, he covered all the mirrors in his house and tore his clothing, and then he turned over a bucket and sat on it for seven whole days. And he didn't even like the man . . ."

By the time I got dressed the Riviera was idling in the driveway. Not honking, on this day, simply idling.

"It's a sad day for all of us," Auntie Hankie said when I got in.

I nodded, willing the sting out of my eyes.

She lowered her cheek, and the Caswell-Massey came toward me as usual. I kissed her, also as usual, and she backed out of the driveway.

"I haven't seen your uncle so gloomy in years. Of course he's just exhausted. He's gone back to bed too. I tried myself, but you know me—I've never been one much for naps."

We headed down Lookout to Laurel Canyon, where we followed the familiar bends in the road, descending the hill and heading toward the city. Where in the city? Where was it so important for my aunt to go on the day that my grandmother had died?

I began to feel an uneasiness even before my aunt turned left at Hollywood Boulevard. It deepened as we continued east on that familiar stretch of road.

At Ogden she turned right and parked across the street from The Apartment. She looked for a moment at the building she had not entered in the years since Huffy had died, except that one time when she siphoned off the furniture and objects she wanted for herself, and then she turned to me and asked me for my help. She and my uncle were going on location with their newest movie, she reminded me. They had been planning to leave for Georgia a week earlier, but with Sylvia not quite right they had decided to postpone their departure. Now they were to leave the next weekend. That gave her a scant five days to *deal with things*. It was a *big job*, she said, and she needed the *most able* hands she knew: my hands.

I listened to all this without quite understanding what she was intending. It was as though the conversation were happening on the other side of a glass wall, or maybe up on a screen. It was only when her car door opened, and she got out and waited for me to open my door and get out, that I realized she was asking me to go into The Apartment with her that very morning, the morning of my grandmother's death, and help her *deal with things*. What things? Deal how? I had no idea. But as usual, even with a tightening stomach, I followed.

I followed her where she had not gone for nearly four years, in between the red brick pillars and up the pink concrete stairs, past the rosebushes and the birds-of-paradise and the camellias, to the front door of The Apartment. She fumbled in her purse for an envelope, which she opened. She took out a key and inserted it into the lock. The door did not open at first, and she asked me to help. I knew the key, I knew the lock, I knew the door . . .

The Apartment was more silent than I had ever before experienced it. And it was dark and cold, as if the very breath had gone out of it too.

Zora had made my grandmother's bed and drawn the curtains, but she had not touched anything else.

When I saw Sylvia's silver-rimmed eyeglasses lying upside down on her bedside table, just where she had set them before going to sleep—assuming she slept (had she slept? had she cried out or known what was happening?)—I felt my heart twist in my chest and I thought, I will never forget seeing these glasses, lying on this table, in this darkened room, in this apartment, on this street, on this morning.

I stood there for the longest time, looking at the glasses, the books by the bed, the bed with its slight indentation in the middle where she had nestled. I looked at my grandmother's robe draped over the back of the self-rocking rocking chair, the dish full of spare change on the top of the dresser, the photographs of my grandfather, the card I had made her, a month earlier, for her seventy-fourth birthday, or rather for the day she decided was her seventy-fourth birthday, which was Lincoln's birthday, because he was, to her mind, the greatest president and the finest of men, and if she could choose when to be born, why not choose to share the day with a human being like that?

As I looked at all this, my aunt stepped over to the window. She yanked the curtains open, and light flooded into the room.

"Let's get started," she said.

She went into the kitchen and returned with a box of large black garbage bags. She took one out, and shook some air into it with a loud snapping motion. It was as though an enormous black raven had just materialized between us.

Swoosh went the raven, and my aunt turned to my grandmother's dresser, bottom drawer first. In big untidy handfuls she took out her sweaters, her hats, her scarves, and she fed them to the hungry black bird while I looked on, paralyzed.

"Won't you at least hold the bag open for me?"

When I didn't move, she said, "What's the matter, Mike? Are you not up to this? It's okay if you're not."

I didn't answer.

"Would you like me to take you back up the hill? I will, you know . . ."

And leave her there, to throw my grandmother's world away? I shook my head.

After my aunt emptied out my grandmother's dresser, she moved on to the kitchen. She tossed out the food from the refrigerator, the spices in the cupboard. Then she began removing dishes and dividing them into stacks: take, give away, donate. She worked efficiently, rapidly, making her way through room after room with no particular pattern or plan that I could discern, but with abundant, I would say almost manic, energy.

I was accustomed to seeing my aunt assemble interiors. The disassembling went much more quickly.

I followed behind her, surreptitiously rescuing from the trash the bits and pieces of my grandmother, of her life, that I thought meant something. The straw handkerchief box that I had bought her for her birthday, earned with my plant-watering money. The notes and drawings my brothers and I had given her over the years. Her favorite sparkly pin. Her hair combs. The book of Hebrew poetry by Hayyim Nahman Bialik that had been inscribed to her by the rabbi at the synagogue where she taught Hebrew for so many years. Her wallet, her bus pass, her pocket mirror . . .

I added these things to a brown Sunfax grocery bag that I hid behind the sofa in the living room. I watched the raven swallow up the rest in its big black maw.

After about an hour the knots in my stomach were making it difficult for me to stand upright. I took the phone from its little niche in the hall, stretched the cord into the back bedroom, Sylvia's former bedroom, and called my parents. "She's throwing all of Grandma away," I whispered into the receiver.

"Who?"

"Auntie Hankie."

"You're at The Apartment?" my father said. "*That's* where you are?"

"Yes," I said, choking up.

"We'll be right there."

They came—both of them together. My father haggard and unshaven, my mother weary, with swollen eyes behind tortoiseshell sunglasses. She had pulled on a sweater over her nightgown, and she was still wearing her slippers.

My aunt seemed surprised to see them appear at the screen door. She looked at them, then at me. Then she appeared to understand.

She said, "Corky and I are leaving next Saturday, as you know." She did not say this with any acknowledgment of how strange it was for her to be taking apart this household on this particular morning. "And it does all, mostly, belong to my mother," she added, gesturing at The Apartment.

"That would be *our* mother, Hankie," my father said. "But today? Really must you start on this today? And with the boy——"

"I asked him if he wanted me to take him back up the hill."

My father said, "We're taking him now."

When I realized that my parents were not going to stop my aunt from discarding my grandmother, that even my mother, with her new look, her new house, and her newly raised consciousness, in her sadness or grief or surprise, or maybe powerlessness—there was always that in the face of my aunt's personality—was simply going to let Hank continue to discard the modest tangible record of this good woman's life on earth, her papers and letters even, maybe also her photographs, I felt a willfulness rise up in me that I had never known before.

"I'm not going anywhere," I said firmly.

"Please, darling," my mother said. "This isn't a healthy place for you. This isn't—" She glanced at my aunt. "This isn't *right*."

The three of them looked at me expectantly . . . and I looked at the three of them in return.

"I'm staying right here," I said.

My aunt's face was ablaze, mistakenly, with triumph. But the triumph, I knew in my heart, was actually mine.

PART II

FIVE

MY UNCLE'S CLOSET (IN MY AUNT'S HOUSE)

Early in the spring of 1969, before Sylvia died, even before Huffy died, my aunt and uncle invited me out to one of our special dinners together, and afterward my uncle took an unfamiliar route home. At the elementary school, instead of heading straight up the narrow streets that threaded through the old part of the canyon, he turned right and followed Laurel Pass to Mulholland. At Mulholland he turned left, and after a few minutes he turned left again onto a newly laid street named Skyline Drive. He drove on its rich, unmarred black asphalt until, near the top of the slope, he abruptly pulled over and parked.

"Let's take a look at the view," he said.

We got out of the car and walked out onto an empty lot. The San Fernando Valley stretched before us, its infinity of gently pulsing lights accompanied by a distant unnerving purr of traffic. It looked unreal, like a projection, a backdrop.

"A sea of light," my uncle said. "You're on top of the world up here. Don't you think, Mike? Mike, isn't it terrific?"

Nodding, I stepped forward to look closer.

Suddenly my uncle's hand shot out to grab my arm. "Careful, Mike. You're about to trip over the sofa!"

I looked down at the raw earth.

"Watch it, that's my desk you're plowing into."

The bookcases.

My reading chair.

Your aunt's bed. (Irving was famous for his nocturnal tossing and turning; they'd slept separately since soon after they were married.)

The toilet. "You don't want to step into the toilet, do you?"

He was giddy, joyful. It took me a moment to catch on but then, *ah.*

My aunt was behind us, pacing and waving her arms around like bicycle wheels. "I see fourteen-foot ceilings," she said. "And columns. And a mansard roof, of course. Palladio. Louis Quatorze. I'm going to call it *La Maison Ravetch. Notre maison!*"

——— ———

The land we stood on that night went way back, as in time-immemorial back. Only three months earlier, there hadn't been any streets on this part of the hill, just California wilderness: live oak, cottonwood, sage scrub, bay laurel—a sea of green and silver and brown, lots of brown, that would become spiked after the spring rains with splashes of pink, purple, and yellow. In late summer it would turn arid and bleak. Combustible. Sometimes, actually, it combusted.

This land was on a hill in a canyon. A near oxymoron, when you linger over the words, because shouldn't hills and canyons oppose each other? But they went together there in Laurel Canyon. Technically the hills were part of a transverse mountain range, a giant fold of land that started way out at Catalina Island and continued past downtown L.A. The earth was composed of ocean sediment, volcanic rock, decomposed granite, all of it millions and millions of years old.

The canyon was cut by a stream, which in the wet season continued to trickle along on the older side of the canyon, where we lived. The stream was fed by a spring whose origin no one could find, and it was topped off with rain and the runoff from sprinklers and garden hoses. Several houses could be reached only by bridges that connected them to the street. Underneath, the water moved sleepily downhill, until it disappeared into a storm drain and found its way to the Pacific.

On our side of the canyon certain houses dated to the turn of the century. Some were built out of stones harvested from the banks of the stream. Others were made of logs or clapboard siding. They were deliberately rustic, simple country retreats. In the olden days (that is, the early part of the twentieth century), when there were mountain lions and the deer were plentiful, Angelenos escaped the pressures of city life and came to these hills to breathe clean air and hike and hunt. In about 1913 a developer began attracting weekenders with a trackless (electric) trolley that brought them up from Sunset Boulevard. He carved the slopes into lots, paved streets, installed lights and a roadside tavern. A hotel went up, then soon burned down. In time the city caught up with the canyon, and the retreats were enlarged or razed, and bigger, newer houses were built. The rusticators were replaced by the silent screen stars, then the talking movie stars, then the musicians. A grade school was established to serve the growing number of families, and the neighborhood grew into a kind of urban suburbia, although at heart it remained geographically and temperamentally isolated from the rest of the city, tranquil and bohemian in spirit if not always in actual fact.

My father was the first in the family to move in. In 1954 he built himself a *bachelor pad*—a name to go with the time. Two bedrooms, a fireplace, hardwood floors, and a slip of a garden that backed up against a steep slope over on Lookout, where a few years later his wife (ever after, in congenial moods, his *bride*) joined him and where I was born.

When the next child came along, my parents built a bigger house farther up the canyon, on a more ample, sunnier lot on Greenvalley Road. Meanwhile my aunt and uncle followed and built their first house over the hill from us on Wonderland Park Avenue; after them came Norm and Linda and the girls. After them came my father's oldest friend, Murray, and his family. Everyone knew everyone, the children all went to school together at the canyon school; we lived in a country village in the middle of a large, complicated city.

Until 1968 the houses simply stopped at the top of the hill, on a street appropriately named Crest View. There was pavement, and then there was chaparral, self-propagating as it always had. In places it was crisscrossed with footpaths, deer paths still used by actual deer or coyote or the occasional mountain lion. Here we explored, my brothers and Barrie and Wendy and I. Here we flew kites, trapped caterpillars, and netted butterflies. Here we knew nature, and felt free.

Then one day the land was developed. It was almost as if the mountain moved. Which in a way it did. The wilderness was erased so completely it looked like it had undergone a military attack. The raw earth was compacted, graded, and cut into lots that were separated by tiny slopes. Curbs, sidewalks, then new street signs were brought in; power lines, storm drains, and sewer connections were buried underground. When the Santa Anas blew, the gravel was stirred into tiny tornadoes, and the air smelled of sage, eucalyptus, and worry. Somebody's future was waiting to unfold.

A later time, another drive. Coming up that same road early in the new year, my uncle gestured at the windshield. On the hill ahead of us a wall, a single wall, was framed and standing.

"Look at that, Mike," he said, again in that giddy voice. "Our new house. It's actually happening."

It happened. Step by step, piece by piece. I loved watching it go up almost as much as my aunt and uncle did. I loved the way truckloads of raw materials were worked into walls, then rooms. I loved the smells of the unfinished lumber, the tar paper, the cotton candy–like (but so toxic) fiberglass insulation. There were columns all right. And parquet floors, and elaborate carved moldings. I learned a whole new vocabulary: pilasters, entablatures, volutes; Doric, Ionic, Corinthian. Plinths. Architraves. Triglyphs, metopes. Rosette, oeil-de-boeuf. Fleur-de-lis. Trompe l'oeil.

You'd have thought we were in Athens or Rome. Or the London of Christopher Wren. Or pre-Haussmann Paris, beloved Paree (*sans* the unlovable French), the epicenter of all that was chic. But this was Los Angeles in the late 1960s, where you were free to make up your own look, your own reality; you could pick and choose from architecture, history, literature—from the gods themselves: Palladio, Mansard,

Le Nôtre, Jefferson. A direct line led from them to my aunt—or so it seemed.

Later on, much later, I learned that she was in fact working within a local precedent. It even had a name, or was eventually given one: Hollywood Regency, self-invented, a fashionable pastiche that—fittingly—derived as much from the precincts of set design as it did architecture. Borrowed, exaggerated, adapted to the climate (high ceilings, large windows, swimming or reflecting pools replenished with curly-haired cast-stone cherubs holding dolphins spitting water), it was a little bit fake and a lot fantastical, like a movie set, only finished on all sides and fully functional. And all too fitting for the screenwriters whose flair for dialogue had earned the money to bring about the maison in the first place and whose complex personal dramas would play out within its hand-stuccoed walls.

My aunt and uncle had engaged an architect, but his job, essentially, was to translate their—predominantly her—vision: rooms that were few in number though large in scale and size; a floor plan tailored to the particular needs of a childless couple who worked together from home and were desirous of peace and privacy; a terrace for entertaining; a pool, of course; and nothing to impede that insistent view.

Joséphine had Malmaison; my aunt had *the* maison. She alone was the unchallenged mistress of the interiors. She maintained control over nearly every inch of every surface of every room, almost as though the physical space were an extension of her body, her face. Indeed the maison was the face she showed the world, layers and layers of accumulated objects, fields of furniture, prints and drawings and paintings, all of it *period*, or if not *period* at least *raffish* or expressing a distinct *flair* or *panache*. Wherever possible each element was the *ne plus ultra* of this or that table or candlestick or chair. France, England, Italy, in that order, were the preferred countries of manufacture. Eighteen-twenty was the preferred cutoff date, the years (the centuries) afterward representing a *falling-off in quality* accompanied by *a tendency toward the vulgar*, with the most asperity of all directed at anything even remotely *mo-derne*. This mass of decoration was assembled locally during my aunt's Saturday antiquing jaunts (Aunt

Trudy having replaced my grandmother as her companion) or shipped over from Yurp following the annual fall trip to London and those exotic hinterlands known as *the continent* and occasionally at auction. Over the years it was refined, weeded out, added to, following such governing precepts as

> *Less is not more; more is more*
> *Go for baroque*
> *Individual objects are boring; collections are what make an*
>   *impact*
> *All the best things come in pairs*
> *Gather ye rosebuds*

Which actually meant gather more things, and which, as my aunt aged, morphed into

> *Follow the pleasure principle—at any cost!*

This, too, equated acquiring with experience and was intended as an antidote to her ever-darker moods.

In the whole of this house my uncle had a voice in only two places. One was the library, where he designed the bookshelves and was master over his desk, the typewriter table that stood at a right angle next to it, and a small low table alongside his reading chair that contained the books and periodicals he had under way. The other was his closet, which was nearly the size of my bedroom at home, and was fitted out with drawers, cupboards, shelves, and compartments of varying widths and heights for different kinds of clothes, manuscripts, and memorabilia.

The scale and intricacy of my uncle's closet, like the maison itself, seemed entirely congruent with the world he and my aunt shared, because everything about the two of them was elaborate and oversized, larger than life. They were charismatic, talented, verbally dexterous, worldly—alternate parents who lived in an alternate reality. Actually, *surrogate parents* is what they called themselves and my brothers and I sometimes called them, without ever thinking that, as we had two viable parents of our own, there was a certain diceyness to this concept; even the words *surrogate parents*, rather like that pairing of hills and canyon, were something to linger over, though for many years nobody did.

My aunt and uncle were sorcerers. They put words on paper that made actors talk and movies move. They envisioned a house that looked like a scaled-down *palais*, and it sprang up out of the earth, just like that. Whatever they wanted, thanks to the impressive sums their screenplays commanded, they had more than enough money to buy. They came back from their travels exuding a sensibility, an aura of knowing otherness, foreignness. To spend time with them was to feel worlds open up, worlds within worlds within worlds.

They were the people who introduced me to painting (but nothing abstract), music (no one beyond Brahms), literature, theater, early movies, all those architecture and design gods, and in time Yurp. In all these categories standards and hierarchies (Matisse over Picasso, Truffaut over Welles, painting over photography) prevailed. They imposed a hierarchy on human beings too, one whereby, following birth order, but for no other evident reason that I perceived at the time, I ranked first.

My uncle was never as overt or as categorical about his feelings for me as my aunt was, but I also felt from him a special life-altering attention. There was an implicitness to his affection, a steadiness and a patience with the indirect and the unspoken that happily drew me to him as to a campfire in a dark wood. He was a man of deeply eccentric habits with a sharp mind, a sparkling sense of irony, and a great capacity for fun. Altogether he was the embodiment of a kind of maleness that was utterly different from my father's; yet it was a conditional maleness, meaning that there was one context in which my uncle repeatedly weakened and faded to the point of nearly disappearing, and that was in the intricate, yin-yangy dance of his marriage to my aunt, which both of them described unironically—more than that, boastfully—as symbiotic.

All the best things come in pairs: this was the axiom they lived by, unfailingly.

——— ———

The rooms in the maison were divided into public and private. You walked into a large entry hall that had a marble floor (white with a brown border), a sixteen-foot-high ceiling under the mansard roof, and a pair of niches that flanked the doors to the living room. The living room, at nearly thirty by forty feet, felt like a cross between a hotel lobby and a private museum gallery and opened directly to the dining room on the left and the library on the right. All three rooms shared the same parquet in a pattern of large amber-hued oak squares set on the diagonal and framed with bands of mahogany. Casements, crown moldings, and baseboards were extensive and elaborate; the windows were long and narrow and looked out over the swimming pool to that shimmering view beyond.

From the dining room you circled back through the breakfast room, kitchen, and several walk-in service closets and pantries, including one that was the size of a bedroom and was dedicated to dishes alone; a small hall continued on to a maid's room and bath. On the other side of the living room, the library led to my aunt and uncle's large bedroom, a hall, and a guest room and bath. Adjacent to the master bedroom was my aunt's bathroom and closet, and between the master bedroom and the library was my uncle's smaller bath and his mysteriously larger closet, the largest closet in the house by far.

"If only it had a window," my uncle sometimes declared as he stood at its threshold, "I might move right in."

He said this within my aunt's earshot, typically on a day in which she had brought more *objets* into the maison. Sometimes she took it as affectionate play; sometimes she would say crisply, "Why don't you?"

She also said: "Your uncle's closet—it's one of the most peculiar rooms I have ever beheld."

And: "Your uncle's closet—I don't know how he got away with that. It's larger than mine by a long shot."

And: "Your uncle's closet—how I would like to get my hands on that room and turn it into something really *charmant*."

Yet it was the one place in the house that remained immune to her decorative fervor. His other precincts had more mixed fortunes.

Every time she passed his desk she said, "That desk is the ugliest object in the state of California. I have to avert my eyes when I walk by."

"It suits me," my uncle said.

"I could find you a period one the same size. Something eighteenth-century and really *good*."

"People were smaller then, Hank, and so was the furniture. I need room to cross my legs where I sit."

"But it's *mo-derne*."

"That's right. Danish *mo-derne*, I believe you call it."

"*I* call it vulgar," she said. "At least let me put these Chinese lamps on it."

"I'm used to the ones that are there now."

"That's because you're a creature of habit. Just let me *try* these, will you, Corky?"

My uncle emitted one of his theatrical six-step sighs.

"And hang a trumeau mirror over it."

"I would prefer not to look at myself when I'm working."

"But you're such an *attractive* man. You attracted *me*, did you not? Anyway after a while it just becomes background."

The mirror went up. The lamps stayed. But so did the desk.

Another time: "If you *must* keep that desk, the accoutrements need to be improved. Do your pencils really need to live in that ghastly wooden thing?"

"It's called a pencil holder, and I like it. I've had it forever."

The pencil holder went too, eventually.

"Do you need that calendar?"

"If you want us to have any sensible professional or social life, I do."

The calendar remained.

"At least that god-awful chair—"

"That god-awful chair is good for my back."

"You're spoiling my pleasure, Corky!"

"Your pleasure shouldn't be so easily spoiled, my love."

The closet was a rectangle of maybe twelve by fourteen feet that had been fitted out according to my uncle's specifications. On the left-hand side were two banks of drawers, graduated in size and depth as they reached the floor. Some were dedicated to clothing, others to papers. Above these drawers was a deep open shelf filled with manuscripts, which had been bound in leather and were arranged in chronological order of their composition. At the left were copies of the five or six plays my uncle had written as a young man. ("All of them spectacular failures," he said with the boastful nonchalance of someone who went on to write so many successful movie scripts.) Next were the screenplays that, beginning in the mid-1950s, he and my aunt had written together.

The other material related to their careers included two cartons of typescripts of light-spirited, O. Henry–esque stories that my aunt produced in her twenties and thirties for magazines like *McCall's* and *Collier's* and *The Saturday Evening Post*. There were also several scrapbooks with reviews of their earlier movies; at some point my uncle gave up tracking this sort of thing. Awards were either tucked away in a drawer or very modestly hung on a strip of wall outside the closet, where they were by intention seldom seen.

There was always a carbon copy of the script in progress, held between a stiff, worn canvas-covered binder, in the topmost drawer. A second copy was kept in the trunk of my uncle's car; in the event my aunt and uncle had to flee the maison in one of those notorious canyon fires, their words would survive.

In front of the bound manuscripts stood my uncle's smoking paraphernalia: the cigars (in their humidor) and the pipes (hung off a special wooden rack), the cigar trimmer, the pipe cleaners, and the leather tobacco box that lent such a strong scent to the room as to the man; a perplexing scent, since as a child Irving suffered from severe asthma compounded by annual bouts of lung-scarring pneumonia and was probably the last person who should have smoked cigarettes, a habit he gave up, with great difficulty and the help of a hypnotist, in his early forties. The pipe and cigar habit that followed provoked a curious justification: "You see, I no longer inhale. I merely *taste* the tobacco. And oh, do I love that taste."

This was very Irving: both the paradox (an asthmatic who smoked) and the fact that he commented, and invited comment, on it. He had

way of regarding the whole of his life—at least the whole that remained apart from my aunt—with a kind of perpetual double vision:
he lived and he observed his own way of living; he accumulated a
basket of odd and mostly endearing habits and made sure that he was
alternately liked and mocked for them; and he told stories about his
youth with such polish and verve, and with a certain darkness of feeling edited out, that I sometimes forgot they had happened to an
actual person rather than a character he had invented.

All this seeing and commenting, much of it infused with delicious irony, was a way my uncle escaped being seen. It was another
reason why I found his closet so captivating: here was my uncle the
man, unmediated by my uncle the narrator—or by my aunt.

Opposite the built-in drawers was a freestanding cupboard with
smaller doors and cabinets, Victorian and therefore definitively *not*
period. How it made its way across the threshold of the maison I
cannot say; perhaps my uncle sneaked it in one day when my aunt
was out so that he could have an extra place to store a few cherished
things.

In this cupboard he kept the tefillin that had belonged to my
grandfather the rabbi. They were buttoned into embroidered burgundy velvet pouches that emanated an obscure, almost clandestine
spirituality—clandestine because of their illogical presence in my
uncle's closet, since Irving was so completely, perhaps defiantly, unre-
ligious. Once, when I was older, I asked him how he and his father
had negotiated the subject of God, if they had. "My father knew that
I felt that a rational man cannot believe in God," he said. "After the
twentieth century? Who are you kidding? He knew that I thought
that, and I knew that he didn't agree with that; he also knew that
I adored him even if I disagreed with him, and we left it there."

As often happened with my uncle, I sensed that the moment might
have been more complex, but this subject, like certain other subjects,
we too left there.

In another drawer in the Victorian cupboard, my uncle kept safely
out of sight two rare, fragile, and cherished photographs of his mother,
my grandmother Sylvia, and her six sisters, which were taken by an

itinerant photographer in Safed, where they had lived until the First World War dispatched her to her fate in Montreal. Nearby was my uncle's honorable discharge from the next war, in which he had served—briefly—as a pipe fitter's helper in the Army until he had the first of several severe asthma attacks and was relieved of his military duties. There was a small box of photographs documenting the first trip he and my aunt took to Europe, in 1946, and a scattering of photographs of us children, all of them given to him by my mother, since after that first trip to Europe, even though they returned there without fail every fall, my aunt and uncle never again picked up a camera of their own.

"Photographs *conceal* the truth; they don't *reveal* it," my aunt liked to say, often in the presence of my mother, who was an ardent shutterbug and lifelong documentarian of our family.

My mother's response, always in private: "Your aunt and uncle don't care about photographs because they don't have children. It's the same reason, if you ask me, they don't keep cards or letters, even the sentimental or significant ones. They have no reason to worry about the personal traces they leave behind, no interest in making a record of their lives for other people to come along and think about later on. Sometimes I wonder if they even care about *remembering* their lives since they get so much of the past wrong."

In a more exasperated mood she added, "They don't care about negotiation or compromise either. Having children teaches you to moderate your expectations. It's one of the many things your aunt and uncle have never learned to do. If only they'd had children of their own . . ."

How many times were we to hear that phrase said about—lobbed at—my aunt and uncle? *If only they'd had children of their own.* Sometimes this was accompanied by *If only they had some real-life limits*, a contribution of my father's that referred to the skewed credit-to-debit balance sheet they lived by that facilitated my aunt's unbridled collecting and was free from such gritty demands as navigating the ups and downs of sustaining a business or raising and educating three children. *If only they'd had children, if only they had limits . . .* they'd have learned to be more reasonable, more pliable, more realistic; to have realistic expectations of actual human beings instead of the inventions that come pouring out of those mixed-up heads of theirs.

My parents were right about the personal traces, the compromises, and all the rest except, arguably, for the remembering, which my aunt and uncle did selectively and with the expert streamlining of seasoned story-builders. And while it was true that my uncle loved to throw things away (cards and letters, bills as they came in and were instantly paid, newspapers and magazines the minute they had been reviewed for material worth reading), I think it may have had more to do with distancing himself from my aunt's acquiring habits. In his case less was purposefully less, and brought on a certain lightness in the physical atmosphere that coincided with a certain lightness in the man.

My uncle did, however, occasionally care about memorabilia that related to the past in a suggestive way—and not only his past. A particular gem in the Victorian cupboard was the diary that my aunt kept when she was eleven, whose entries he delighted in whipping out and reading aloud:

" 'June 13, 1934. Practiced for the Rose Festival dance. I am very tired. June 14. Performance last night. Was stupendious. People were very inthusiastic'—*in*thusiastic."

Or: " 'August 22. King Alexander of Yugoslavia assinated while in France.' Sweetheart, I see that your spelling has remained quite consistent over the years."

My aunt missed the uxorious impulse that so clearly stood behind my uncle's gentle mockery; here, as often, she failed to see the humor, period. She pouted, stuck her nose up in the air, and said, "I really cannot understand why you two are so tickled by *stupendious* or *assinated* or anything else in those juvenile pages. The child is not, you know, the measure of the man—or woman, as the case may be."

Undaunted, my uncle found another savory entry to read from and be amused by, at least until my aunt's pout crossed over into less playful territory; then he beat one of his famous strategic retreats.

Irving was a master of the strategic retreat, as he was of the theatrical sigh, the dry aside, the raised eyebrow, the dissent telegraphed with the mere refocusing of a stare or a glance or a gesture he made with the crook of a finger, the back of a hand. It was no accident that, as an undergraduate, he had acted at UCLA and believed, for a time, that performing was to be his destiny. Yet for the most part, all this visual and gestural commentary was fundamentally benign, more Fred Astaire (a particular hero) than Ingmar Bergman (another hero, but only selectively welcomed as a household deity at the maison, where, arguably, he was a better fit).

Benign or consequential, my uncle's oppositions to my aunt were generally offered within his steadfast embrace of her. This was a man, after all, who on the occasion of their silver anniversary bestowed a trophy on his wife engraved with the words "For my darling Harriet, in commemoration of twenty-five years of unmitigated bliss" and, what's more, believed, at least at that moment in the engraver's shop, in the viability of those slippery words.

——— —

My uncle's devotion to my aunt was reflected in the closet, where the object that was given pride of place was a portrait of her by a man called Mischa Ashkenazy, a Russian immigrant painter who once had a certain following in Los Angeles and had been the lover of my grandfather Sam's lover—but presumably not at the same time. (Once my grandmother looked for love outside her marriage, she encouraged my grandfather to do the same. Given the internecine workings of these people, Sam's most sustained affair was with the painter's ex-girlfriend, who also happened to be the sister of one of Huffy's best friends, another intertwining that was so quintessentially Mighty Frank.)

And there was more: the painter Ashkenazy had a daughter, Dorothy Irene, nicknamed Mock, a woman with whom my aunt had a long, passionate friendship that, as with many of her friendships, ended when Hank, feeling injured, abruptly severed all contact overnight. These excommunications of hers were formidable affairs, enacted either by explosions in person or on the telephone or by brutally detailed, elegantly cadenced, rapid-fire letters that left no opening for negotiation or rapprochement, even after a connection of twenty or thirty years. They were alarming not only to the people, usually but not always women, who were banished but also to those of us who watched them go and wondered when our turn would roll around.

I always sensed, as I had with the tefillin, a special charge around this other portrait of my aunt. I could not figure out why the maison was jam-packed with eighteenth-century paintings of English and French aristocrats, while our very own aristocrat—to use the word as my aunt and uncle did, meaning someone who was cultivated and displayed a refinement of intellect and taste and whose ethics were irreproachable—had been sequestered in the closet. Was it because of who the painter, or maybe his daughter, was? Or was it because my aunt did not like living openly with an image that depicted her as she no longer appeared: young, inevitably, and with her hair spilling over her shoulders (the day she turned thirty, it went up and never came down again) and with a kind of beguilement in her eyes that made you understand why my uncle found her so devastatingly beautiful when they first met at MGM in 1945?

The portrait was neither as large nor as sober, nor as suggestive of her dark side, as the other portrait of her, the one done by my grandmother's cousin in Belgium. This one had more sweetness; it was executed in a style that you might generously say evoked Manet (on a sleepy day). Raphael Soyer (on a good day) might be closer. The paint was loosely applied in small rounded strokes and the palette had a rather greenish tinge, yet the woman—the girl of twentysomething—in the pale carved frame had an aliveness and a softness that made her feel like Hankie's kinder doppelgänger.

Depicted in three-quarter view, my painted aunt did not have those unnerving portrait eyes that seem to follow you around or hint, as in the later painting, at alarming interior chasms; their attention, instead, was light but fixed—on my uncle's closet. Might *that* have been the reason my uncle placed the portrait where he did: to compel my proxy aunt to take note of the one place in the maison that captured something of who he actually was?

Directly in the gaze of these portrait eyes my uncle had set an enlarged studio photograph that had been taken of him in 1921 in Newark, New Jersey, where he was born. In this photograph Irving the year-old baby lies on his stomach, naked on a bearskin rug, a glittery-eyed sepia-toned putto who smiles as he looks off into space, or his future.

See me naked, see me whole. Or as whole as the surfaces of a room, the contents of drawers and shelves, all of them curated with intention, permit. Is that what this tableau said?

It did to me.

As for the rest of what this longhaired Hankie looked down on, next to the Victorian chest was my uncle's one filing cabinet, intentionally left unlocked with, at the front of the top drawer, a manila folder marked WILL? That question mark was oh-so-very Irving. To find the answer, you merely had to dip an index finger between the cardboard, where on a sheet of yellow paper—yellow being my uncle's preferred color for all first-draft typescripts—a simple instruction was written in his distinctive loopy printing: "Contact lawyer."

A name and a telephone number followed.

Such a dry, you might say even sly, touch was very like Irving and very unlike my aunt, who as she aged began referring to that particular document with the threatening frequency (*she is in . . . he is out*) of a well-heeled dowager in Balzac or Dickens, the line between literature and life never having been so well delineated for her.

To the left of the filing cabinet was a shelf, at a friendly height to a boy, that was particularly important to me. When I was younger, it was here that my uncle left me his shirt cardboards so that I could use them to draw on or for arts-and-crafts projects; when I was older, on this same shelf he left me his reading discards, meaning the books he had read and disliked, or the books he had read and liked well enough but didn't think belonged in his permanent library, or the books he had read and loved and thought I, too, might love—which is to say a lot of quite wonderful books.

To the right of the filing cabinet was a run of shelves, each angled and built with a cleat to catch the heels of my uncle's shoes. In the middle of the room was a chair with a caned seat on which my uncle sat to put on those shoes. And the remainder of the room, as in a more conventional closet, held my uncle's clothes.

In clothing my uncle had beautiful, at times rather flamboyant, taste. Returning from one of his annual fall trips to London, he once said to me, "I had to do *some*thing while she was out antiquing." This was his way of explaining (or maybe, as a child of the Depression, justifying) the Jermyn Street jackets, the cashmere sweaters (V-neck, round-neck, cardigan, shawl-collar) that rose in such rich Gatsbyesque stacks, the DAKS pants, and the Aquascutum raincoats that he would buy or have made for him during each of these London trips and wear so gently that by the time he had reached the sweatpants phase of life, meaning his eighties, and was ready to give them to the one person who was built exactly as he was—that is to say, me—they were scarcely used. My uncle's clothes fell onto my body as if they had been made for me instead of him—even if they didn't manage to transmit his aplomb.

The clothes were one thing we came to share, if nearly too late. In my adolescence and twenties and even thirties I was far too timid to accept, let alone to understand, my uncle's exuberant Liberty floral shirts (some with neckties sewn in a matching fabric) or his swinging Austen Reed Eisenhower jackets; but as usual it was more important to me to *see* them than to *have* them, because I enjoyed categorizing my uncle's sartorial quirks as much as I enjoyed archiving his other habits. I paid close attention to everything: The way he would order his everyday chinos from L. L. Bean along with the slippers he put on the moment he walked into the house. The way he would bleach his socks so they would stay white. The way he cherished, though only occasionally wore, the leather belt with the words *Buck Ravetch* tooled into it by a genuine cowhand on the set of *Hombre*, a western he made in the sixties with Paul Newman. The way his shoes were infrequently polished because polished shoes, he maintained, meant you were trying too hard, and one should never appear to try too hard. The way the buttons on his bespoke suit-jacket sleeves actually opened and transmitted a secret signal. The way he eschewed blue jeans because he was of a time and generation that couldn't comfortably pull them off. The way the knit ties he wore, on those rare occasions when he was obliged to wear a tie and one of the Liberty numbers was too outré, dangled floppily from his shirt collar. The way he kept his gold Rolex sitting among his pennies in a saucer until it was stolen (he merely shrugged off the loss and afterward ordered an inexpensive field watch from L. L. Bean). The way he insisted a gentleman's wallet always be thin. The way he carried a handkerchief like men in old-fashioned haberdashery ads and stockpiled sleep masks in his top left drawer because he maintained that his left eyelid never stayed completely closed when he slept. The way he had stacks of tennis whites during the years when he still played yet only one bathing suit, a pair of hideous mustard-colored trunks, because, although he loved to swim, in his own pool he skinny-dipped in front of anyone and everyone.

"Yes," he would say when we looked, "it's red"—*it* being his hair *down there.*

How I loved to follow my uncle into his closet as he put away his dry cleaning, or showed me a new shirt, or talked to me about a new book. How I loved that room, that place of tobacco-spiced stillness and cocooned quiet and information left there out in the open for the raking in.

My aunt could never grasp my affection for the one room in the maison that had escaped her touch. She pronounced it an aesthetic carbuncle and regarded it with deep suspicion.

"What do you two find so interesting in there?" she said nearly every time Irving and I disappeared for a few minutes.

Or: "Why don't you come out of the closet and spend time with *me*?"

Or: "What is it that you two *do* in there all the time?"

She made these visits to the closet sound illicit—forbidden, threatening, faintly sexual. There was nothing sexual about them. Threatening maybe, but only because they excluded her.

——— ———

In each and every corner other than the closet, the maison was my aunt's most sustained work of art—though performance art may be closer, since its surfaces were ever changing, being rethought, rejiggered, remade; it was her stage, and here she acted as writer, decorator, hostess, friend and excommunicator of friends, wife, aspiring matriarch (even if she was actual mother to no one), and all-around wizard of the domestic.

Her gifted touch could transform something as simple as a sandwich: by cutting it in half on the angle, she instantly differentiated herself from my mother, who cut hers on the square. The angle was special—but why? Her salad dressing tasted better than my father's, though it was ostensibly prepared following the same old family recipe. Her trick? She sugared it, just as she improved her brownies, which were richer and better than anyone else's, by tripling the butter.

She knew the techniques, the sleights of hand. *Make beauty at all times*—it was one of the precepts. We came over to swim on hot summer afternoons, when the bowl of the Valley cupped a sea of bilious brown air and the asphalt in the canyon was softening, reverting to tar. After an hour the French doors to the dining room would swing open, and we would hear the sound of ice cubes tinkling in a glass pitcher. We would lift up our goggles to see my aunt lowering a large tray onto the garden table: little decrusted tomato-and-cucumber or egg-salad sandwiches cut, at this hour actually quartered, on the diagonal; a basket of fruit; a plate of cookies from Weby's; a bowl of foil-covered chocolate eggs.

What's the point of eating just one cookie? There's no fun in that. Have two—have six. Have sixteen if you like.

Everything was topsy-turvy, rule-breaking, extra-indulgent. The aunt's prerogative—*this* aunt's prerogative.

Hank and food: here, too, she was the inverse of my mother, who managed to put nourishing, if workaday, meals on the table six, seven days a week, tri-tip roasts and chicken baked in onions and carrots, now and then a take-out pizza from Barone's in the Valley. Our aunt, instead, was free to sweep us boys up and take us to the Farmers Market, hand us each a wad of cash, and tell us to choose whatever we wanted from the array of food stalls—*keep the change and double dessert a must!*

At home her Sunday dinners were masterful, a spectacle. I often went over early to help. "I could never do all this without you, Lovey." Of course she could. She didn't need a helper; she needed an audience.

What is the point of making beauty if no one is there to perceive it? I stood by, dazzled, emptying the sink of its vegetable tossings, maybe sometimes peeling the carrots while she chopped, minced, whipped, mashed, roasted, baked, and stewed with high energy, like a cartoon chef in fast motion, now and then pausing, but only briefly, to confer with Julia or Mrs. Knopf. To conjure these meals she drew on her extensive collection of cookware, much of it assembled from Skillets, a favorite high-style kitchen store on Sunset Boulevard. In this atmospheric emporium my aunt shopped for pots, pans, knives, and, with more pleasure still, dishes, glasses, tableware, napery, much of it—*bien sûr*—French. New pieces were regularly introduced to the room-size dish closet, from which she constructed tablescapes that were mini-theatricals of their own. She never repeated the same setting or centerpiece, which was often so tall you could not see around it to speak to your fellow diners. You didn't look at one another; you looked at her elaborate towers of fruit, flowers, and *objets*. Like her, like her coiffeurs, they drew attention to themselves and were always the first subject of conversation at every meal.

"You've outdone yourself this time, Hankie."

"It could be in a magazine."

"A movie."

"A painting. It *is* a painting."

Once she even copied a seventeenth-century Dutch still life she had bought years earlier in London and had propped up on the dining room counter nearby to see if anyone would notice. Of course everyone did. It was a kind of movie effect brought to life: a blue-and-white delft jar (better yet, an actual Duveen delft jar, with a wax seal on the bottom attesting to its provenance) that so closely resembled the one in the painting that it might have been its twin. She arranged in it the same overblown peonies and faded roses; following the painter, she had even found a ladybug (albeit plastic), which she'd attached with florist's clay to a leaf that had fallen to the table just so.

My aunt's meals were lavish and delicious, and always abundant. No ravenous adolescent boy ever left her table unsated. *Go back for seconds. Thirds. Less is not more, children; more is more!*

The conversation sparkled and flew by at warp speed. Its contents varied, depending on the guests, their ages, and whether they were part of the inner family circle (for a long time this meant us canyonites exclusively) or the inner circle of cultivated like-minded friends.

If my aunt and uncle had a movie under way, they would talk about how the filming had gone during the previous week, since they were often on set, either as producers or on account of the special relationship they had with Marty Ritt, the director with whom they most often worked.

Another frequent topic was politics, but because there were no real dissenting voices, mostly there was my aunt, often egged on by my uncle, delivering one of her impassioned diatribes.

"You are not going to say that man's name in this house on a quiet Sunday night, are you?" Half offended and half delighted, her eyes shooting out sparks and her fist pummeling an invisible punching bag, my aunt would *raise hell*: "Richard *Milhous* Nixon! Why, it makes my *blood boil* to see this country, the land of Adams and Jefferson and Lincoln and the great FDR, succumb to *the darkest days since the war years!*"

And this was pre-Watergate too. Later there was *venal fascist* Nixon, the *blot upon America* that was Vietnam, Ford *the buffoon*. The fulmination that Reagan provoked (*a brainless B-movie actor, the lowest of the low*, etc.) would often spread more widely to all thespians, whom my aunt and uncle, with few exceptions, did not hold in very high esteem. *Without dialogue, actors scarcely have an idea in their heads! Who makes them sound so clever? Your unc and I, that's who!*

There was something bracing, to be sure, about all this conviction. You knew where these people stood. You knew what it was to have a committed take on the country you lived in and to hold the people in authority up to reasonable standards of behavior. And you felt a certain freshness in being free of the more obvious kinds of celebrity worship: *Mind you, actors put their pants on one leg at a time, just like everyone else—and I should know, I've worked with piles of them.* Yet all the same, to a child there could be something withering about this juggernaut of unstoppable opinion. Did a boy dare speak up, ever? Sure he did. He spoke up to parrot and assent, agree and confirm. It was the only way.

A kind of celebrity worship *did* prevail at the maison, though it was probably closer to idolatry—idolatry of The Greats. Starting when we were children and continuing with increasing frequency as we became adolescents, the conversation at dinner and especially in the library afterward was more and more dedicated to our further induction into the world of Our Personal Heroes.

Equipped with some inner sturdiness, or maybe just plain common sense, my brothers early on chose to opt out of this particular indoctrination. I, however, believed—or worried—that I was obliged to participate, or else. Or else I wasn't educated, I wasn't cultivated, I wasn't *one of us*; and being *one of us* was central to me then, essential. Certainly I did not want to be a friend or a relation, one of those other, outlying nephews who was *not our cuppa* or who *came up short* or—worse—*didn't live up to his early promise.* And so I learned to love, and learned why I should love, Colette, Trollope, Matisse, Mozart. I read *Great Expectations* without perceiving the Havishamian cobwebs beginning to send out their earliest tendrils, and I read the ghost stories of beloved Henry (as in: James) with a feeling for, but little understanding of, the familiar foreboding of the milieu. Certain of the gods were undeniable, unchallengeable. Shakespeare. Proust. Virginia Woolf, and Leonard for being *the most stalwart husband imaginable*—*stalwart*, in husbands or friends, like *forthcoming*, in friends and relatives, connoting the highest possible praise. Jean Renoir, but not Pierre-Auguste (*too many pink behinds!*). The Renaissance, never the Middle Ages; likewise Periclean Athens but not those *death-obsessed* and *stylizing* ancient Egyptians or *those copyists and engineers* the Romans. Faulkner (two of whose novels my aunt and uncle adapted into movies and whose mistress, Meta Carpenter Wilde, had worked on one of their movies as a script girl and briefly become a friend) but not Hemingway (except for the short stories) and certainly not Fitzgerald, who was a *drunk who drove his wife mad* and had *one good book in him*—*plus who knows, maybe Zelda wrote it, that wouldn't surprise me in the least. You realize, don't you, that behind every great man there stands a woman who is sometimes more than his helpmate in every sense. Of course in our case it's different, it's clear as day: line for line, dollar for dollar, I am one hundred percent your uncle's equal partner.*

The list went on. Fred, not Ginger (*a ditz and a Republican*). Hepburn, who had been fond of my grandmother, even though, à la Tracy Lord—at least Tracy Lord at the beginning of *The Philadelphia Story*—she was *limited by her froideur.* Garbo, but mainly for Ninotchka and Anna Karenina, certainly not for her later-in-life faux-recluse shenanigans (*who does she think she's fooling, swanning down Madison Avenue in that dreadful hat?*)—though my uncle did like to remind us that in 1930, when he was ten, he had walked under the words GARBO TALKS on a movie marquee advertising *Anna Christie* (otherwise *a dud*) in New York City: it was the first grown-up movie he had ever seen.

Lubitsch. *Scarface.* Buster Keaton. De Sica. Fellini (early only). Bergman, but the sweeter, more autumnal Bergman of *Wild Strawberries* and *Fanny and Alexander* (the arguably more relevant *Scenes from a Marriage* was *too plodding and claustrophobic*). *Upstairs, Downstairs*, when it debuted, was reveled in religiously every week for its entertainment value and *panache*, as were, in a similar vein—and as long as you were clear about their decisively lower ranking in the pantheon—*The Forsyte Saga* (both the novels and the television series), the Lucia novels of E. F. Benson, Nancy Mitford (the novels, also the biographies of Mme. de Pompadour, the Sun King, et al.), and Evelyn Waugh, even though he was *a pig and an anti-Semite, like far too many of the bloody English of his time and class.*

The Founding Fathers. Ella Fitzgerald and Cole Porter. Tennessee Williams (before he *went to seed—too much alcohol, too many indulgences of the flesh!*). Frederick Lewis Allen (who was very dog-eared, because he wrote about the twenties and the thirties, the decades in which my aunt and uncle originated, and which formed them). The Durants. Delmore Schwartz. Emerson. Dylan Thomas. All of Bellow but only some of Roth (The Breast.? *What was he thinking?*).

Katherine Mansfield was a special case. She was *a lustrous talent* whose life was *tragically cut down by TB.* She might have gone on longer *if only she hadn't fallen in with that fraud Gurdjieff* and *if her husband, Middleton Murry, hadn't been such an exploitative bastard. I could just kill that man!*

My aunt and uncle approached these figures as though they were themselves members of our actual family or their circle of like-minded friends, very selectively picking and choosing what qualities to esteem or ignore (there was just as much anti-Semitism in James as in Waugh, one might argue . . . if one dared), but when it came to *poor Katherine,* the interplay of the personal and the literary-critical had, I eventually understood, a special resonance for my aunt.

Just as listening in went with listening, so, too, as I grew older, did sleuthing go with observing. As I became more and more per-plexed and, later, troubled by my aunt and uncle and the power they held over me, I took to "exploring" the maison when they were out of town to find some documentary evidence that might help shed light on how they became who they came to be.

Decoding through investigation supported by forensics: what piv-otal training for a writer, though of course I did not think of it that way then. I did not think so deeply at all, really; I simply felt driven to keep my eye on the calendar, and when my aunt and uncle left for one of their Palm Springs weekends or (better, because longer) fall trips to Yurp, I took my set of keys, bestowed upon me earlier when I was relied on (so unequivocally and unsuspiciously relied on) to look after their house and houseplants while they were gone, and I let myself into the darkened maison.

If my aunt's portrait eyes used to follow me on Ogden Drive, on Skyline there was a small city's worth of eyes to track my surrepti-tious investigations. There were the eyes of Voltaire and Madame de Sévigné, who had transferred uphill from The Apartment along with her onyx column; Dr. Johnson and Napoleon, for whom my aunt had a lifelong passion—*not because he was a dictator, mind you, but because he wrote the most beautiful love letters and freed the Jews from the ghetto.* (We all knew that it was as likely because he was obsessed with neo-classical architecture and decoration, as she was.) There were the eyes in the bewigged, red-coated English gentlemen in their carved and gilded frames . . . the eyes in the steel engravings of eighteenth-century notables . . . the eyes in the robed Chinese ladies on porcelain bowls—all these multifarious eyes tracked me as, with a thumping heart that constricted every time the house creaked or a passing car rattled a window or, God help me, the phone rang, I sifted through boxes and drawers and cupboards; they tracked me, but they were powerless to stop me from coming across sentences like these, written from my grandmother to my aunt:

> My darling, I have said it before, I will say it again, I believe you have the talent of a Katherine Mansfield, I know it in my heart, in my bones, if only you would *apply* yourself, not always go for the juicy assignment, the easy effect.

And:

> Dearest, I of all people know what it is to be without money, to yen and yearn for it. But you, you and Puddy both, are so well-established now in the screenwriting line . . . why not take a stab, once more, even if it is for the last time, at writing out of the full depths of your gifts? The full depths of *you*? You remember how I used to compare your work to darling old K. M.? You haven't forgotten the poor waif, that poet of the soul we once loved and communed over? She was our compass, once. Never settle, my angel. Surely you must remember that too.

The language in these letters was at odds with the version of her mother that my aunt had begun to live by in the period after my grandmother died, when Harriet senior became the all-loving, all-praising mother *who with the exception of Corky of course embraced me more fully than any human being on this planet ever can or will* and gradually became larger than life, more character than human being, another household idol, this one with her own shrine where that daily, or every-other-daily, flower was placed just so.

It was at the same time (I can add with the leveling effects of distance) unfair to the quality and quantity of work my aunt, in collaboration with my uncle, *did* do, even if I think my grandmother perceived early on what emerged as the essential puzzle of my aunt and uncle's creative life: why it was that they always looked so far outside themselves for stories to tell, meaning to the West or the South, to Faulkner (*The Long, Hot Summer*; *The Reivers*) or Elmore Leonard (*Hombre*) or Larry McMurtry (*Hud*), or to the plight of schoolteachers (*Conrack*) or factory workers (*Norma Rae*), rather than choosing subjects that came out of their own blood, their own guts.

Story wizards who lacked interiority: it was an interesting conundrum but one that did not occur to me when I was young, and my aunt and uncle together simply constituted an alternate school, a second school. Actually, no, that's wrong. It was the *central* school of my youth, the school of culture, of aesthetics, literature, music, movies, architecture, and design. Learning by reading, learning by doing; learning by sitting at the feet of one's cultivated relations, preferably of course these particular two. *Truly intelligent people don't need teachers; they simply choose the right people to spend time with, and they read themselves into education. Writers write, critics criticize. If you wish to paint, buy a brush. If you wish to write, pick up a pen.*

The thing was . . . this alternate/central school of my aunt and uncle's was governed by a set of rules as intractable as those at any formal pedagogical institution. At first I obeyed these rules without even knowing what they were, without, for all my looking, even seeing them very clearly. The maison offered such an alluring contrast to life on Greenvalley Road that for a time, a long time, I didn't know where my aunt and uncle left off and I began. I might have turned to literature for guidance—if only I'd been awake enough to benefit from what I was reading. Beloved Henry (as in: James) might have helped, but I wasn't clever enough to see the parallel between my predicament and that of the Maisies, the Pansys, the Mileses and Floras or their kind. Instead I merely provided what was expected, and endlessly. Just as the mirrors in the maison reflected my aunt's interiors back at her, I reflected back the love. I agreed, I celebrated, I praised. I made conversation by parroting, or cutting and pasting, what I heard and read and was taught or told, rather the way a moderately lazy middle school student used to read an entry in the *Encyclopaedia Britannica* and restate the argument "in his own words." Only they weren't my own words, or anything close. I didn't know what my own words *were*. Or if I knew them I couldn't figure out how to link them together in my brain and get them out of my mouth. I had learned to be so adept at supporting the prevailing point of view because it was evident that dissent, independent thinking, divergent tastes (late Fellini, dark Bergman, *The Sun Also Rises*, Jackson Pollock, mummies!) did not grow the mind; it threatened to end the conversation—and eventually the relationship.

This mirror-meld was all-encompassing. It ranged from high to low, from ideas to practicalities to the most superficial evaluations of the most basic things. When I was asked for my opinion—and I often was—I either concurred or offered a disagreement that wouldn't stand up to the ricochet of a few lively back-and-forths. When I was asked a favor, I complied. And when I was summoned to the maison, I went—ideally within minutes.

Lovey, I have pictures that need k-nock-k-nocking (which meant nailing into the wall; the *k* was always pronounced) . . .

Furniture that needs moving . . .

A blue day that needs cheering . . .

Let's make fall—which took the form of tricking out the maison in twigs and appropriately dyed silk leaves and planting all the urns with chrysanthemums. *Spring. Christmas.*

Let's light a fire and sit and discuss, other calls would begin . . .

The Seagull . . .

Of Human Bondage *(I really do think there's some of Philip in you, Mike)* . . .

The sonnets (an educated person learns yards of Shakespeare by heart, you realize).

As she did, lines and lines of it.

So I did, lines and lines of it.

" 'Shall I compare thee to a summer's day?' " I learned to recite—to my aunt. " 'Thou art more lovely and more temperate.' "

" 'Rough winds do shake the darling buds of May,' " she recited back to me, her eyes sparkling. " 'And summer's lease hath all too short a date . . .' "

She took my hand, which turned clammy in hers. "You know,

Lovey, you and I really do understand what it is to have a marriage of true minds, do we not?"

When I didn't answer, didn't know how or what to answer: "Lovey? Don't you agree?"

Those eyes burning into me, wide, electric; causing my heart to thump uneasily.

"Aren't we lucky?"

Lucky . . . clammy . . . thumping . . . compliant . . . in the moment summoning an equivocal *mmm* that seemed to do the trick as far as she was concerned. Meanwhile, at home at night in bed or in the early morning before school or sometimes at school, I was doubled over with a tightened stomach, but never at the maison. Never there, where, arguably, these stomach pains originated.

Let's toodle down to the Vagabond, other calls began, *and see* . . .

Top Hat . . .

The Front Page . . .

Auntie Mame (which was proposed without a pinch of irony, and correctly: the celluloid Mame was a meringue by comparison) . . .

La Grande Illusion . . .

The 400 Blows . . .

And I went, and did. And read and watched and discussed (= agreed).

I loved being in this world. It was a world that had its own motto, *Ad astra per aspera*—through hardships to the stars—which was often cited by my uncle, who never really specified what, exactly, the hardships were. It had its own songs too. One, my uncle's alone, was sung whenever he was in particularly high spirits:

> *Lady of Spain, I adore you*
> *Right from the night I first saw you*
> *My heart has been yearning for you*
> *What else could any heart do?*

The other was sung religiously every time my aunt and uncle set out on a journey, even a brief road trip to Palm Springs:

Roodly toot, roodly toot
We are the boys of the institute

Then again three, four times, in a progressively softer voice,

Roodly toot, roodly toot
We are the boys of the institute

Who the boys were, and what institute they belonged to, like the hardships that had to be overcome before reaching the stars, was never clear, but no matter. This nonsensical ditty was the theme song to a serious world that opened me up and brought things into my life that would not otherwise have been there—books, objects cast off from the collections at the maison, knowledge. I loved knowledge, just as for years I loved being singled out and loved by my aunt. I loved her worshipfully, deeply, obediently. I loved the magic of her love, the magic of her magic, the magic of her world, our world. As for the rest, the feelings and worries that did not dovetail with the magic, I merely drew a fence around them, closed and locked the gate, and hid the key away.

One Saturday afternoon in the early 1970s my aunt was driving me home from one of our special dates together when we ran into my father, who was riding his Vespa to the tennis club at the top of the hill. She pulled over. He pulled over and took off his helmet.

Just as my mother's appearance had changed in these years, so had my father's. He'd grown his hair long and allowed his sideburns to turn thick and bushy; they were like two dark commas framing his face. And he'd traded his black-rimmed glasses for a pair of more stylish aviator frames, whose tint, dark at the top of the lenses, turned lighter and more transparent at the bottom. In the light part of his lens I could see his eyes, and I saw them look first at my aunt, then at me, and then at the backseat of the car.

He tilted his head back in a way that I had seen his mother tilt hers many times over the years. The tilted-back head was as much language as these siblings needed between them.

"It's an old junkery table, Martin."

Martin was never auspicious.

He nodded; but this was no affirming nod. "It's just that the boy . . ."

"Should not have lovely things, civilized things to live with?"

"His room——"

"I paid five dollars for it years ago."

"It's not the price, or the value. It's——"

"It's what? You want him to be *average*? You want him to live in a *bunker*?"

"Our home is not a bunker."

She sniffed. "It's to go by his bed. For his books. And to hold a good strong reading light. You can't find fault with books and reading, now can you?"

"Of course not, but——"

"But nothing. You're spoiling his pleasure, Martin—and mine."

With this she rolled up her window and started the engine. I looked back over my shoulder and saw my father sitting immobile on his Vespa, thinking.

We continued down the hill in silence. When she pulled over at our house, she said, "Do you need a hand, Lovey?"

"I'm okay," I said uneasily.

"Martin has no concept of the pleasure principle. He never has. Not to worry, though. I'll see to it."

When the phone rang as we were finishing dinner that evening, I was filled with an instant sense of dread, which was only amplified when my father went to answer it in private.

As soon as my mother was busy with the dishes, I managed to slip upstairs to listen in at the door. My father was speaking in the kind of deliberately flat voice he used when he was trying to keep his temper under control. ". . . Just a little less often, just so that he might fit in better with his peers, and be more . . . more normal. Develop more normal interests, I mean. The boys he goes to school with, they're just not reading Trollope, or watching French fil——" There was a pause.

"*Movies.* And it's not *only* that. We're concerned about how Danny and Steve must feel, always being left out. You must see——"

My father might have been speaking softly, but his interlocutor was already yelling at such a pitch that *her* voice, traveling along the phone line, over the hill, down into our part of the canyon, into our house, up into my parents' room, and out through the telephone receiver, which my father was presumably holding away from his ear, seemed to be making the very glass in the windows rattle and buzz.

One thing has nothing to do with the other——

Normal? Since when is that something to aspire——

After all I have given——

Martin, he is my blood too.

My family.

My boy.

Mine!

"He's not *yours.* He doesn't belong to anyone other than himself. And besides, Hankie, one thing I'm absolutely asking——no, actually, I'm *telling* you——is to start including the other boys. Otherwise——"

Otherwise what? My aunt did not remain on the line long enough to find out.

The next evening my father came into my room for a talk. My father never came into my room unless he wished to speak to me in private, usually about something I had done wrong. The very sound of his heavy tread on the steps was alarming. The knock——there was always a respectful knock first——tightened my stomach. Yet there was awkwardness, too, in the way he stepped into a room that did not seem to belong to the house that he himself had built, the bedroom of his first-born, tricked out *à la Maison Ravetch.*

There he found his son, sitting at his (period) desk, under an (engraved) portrait of Shakespeare, lost in a (Victorian) novel. At least I wasn't reading by candlelight——though I'd been known to try.

"Mike, do you have a moment?"

I couldn't answer no to such a question. I nodded. He sat down on the corner of my bed.

"Your mother and I"——this by itself a worrying phrase, a phrase that suggested decisions already solidified beyond negotiation——"we have been talking. And we have a favor to ask you. Well, it's not exactly a favor. It's a new . . . policy. Here in our house. The house of our family, *your* family, here on Greenvalley Road."

He paused. I waited with a rumbling stomach.

"We have decided that, from now on, when your aunt or your uncle, together or separately, invite you to go out with them, day or night, no matter where, you are to invite your brothers along. You are to tell them that you are going, and you are to include them. Do you follow me?"

I nodded.

"There are to be no exceptions to this new policy. Even if you are just running down the hill to buy a quart of milk, or pick up the dry cleaning. It's you *and* your brothers, one or both of them. Understood?"

Again I nodded.

"I'm sure you understand why."

I shook my head and spoke for the first time. "No, I don't."

"Well," he said, "we feel, your mother and I do, that sometimes your aunt—your aunt and uncle—don't always take into consideration your brothers' feelings as much as they should. They're always singling you out . . . and taking you places . . . and giving you things. As you well know."

"But how is that my problem?" I asked in frustration.

He paused. "It's not your . . . problem, exactly. But it is a situation you, we all, find ourselves in. And it can be hard to get your aunt and uncle to see things from another point of view. Which is why we have decided to make our feelings very clear. It's just not right—certain things are just not right."

My father's blue eyes looked very dark to me all of a sudden. "Do I make myself clear?"

I nodded. And I wondered why he did not say anything about trying to make me have those more normal interests, or become more normal. Was it because he did not want to say to me, in plain words and to my face, that he thought I was *ab*normal? Or show that he knew (did he?) about the problems I was having at school?

This was not an easy conversation for him to have. I could tell that much. After another brief pause, my father looked around the room. I had the impression that he was looking at it for the first time in a long time. In years maybe. He looked; he sighed; he left.

The next day was Saturday. My aunt phoned in the morning, and I answered.

"Lovey," she said. "How do you feel about a trip to Pasadena this morning?"

Pasadena was one of her favorite stomping grounds.

"We can noodle around and have lunch. How quickly can you be ready?"

"I'm ready now."

"I'll come pick you up."

I hesitated.

"I can walk over," I said, my heart racing. "I like the walk."

It was early. I peered into the bedroom next door. My brothers were sitting on the floor playing with Hot Wheels without me as usual. I slipped stealthily past their door and down the hall. Every step I took was saturated with anxiety. I made sure that my foot touched the stairs with extra lightness so that they wouldn't creak. I inched through the front door and closed it behind me.

"You disobeyed me. What were you thinking?"

My father's voice was edged with fury, the way it sounded before one of his eruptions. He was working to keep the anger down, though, controlled. I think, for once, he truly wanted to know what I had to say.

How could I explain? I couldn't say, I have been bewitched—possessed, almost. I did not have the language or the insight, the freedom such language would have connoted.

I couldn't say, She has power over me that I do not comprehend. Or: The threat of losing this love terrifies me and keeps me in check, in chains. Or: I am bullied and beaten up by my peers because I am so different from them and I do not know how to be friends with people who are so different from me and somewhere, deep down, I feel I probably deserve to be bullied and beaten up *because* I am so different. Or: I don't understand why she prefers me to my brothers, yet at the same time I love it; I love the attention and the gifts and being made to feel special, and I don't know who I would be if I were not at the same time both singled out and outcast, a victim who is also, as it happens, a prince.

"I don't know what I was thinking," I said honestly.

We were in his room this time. The room he and my mother shared. The door was closed. Tight. He was sitting forward on his brown vinyl club chair, a big, ugly, boxy thing that had previously been in the bachelor pad over on Lookout and had somehow escaped my aunt's redecorating impulses.

I was half sitting, half leaning against the bed, fighting tears, and now mute.

He ran his hands through those thick sideburns of his. "You must have been thinking something. You remember what I asked you?"

I nodded.

"You remember but you forgot? You heard me but you ignored me?"

"They . . . were busy."

"They—your brothers?"

I nodded.

He crossed his arms. "Busy doing what?"

"Playing."

"Did you ask them to come along?"

I felt my face turn tomato-colored. "I—I didn't think that they would want to."

My father sat back in his chair. Just as before, when I felt him looking at my room as if for the first time, now I felt him looking at me, at me and my aunt—not for the first time, surely, but more deeply, more diagnostically, than he ever had before. As if he was looking at a problem that was larger than he was; beyond him, perhaps. A problem that was woven into the whole nature of our family, brother and sister and sister and brother and all that, and the grandmothers, and my parents' peculiar second-tier status (but assigned by whom, decided by whom?) within this group of people, which likely had something to do with the fact that my aunt and uncle were far richer and more flamboyant and more dramatic and attention-seeking (and at the same time, of course, attention-starved) than my parents, who remained the perpetual younger siblings utterly lacking the arty and exotic

Hollywood wattage of their older brother and sister. Or maybe it went back, further back, to the time when my mother first met my aunt and was just a girl herself and was as bedazzled by her as I was and had never quite been able to grow out of that dependent, younger, smaller, lesser, obeisant role she had fallen or been cast into. One thing seemed pretty clear to me: my father had begun to realize that the spell my aunt had cast over me was something he might not be able to break so easily, whether through reason, or anger, or pressure, or new family policies.

He gazed out through the large window that faced the big green canyon, the beloved canyon where he had been instrumental— pivotal—in bringing these people to live so closely together so many years earlier, and he said, "Your mother and I, this morning, Mike, when we realized that you had expressly disregarded my request and had gone out without your brothers, we had a talk. And we made a decision, both of us together, that for the next month you are not going to be able to see your aunt. I have spoken to her, and she understands. Well, let's say she complies, at any rate. Tonight, as you know, your cousins will be there for dinner and we are invited, but you and I, we will not be going. We will be home, just the two of us. I hope it will give you some time to think."

I was stunned. "A month," I said. "That's not fair. That's not *just.*"

"I'm sorry if you see it that way, but this is non-negotiable. And it's exactly how it will be whenever there are invitations in the next month. That's thirty days, beginning today. No exceptions, no further discussion. Period."

It was summer. Such a punishment was all the more consequential in summer, when the days were long and unstructured. A muddy haze dimmed the July sky, and in the absence of rain the green faded out of the canyon's slopes until they became drier and more and more brown and crisp. Dangerously crisp. Fire warnings were nailed on telephone poles throughout the hills, and whenever I heard a siren, I ran to the window to see if there was any smoke or flame.

I had seen flames before out my bedroom window, in similar

weather one evening several summers earlier, terrifying orange tongues licking at a patch of chaparral within hiking distance of our backyard. My father and other fathers in the neighborhood climbed up on their roofs tugging garden hoses behind them and called down to their wives or older children to turn on the water full blast. Standing up on peaked or gabled or even flat roofs, these men looked like they were steering, or sailing, their homes away from a sea of diabolical flame. They sprayed the shakes, the tar paper, and the tiles and monitored those orange tongues well into the night, long after they had been reduced to embers and the sirens and the firemen had come and gone.

There was no actual fire that month. Only the threat of it, and of a different kind of fire, the fire of anger, meaning the Bergman Temper, sizzling between the two houses, Greenvalley and the maison. It was like that static electricity that sometimes accompanies a Santa Ana wind. I felt it in the air, the danger and worry of it spontaneously combusting at any moment; exploding.

But something even stranger and more alarming happened: there was complete silence. No family dinners, no triple-butter brownies, no conversations about Faulkner or Fellini in the library; instead, nearly a month of complete silence between the two families who otherwise visited and spoke (or argued) every day, pretty much without fail, and dined together twice a week, either at home or in a restaurant, all year long.

Like an athlete training between games, I read so many books that I had to start in on the first of my great-grandmother's thirty volumes of leather-bound Balzac, which, after Huffy died, had migrated to our living room bookshelves. I put in so many hours in my room that I was convinced I could see the Japanese elm out my window adding more leaves to its thick canopy.

And I kept close count of the days.

Day 4.

Day 13.

Day 21.

On day 25 my mother came to my door to say that there was a call for me.

"Lovey, we've been given a reprieve! Five days off the sentence. What are you doing right now?"

Reading, I told her.

"Well, mark your place and come on over this very minute."

I put down the phone and ran back to my bedroom for my shoes. I hurried into them, knotted the laces, and flew down the stairs.

My mother was waiting by the door. Her head was tilted to one side, at almost the same angle that Sylvia used to tilt hers when she was thinking something through.

"Do I have to invite Danny and Steve this time?" I asked.

She paused for a moment. "Not this time," she said with a sigh.

I ran out of Greenvalley and up the hill and across the canyon. At the front door of the maison my aunt and I fell into each other's arms like—like lovers? Is that what this was? Between aunt and nephew, a woman of fifty and a boy of thirteen? How could that be? It couldn't be; it wasn't . . . exactly. I *was* happy to see her, giddily, relievedly happy, even as I was aware, dimly aware, that this connection—this reconnection—wasn't quite, or at all, reasonable. Or healthy. When she swept me up into her arms at the front door, I felt an intensity and a desperation emanating from her that evoked her desperation the day Huffy died three years earlier, when she pulled me toward her and held me so tight that I was nearly unable to breathe, nearly unable to remember that I inhabited my own individual life, that I had my own feelings, my own grief (or absence of grief), my own self—whatever that was, *wherever* that was.

These two days felt linked by more than this physicality, though. I couldn't say what it was, but I knew there was a link. I felt it. It was a kind of bone knowledge. My grandmother died and left a black hole. My aunt pulled me toward her and into it. Nearly into it, because if I had truly fallen into the blackness I would not have known that I was falling into the blackness. Not in this way. Not in the moment. And not with my eyes open, my mind registering.

That was what I told myself, anyway. There. Then and there. Making deductions, pairing up feelings, situations, had to be how you pulled yourself out of them. Or so I believed. Or hoped.

We went into the house. She showed me all the changes she had made to it during those twenty-five days. She had been busy repaint-ing, rearranging. When my aunt and my uncle were not at work on a script, the house underwent more frequent changes, but this time whole rooms had been redecorated and flipped around. And for the first time the formerly all-white walls had been painted deep, saturated colors. The living room was a mustard yellow that verged on gold, the dining room terra-cotta, the library red. My aunt had reupholstered much of the furniture to match. Throughout the house there was more fabric, darker colors, more and more objects, which she pointed out as she took me on a tour, room by room; though of course she didn't need to point out the changes, since I was as close an observer of the maison as I was of the people who lived in it, and whenever an object was moved or added or subtracted, I noticed at once. But even so, the newly intense coloration of the rooms took me by surprise.

"So, Lovey, what do you think? You're my best critic. Yea or nay?"

"It's all so . . . different."

"Different good or different bad?"

"Different good."

"So yea, then?"

I nodded. "Yea, then."

Her face rearranged itself into a big buoyant smile. "I knew he'd be pleased," she said.

I looked around for my uncle, thinking that she was addressing him. But she wasn't. She appeared to be speaking to the walls, to the maison itself.

"Don't forget to say hello to your unc," she said next—but this too was strange, since I always went to look for my uncle. I didn't need the prompt.

Irving was two rooms away, in his usual reading chair in the library. Unable to look at my aunt, at her eyes, I went to join him there.

I sat down across from my uncle in my usual chair, and after a few minutes my aunt appeared with a tray of cookies and lemonade. She stretched out on her daybed, Field Marshal Montgomery's daybed, it was said to be, bought in London some years back.

No one mentioned The Punishment. It was as though it had never happened. Instead we caught one another up in the way we did after they returned from one of their European trips or I returned from a ski vacation with my family. We talked about what books we had been reading, what movies they had seen, when they were planning to leave for London that fall . . .

At one point my aunt looked at me with those bright glittering eyes of hers, then she turned to my uncle.

"Don't you wish he were ours?" she said, her voice cracking and her face suddenly full of desire. Saturated with it, the way the walls were with color.

My uncle—for just a moment—took in a sharp breath, those ever-so-communicative eyes of his communicating . . . nothing.

He said nothing.

She said, "Let's steal him!"

In the novel version she would have. In life she already had.

SIX

OFF THE HILL

Not long after The Punishment was rescinded my aunt and uncle took us—all three of us boys—to dinner one night at the Hamburger Hamlet on Sunset Boulevard. The Hamlet (with its self-proclaimed "simply marvelous food and drinks") was a favorite casual eatery of my aunt and uncle's, family-friendly, and one with a ready-made Shakespearean motif, no less.

Hanging above the plush red leather booth where we were seated that night was a gilt-framed engraving of actors dueling—Edmund and Edgar—and alongside it another of black-clad Hamlet himself, standing at a distance from Claudius, with a caption from the second scene of the play:

> King: How is it that clouds still hang on you?
> Hamlet: Not so, my lord. I am too much in the sun.

Too much in the sun/too much in the son: even the material world was providing me with accidental clues and revelations, little though I recognized them at the time.

After my brothers and I had politely ordered our hamburgers, the waitress turned to my aunt and uncle and said, "You have such well-behaved children. I must say we don't see so many like them nowadays."

"Why, thank you," my aunt said with a proud smile. "We're pleased with them ourselves. Aren't we, Corky?"

"Excessively," concurred my uncle.

After the waitress left, my aunt leaned in. "We could pretend, you know," she said to us. "Just for a lark. Just when we come here."

I alone seemed to notice the worrisome sparkle in my aunt's eyes, and I alone seemed to hear a worrisome warble in her voice.

Danny had just turned eleven and at once fell in with the game. He pushed his ever-smudged gold-rimmed aviator glasses back up on his nose and said, "Mom, would you pass me the salt? I'd like to have some right here when my french fries come."

"Of course, son."

From Steve, my little brother, who was about to turn nine: "So tell us, Dad, how was your day at the office?"

My uncle at an office? It was hard to envision. "Exhausting," he said. "Clients. Meetings. Adding machines. Shoes!"

From the younger two, laughter. From me, anxious silence.

The waitress brought our salads. "Now I forget. The Thousand Island is for . . ."

"Dad," piped up Steve.

"And the vinaigrette?"

"Mom," said Danny. "She's going to ask you for some sugar now. Mom *always* puts sugar in her salad dressing."

Sheila was the waitress's name. We saw her the following week, and the week after, and the one after that. Did it mean something that, out of the repertoire of restaurants my aunt and uncle liked to take us out to, we kept returning to the Hamlet, especially when it was likely to be Sheila's shift?

"Ah, my favorite family."

"Ah, those well-behaved children."

"Ah, it's Mrs. Ravetch, the mother who likes to put sugar in her salad dressing."

"Please, my dear Sheila, call me Hank. All my friends do."

I found these evenings—these little performances—deeply uncomfortable. The game was too close to be fun, to be a game at all, for me, because there had been times in my very early childhood when I had certain strange haunting thoughts that fell somewhere between dreams and worries, and they had returned to me later on around the time of The Punishment, when I found myself wondering why it was, really, that I was so much more like my aunt and my uncle than was my parents; why I shared so many more interests with them; why I shared The Eye with my aunt while no one else in my family did; why I read what I read and as much as I read; why the time I spent with my aunt and uncle was so extended and why it provoked such intensity of feeling in both my mother and (more surprisingly, for a man otherwise so remote) my father; why my aunt and uncle singled me out from my brothers and loved me as ardently as they did.

Why it was my aunt wished she could steal me. Steal me? Steal a human being, a child, by now a boy turning into a teenager, away from his parents and his siblings? And his home, his world? How was that so different from her despised uncle Mark and aunt Zeena, Sam's childless brother and his wife, who when my father was born had offered to buy him from my grandparents for one hundred thousand dollars? *Our own Flem Snopes*, my aunt called Mark. *DE-spicable.* With the emphasis on the first syllable, where she maintained it belonged.

Was it merely that this game made me uneasy, went this secret worry of mine . . . or was it perhaps not a worry so much as a fantasy? That I was in truth *their* son, given (loaned?) to their younger siblings to raise, the way children were in fairy tales and legends and eighteenth-century novels—but given (or loaned) for what reason? So that they could pursue their busy screenwriting careers? Dine with actors? Travel to Yurp every fall for weeks or months on end? Live in perpetual unsated hunger for the one experience that was missing from their lives?

Or maybe it was because they were unfit; known to be unfit, incapable of raising a child. They? She. Maybe she was not quite up to the task. Not quite *right*. In her head. More than that. Broken. Ill. During one of my recent listening-in sessions I had heard my father speak more explicitly about Auntie Hankie than he ever had before. "My sister is not reasonable, Merona," he told my mother. "Her thinking, her behavior, the scenes she makes, the people she banishes—it's less and less *sane*. I worry for her and for Irving. And for Michael and the boys, for all of us . . ."

Maybe that was the missing clue, the key that would unlock the whole mystery: my aunt had some kind of gradually deteriorating mental condition that was bringing on these fantasies of hers (yearning to steal me, to pass with Irving as our parents). Maybe *this* was responsible for the way she had started speaking to the walls ("I knew he'd be pleased") and the change in the way she began to speak to me when we were alone—

Sometimes, Lovey, affinity trumps blood—do you know what I mean by that?

I am a believer in making your life what you want it to be, the way my mother did before me. Your life and your loves. Do you know what I mean? Surely you of all people know what I mean. Surely you and I of all people know . . .

Too much in the sun/son: even in play I could not call them Mom and Dad.

The phone calls began to come more and more often.

I have pictures that need k-nock-k-nocking . . .

Furniture that needs moving . . .

A blue day that needs cheering . . .

I began, tentatively, so very tentatively, to test the boundaries. I was beginning to wake up, just slightly.

Now and then I would finish whatever I was doing at home—schoolwork or reading a chapter in my book—before walking over to the maison.

When I arrived I would find a dark face on the other side of the door. Her language was straightforward, but her delivery was full of reproach.

What on earth kept you?

I was scared something happened to you on your way.

Don't tell me you fell back asleep. You haven't forgotten that there's plenty of time to sleep in the grave?

Even when I did comply, and hurry, and go, see, do—play house, talk books until there were no newly read books to talk about, *k-nock-*

k-nock until there were no more pictures to put up on the wall—the next morning or, if it was a school day, the next afternoon the call would come again, and again I would return, and it was as if I were starting from scratch, over and over trying to lift these increasingly not blue but black moods of my aunt's. It was like pouring sand onto the beach. Time, effort, energy, nothing *accumulated*. It didn't matter whether you brought one grain or a million, after you left, the landscape reverted to its former unaltered (unalterable) self.

If I said I could not come for an hour or (worse) at all that day, the goodbye would be swift and the phone would hit the cradle with a bang. And when I did eventually resurface, there would be a faraway look in her eyes, the head tilted back, the nose up in disapproval or hurt or ire. And it would not take her very long to find her words, which became more and more biting:

You're a very sensitive boy, but sometimes, I must say, you're not sensitive to other people.

Sometimes, in truth, you're actually quite a heartless child.

You're like your father.

Worse: *You're like* my *father.*

——— ———

For a time, very gingerly, and not entirely conscious of what I was doing, I tried to make a few fraidy-cat forays into a separate life; just a little bit separate. Afterward I dutifully reported in, as I reported all things to my aunt and uncle.

When I peeped—just once, maybe twice—about a girl I might possibly have been able to think about liking (on those rare occasions when I found one at school who would even speak to me), my aunt's arms wound themselves into a knot at breast level, and the nose shot up into the air as a grave inquiry was instantly lobbed: "But is she up to the standards of the Mighty Franks?"

Those glittering vibrant eyes fixed on me as she persisted, "Is she, Mike?"

"I think so."

"You *think*? You need to *know*. To take her measure. For example, whom does she read, what captivates her? Is she imaginative, creative, an original like you? A joiner, an iconoclast, a rebel, a conformist? What's her house like? The house says so much, as you well know. Describe it to me. Go on . . ."

Another time I mentioned a new boy at school I thought I might start hanging out with (on that unprecedented occasion when I found one with whom I had something in common, in this case fossil collecting, and who did not bully me or call me names): "But whatever *do* you do together? Play sports? Pick through those old rocks of yours? Watch television? Please don't tell me you are watching television. Please, not that."

No sentence was more disconcerting than *Bring her*—or him—*by. I am always interested in meeting new young people!*

Even plucking references out of the current atmosphere could be loaded. *Cat who? Simon and what-funkel?* The face, darkening; the throat, clearing. Then: *I didn't think you, Mike, of all people would cross over.* Then behind a cupped hand, stage-whispering to my uncle, who was in retreat, more and more often, in the cocoon of his library chair: *Did you ever think he might cross over?*

Become one of them.

Mike, one of them? *Not possible. It simply cannot* be.

My aunt's circlings had a clever hawk-like quality. She began wide, maybe a little off subject and with the appearance of normality; her probings and inquiries always seemed innocent at first, superficial and apparently unimportant, but that was only if you ignored the tone, or if you didn't understand Hankspeak, a language in which I was fluent.

Your mother, does she like the cachepot I sent over? When I was there the other day I didn't see it out with flowers in it, as it should be. I chose it for that table in the living room. You know, the one with the funny little drawer that belonged to Mamma and, thank God, is still on grudging display.

Your mother—*is it possible that with all this new interest in decorating of hers, her taste is going too far toward country?*

(*Country* was said in the same critical tone as *mo-derne.*)

Doesn't she become bored *with Americana? I mean, all that primitivism—it's so repetitious. Shaker-shmaker. It reminds me of the Egyptians.*

All this was in code, but it was not difficult to decipher. It meant: Your mother doesn't like my gifts, so she doesn't like me. She doesn't share my taste, so she has inferior taste; more than that, she is an inferior person. A person who likes primitive things is herself in some way primitive. I'm a Greek; she's an Egyptian. I'm worldly; she's not. I'm a cultivated screenwriter; what is she, what has she achieved with her life? Other than you boys . . .

Honestly, I have no idea. How does your mother spend her days? Whom does she talk to?

What does she read?

Who is Merona, deep down inside?

The only way I could think to respond was with neutral, evasive mutterings and reassurances; half-answers and half-truths. Yes, the cachepot, she put a yellow ranunculus in it just the other day. Of course she still likes formal things. She's reading a novel now, it's by a woman, Doris somebody. I forget the title.

But these answers never satisfied.

Lovey, there's something I strongly believe. I believe it's essential to know a parent, a mother, the way I knew mine. To the very innermost parts of her being, her heart and soul. You remember how I guessed that my mother was in love with Henry when I was eleven years old? There were scores of other things I guessed or understood or knew about Mamma, just knew in my flesh.

Can you say that you know your mother in this way?

This question I never answered, I only listened, mute and with a tightness in my chest.

And can you say that she knows you in this way too?

Can you, Mike?

Mike?

My father presented a more complicated case. During their childhood he had been her cherished younger brother, her Magoof who had been their mother's *great supporter* in the *grim, unhappy* Portland years as *the world crumbled around us* and *that absurdity of a marriage showed its true loveless nature.* He grew into a handsome teenager who went off to war and returned a responsible, sober young man, an ace athlete and ambitious student of economics at UCLA. He had a *big brain* and *such a knack for business—a marvel to me, since I cannot even write a check or address an envelope.* (Both tasks fell to my uncle.)

Around the time Hank threw away Sylvia's things that day in The Apartment, Marty began to withdraw, as much as he could in this elaborately intertwined family, from his sister's particularly charged world. And then began . . .

Your father, I never hear from him anymore.

I first heard this when I was maybe fourteen. I went on hearing it for decades.

He is not the brother I grew up with.

Had such high hopes for.

Respected so much—once.

He's such a Goldstein—he thinks only of himself.

You don't want to be a Goldstein. The Goldstein men were heart-less, closed, and selfish. They were cheap and mean-spirited. The worst kind of men. I had hoped Martin would be an exception, but alas the apple . . .

——— ———

I returned from school one day to find both parents waiting for me in the living room and my brothers parked at friends' houses. Taken to-gether, a curious sign. My father was still wearing his work clothes. My mother had her shoes on in the house. Like my uncle, her brother, she never wore shoes at home.

"We have an appointment this afternoon, Mike," my father said, "and we would like you to come with us."

"What kind of an appointment?" I asked in a worried voice.

"With a man we have gone to speak to," my father said. "He is helping us understand some things."

"What things?"

There was a moment of silence, then my mother spoke up. "Things to do with our family . . . and your aunt and uncle. And to do with you . . . and school."

So they did know. Did they know? How and what did they know, when I had been so careful to hide every sign of bullying, every mark on my body, every scar on my self?

"Is it a psychiatrist?"

"Psychologist," my father said.

"Where did you find him?" I asked.

"Through a friend," my father explained.

"So you think I need a doctor, a head doctor?"

"It's not *you*," said my mother. "It's *we*. All of us. We all, as a group, don't seem able to——"

"You can go without me," I declared.

"We already have," he said, "but he wants to meet you. Talk to you."

I crossed my arms in front of my chest.

"Mike, we're trying to help."

"Help with what? I don't need help, and I am not coming with you. Sorry."

I went upstairs, and for good measure changed out of my clothes into my bathing suit. My parents would never make me go see this man in my bathing suit. I flopped onto my bed and opened *David Copperfield*, the novel I had under way.

Before long I detected the heavy sound of my father's tread on the stairs. I heard him when he was still at the low end, down around stair two or three. Instantly my stomach tightened. His steps grew louder, angrier. He didn't knock on the door this time. He simply swung it open, his nostrils already flaring.

"I understand you were not so open to coming to see me this evening."

He was my father's age, maybe a few years older. Balding, with thick black-rimmed glasses. His hands were oddly large, out of proportion to the rest of him. In another context, the hands of a musician.

"Who told you that?"

"Your parents—your father just now. I'm curious. How did they convince you?"

I was wearing my bathing suit under my jeans. This was my rebellion. My dissent. As I shifted in my chair, I could feel the bulk of extra fabric, the mesh liner; my own personal hairshirt.

"They just did."

"Can you give me a little more . . . information?"

My father had one of his temper tantrums—is that what you want to hear? He raised his voice and banged on my desk. He yelled so loudly the pictures on my wall began to tilt. My mother stood in the doorway, the tears welling in her eyes, begging him to stop. But he just kept screaming, and so I put on my pants and my shoes and I got into the backseat of the car, and that is how I came here. If you must know.

"I sense that is not something you would like to talk about."

I nodded stonily.

"Maybe we could talk about school. Tell me, do you have many friends there?"

Did he—did my parents—think I was an idiot?

"Sure. I have friends."

"Tell me about one."

"Why?"

He let out a sigh.

"I am here to help, you know."

"Help with what?"

"Is there no one at school, no situation there you would like to talk about? An uncomfortable situation?"

I remained silent.

He paused. "Your parents tell me that you have a close relationship with your aunt and uncle."

When here, too, I said nothing, he continued: "Your aunt is your father's sister, is that right? And married, also, to your mother's brother. It's not the kind of family configuration you come across all the time, and I come across all kinds of families in my work."

He paused again. "They have no children of their own, and they live near you, yes?"

"If you know all this already, why are you asking me?"

The pause was longer, more ruminative this time. I was aware of his eyes, behind those thick glasses, working, searching. "I can see that you are an intelligent young man," he said. "So I will be open with you. Obviously I have met with your parents. They are concerned about some aspects of the relationship you have with your aunt. It's not just you. It's the whole family system."

The whole family system? He must have seen some consternation or, worse, disgust on my face, because he retreated.

"At this point all I am trying to do is engage you in conversation."

"But I don't want to talk."

"Yes, that's clear. Only . . ."

"Only what?"

"It might possibly help you."

"Which 'it'? The talking 'it'?"

"Yes, *that* 'it.' Talking to me."

"Why you?" I said insolently.

"Because it's my life's work to talk to younger people. It's what I studied at school, what I have been trained in, and what I have done for many years now. I like to think I can help them."

"Help *them* how?"

He considered for a moment. "To be more comfortable in themselves. In their lives. For example, I understand you have been having some stomach pains."

I began to have one just then.

"And I understand that doctors, medical doctors, have checked you out thoroughly and that they have not been able to come up with a diagnosis."

"I refused to drink the liquid."

"Why is that? Why would you do that? Why wouldn't you want a physician to look into your stomach?"

"It disgusted me."

"The idea of a doctor looking?"

"The taste of the white liquid."

He smiled. "Either way, I think I can understand."

"Well, if you understand this, all this, then you don't need to ask me about it, do you?"

"When I say I 'understand,'" he said, overlooking my tone, "it doesn't mean I get everything. It means I have an idea, I would like to know more. I don't mind telling you that."

Silence opened up between us. He just looked at me with clear eyes that later, much later, I might have described as expressing a combination of puzzlement and concern. In the moment I found their penetrations offensive. More than that, indigestible, as repulsive to me as the white liquid the stomach doctor had wanted me to drink.

When I first came into his office, I had noticed a large sandbox pitched at table height and on the shelves behind it an array of tiny figures made out of wood and plastic and metal in every form imaginable. There were firemen and policemen, soldiers and street sweepers, kings and queens and peasants; there were animals and monsters, mothers and fathers, boys and girls, black and white, dressed and naked; many were in multiples, and they were all lined up in tidy rows, an out-of-place treasure trove of a toy store.

He turned to face the shelves now. He took two men and two women and three boys. He set them into the sandbox. He said, "Maybe you want to arrange these figures in a way that could help tell a story. Sometimes kids find it useful to have something . . . tangible. They tend to be younger than you are, but I've found it effective with people all the way into their twenties."

And he had called me intelligent. I stared at him.

After a while he began making little circles in the sand with his index finger. I shrugged, then began to do the same. He circled and I circled, I was silent and he was silent. When fifty minutes were over, he stood up and I stood up. He opened the door, and my parents and I exchanged places. I sat down in the waiting room, my arms tightly crossed against my chest, while they disappeared into his office.

In the car on the way home I asked what he had said.

"He said you were very resistant," my mother told me, emitting a long sigh.

"Do I have to go back?" I asked.

"No," she answered with another long sigh. "You don't have to go back."

Alfred, as we grew older, had become more creative in his bullying, which followed me from Wonderland Avenue Elementary to Bancroft

Junior High like some kind of malevolent shadow or curse. He did sometimes continue to pounce on me physically, but more and more often he worked behind the scenes, a diabolical puppeteer.

I should have known better than to think that the transition to junior high would bring about some kind of change in Alfred and make it possible for me (both of us) to have a fresh start in a new school. Such naively wishful thinking underwent an abrupt revision when, within the very first week of junior high, I had been approached by a group of ninth graders who closed around me threateningly to ask if it was true that my name was actually Suzie as they had been "informed."

It devastated me to hear that name pronounced so early on in this new setting, because I had hoped, or dreamed, that I might be able to let my guard down finally; and because I was tired and increasingly lonely, even if I covered my loneliness by doing perfect work at school and by always being busy, reading or writing or drawing; and because going dead had become a plainly awful, restricting, and stultifying way to navigate the school day. And here I was now having to gear up—suit up—for a very wearying kind of battle all over again.

What was it about me? Hadn't I learned to conceal my sketch pad in a plain brown wrapper, folded and tucked just so, the way we were taught to wrap our textbooks in homeroom? Didn't I sit off by myself at recess and lunch hour? Was I not careful to walk with my gaze averted, never making eye contact, never letting anyone see how humiliating it was when, season after season, I was chosen last for whatever competitive sport's team was at that moment being assembled?

And didn't I do everything I could think of to keep my distance from Alfred during the school day and—increasingly—afterward?

This may have been the problem, or part of the problem. I no longer made myself available to trade stamps or baseball cards or to play handball against our garage door—I had become exasperated by the like/hate, attract/repel, hang out/beat up approach to young male "friendship" that was on offer. The curious thing was, though, the more I avoided Alfred, the more he came after me. I was *his* sport, all season, full stop.

In the junior high school years Alfred tended to reserve his physical assaults on me for our bus trips home, when we were among the last kids to be dropped off, or just afterward, during the walk home from our bus stop. I dreaded the stretch of Greenvalley Road that led from the bus stop to Alfred's house more than any piece of street, anywhere, since often, all too often, it was empty except for Alfred, one of his sidekicks, and me; or just Alfred and me.

Alfred and those fingernails of his and me: he looked after them the way a master chef tends his knives. And now that he was older and bigger, when his nails dug in, they dug in deeper, and took more flesh, and brought up more blood—so much blood that there came a day finally when I could not conceal the marks on my hands from my mother as I came in through the front door and made a beeline for the bathroom sink.

My mother glanced at the red streaks streaming down the backs of my hands, and she knew. Probably she had had some inkling, or more than an inkling, all along. Wasn't that one of the reasons she and my father had taken me to the man with the sandbox? Hadn't he asked about school, someone at school? If she had known, it would appear that she had been at as much of a loss as to what to do about Alfred as I was. That day, though, she did see something. She waited until my father came home from work and then showed him my hands, and together, with scarcely a word passing between them, they walked across the street and down two driveways, where they found Alfred playing ball by himself.

You could hear my father's voice all through the canyon. The Bergman Temper, deployed appropriately for once, brought out a thundering threat: "If you ever lay another hand on my son, Alfred Druckerman, I personally will see to it that those hands of yours never touch a basketball again." Even my mother, generally so soft-spoken, joined in, saying in a loud, high voice, "You are a bad, foul piece of garbage, Alfred! Everyone knows it and has for years! You belong in juvenile detention, not Laurel Canyon. Stay away—do you hear us? Stay away from our son, stay away from our house. Stay *away*."

I stood out of sight, hiding behind a corner of our garage. I was mortified, grateful, and scared—more scared than anything, because much as part of me was relieved that my parents understood, finally, what had been going on and had tried to help, another part of me knew better how kids worked and realized that there would be consequences.

We sat down to dinner as on any ordinary night. No one mentioned Alfred's name. Afterward I went to bed unable to sleep, dreading what would happen at school the next day.

In the morning Alfred and his henchmen were waiting for me in the school yard, with a taunt already prepared: *Suzie needs her mommy and daddy to do her fighting for her. Suzie can't stand up for herself—she really is a girl, now we know it for sure . . .*

They went on in this vein until the bell rang twenty minutes later. They did not touch me, though. Not that day.

On the bus ride home Alfred kept his distance, but once we got off he started again, coming up close to me, half whispering and half spitting into my ear, the same old faggot-sissy-Suzie refrain.

Finally, I turned around to face him. "Hey, Alfred," I said evenly, "you want to come trade stamps or something? I've got some new stuff."

Immediately old Janus swapped faces. "Sure," he said with a shrug. "I've got some new ones too," he added. "Important ones. From my uncle." Alfred's uncle was a "real" stamp collector according to whom— Alfred had once told me—Alfred had advanced to the sixth grade of stamp collecting while I was stuck back in nursery school.

"I'll wait for you," I said. And I did wait for him, very patiently on the side of our house.

It was fire season in the canyon, and my father had recently bought a new power hose that had an extra-long reach and a nozzle with an extra-strong, extra-sharp spray. I glanced at the hose and in a flash I knew what I was going to do. I bent down and turned the spigot on full blast, which allowed the pressure to build up behind the nozzle. It felt like I was holding something alive in my hands; stiffened with water under pressure, the hose was like a snake getting ready to strike.

Alfred came up the hill and across the street. I stepped around the corner. He saw me and froze.

I pulled the lever and released a blast of water so powerful that it knocked him down and sent his precious "advanced" sixth-grade stamp collection flying.

"Hey, what the—"

I stopped up his speech with even more water, aimed at that

mouth of his, which had said so many horrible things to me over the years . . . his mouth, his nose, his eyes. He groped around and somehow got hold of his soggy stamp album and half crawled and half staggered across the street. Even after he stood up and started hightailing it for home, the water found him. I sprayed his feet, his thighs, his butt, his receding back. I chased him across the street and down the hill. That new hose of my father's had a long run—seventy-five feet, maybe a hundred, and that powerfully spraying water reached another thirty feet, easily. The water pursued Alfred all the way to his driveway, where his mother, hearing him shout and cry for help, had come running. I blasted her too, for good measure—for interfering with my revenge, for giving birth to her beast of a son, for knowing or not knowing, it no longer mattered, what a terror he was, for never reining him in. "You crazed boy, stop it right now!" she gurgled shrilly, her waterlogged voice at a decibel that did nothing, meant nothing, said nothing to me. I was spraying, dousing, *soaring*; even after the two of them ran inside and closed the front door and drew the blinds, I was my own personal tempest. I saturated the driveway, the plants, the car, the mailbox with its newly delivered mail . . .

Finally I went home, turned off the hose, and wound it into a precise coil. I went upstairs and changed into dry clothes. Then I put away my stamp collection for good.

On the following Monday Alfred was back to Suzie-ing me, but either he had lost some of his grit or, more likely I now think, taking action against him had made me less vulnerable to him, and his words flew past me like the wind. No, not as much as that. A breeze.

——— ———

Gradually I began to spend more time with my uncle. How this happened, and whether my parents had anything to do with it, I had no idea. But after the visit to the therapist's office, and after they marched across the street to yell at Alfred, something in our wider family rhythms shifted.

My uncle's reaching out to me developed in tandem with certain changes in my aunt. More and more she had begun to go beyond her circlings and had started angling for open fights. Her targets were indiscriminate and unpredictable: family members who disappointed her, friends who were less stalwart than she demanded, colleagues who were found wanting in deference, or mettle, or creativity, or spunk. And when my aunt felt offended or hurt, no matter how unreasonable her complaint, my uncle—when he was with her—simply backed her up: what Hank felt was just; the way Hank saw the world (increasingly against her, or them) was the way the world was. When she became disaffected, that was it. Depending on the form the excommunication took, Irving was the one to dial the phone number or address the envelope or (more than once, memorably) dispatch the telegram. Just as had they merged their writing styles into a single voice, so it appeared they had merged the way they felt about the people they knew. Gradually they went from being Hank and Irv to HankandIrv.

"Irving," my father said with crisp disapproval, "is a hold-your-coater."

"My brother has vanished," my mother said. "I no longer know who he is. Who *is* he?"

All this was true, nearly 100 percent true, when my aunt and uncle were together, and it made them increasingly difficult to be around. But my uncle, being my uncle, managed to maintain a certain sly distance, possibly a life-saving, sanity-preserving distance, by claiming a sliver of every day for himself. In doing so, for a piece of each day, he again became Irv apart from HankandIrv.

This Irving was not an at-home Irving but an out-in-the-world Irving.

This was not a morning or midday Irving, but an afternoon or evening Irving.

This was not a quiet or contemplative Irving, a reading, writing, or reflecting Irving, but an active Irving who needed to be busy doing . . . pretty much anything that did not involve my aunt.

This Irving needed wheels. In the first part of their marriage, for nearly twenty years, quite amazingly my aunt and uncle shared a single car—in the canyon, where the only place accessible on foot was more canyon. When Huffy died in 1969, my uncle inherited her dark blue Oldsmobile, a big old battered boat of a vehicle that did not particularly jibe with his style, though it did free him to go out on his own. After a few years the Olds was replaced by a sporty white Thunderbird, and after that an even sportier hunter-green Camaro.

But the car I most associate with my uncle was "a perk," as he giddily described it, that was part of a two-script deal that their agent, Everett Ziegler, negotiated in the mid-1970s with David Begelman, who was then head of Columbia Pictures. The car was a chocolate-brown two-seater Mercedes 450SL coupe with an alternate canvas convertible top (which he never used) and beautiful aromatic caramel-colored leather upholstery. It rode so low to the ground and with such a cant to the seats that my uncle almost seemed to be reclining as he drove.

My uncle loved that car. He did crazy, un-Irving, extra-thrilling things in it, like hitting one hundred miles an hour on the open highway between Palm Springs and L.A. or swinging into an empty parking lot and saying, "Kid, how about if you take it for a spin?" He kept the car immaculate too, as gleaming as his white socks and the kitchen floor, which he insisted on mopping every evening after dinner.

In the garage he parked it as far from my aunt's Buick Riviera as possible, so that when she opened her door she would not risk scratching his, and every week he had it washed and hand waxed; yet for all this the car as object was less meaningful to him than the car as a form of liberation that sprang him from the maison. Every single day after he and my aunt were finished writing, and he had finished retyping (thereby polishing) the morning's work, and had eaten his lunch, which every single day consisted of fresh fruit, cashews, a glass of milk, and three or four graham crackers, my uncle would get in his Mercedes and disappear.

"Where is it that you find to go every afternoon?" my aunt often inquired.

"Out."

"But where 'out'?"

"To do errands."

"What kind of errands?"

"I buy paper towels. I take the sheets down to Sol. Every three weeks I have my hair cut."

"How thrilling."

"Would you like to come along, darling?" (This was asked in a voice that clearly anticipated the answer.)

She made a horizontal slicing motion in the air with her hand. "Corky, when I finish work I do *pleasurable* things. I go antiquing. I go down to Skillets to look for new dishes. I noodle around in Pasadena. I do *not* go to the *super*market."

My uncle would then turn to me and say, "What about you, Mike? Would *you* like to tag along with me this afternoon?"

He knew the answer to this question too. Of course I wanted to tag along. I was happy to go anywhere with him.

And where did we go? We did indeed make a trip to the supermarket for the mundane items my aunt never bought, like the aforementioned paper towels, toilet paper, and (of course) cleaning solvents, especially those dedicated to washing floors.

Or we went to the dry cleaner's—Sol's, on Sunset Boulevard just down from Schwab's, where he insisted on taking his sheets to be ironed, because after years of staying at "the Dorch" in London he had grown accustomed to the pleasures of an ironed sheet.

Or we headed down to the public library at Hollywood and Ivar, or on special occasions all the way to the central library downtown, where he liked to point out the 1930s-era murals—"my period"— that depicted the history of California. This was a semi-professional excursion, since he was always on the lookout for material to adapt into screenplays, and one source was the happenstance of the local library, where his attention could run casually along the shelves.

Sometimes we drove out to the smoke shop—in his smoking years—in Santa Monica, a small, fragrant old-world emporium on Wilshire Boulevard where he replenished his pipe tobacco and paraphernalia (the Cuban cigars, however, came from a secret source, never disclosed).

Or we went to the bank for his weekly infusion of cash, thick stacks of twenties from which now and then he would pluck a bill and say, "Would you like one, Mike?"

The verve with which my uncle approached these chores suggested that they held a place of particular importance in his day, possibly his life. I felt it in the way he slipped into Yiddish with Sol, or asked the barber to tell him about his childhood in prewar Warsaw, or how, when he was faced with a shelf packed with floor solvents, he would hold up to the light first one bottle and then another, evaluating them in mock imitation of the way other men might evaluate a fine burgundy.

These rounds of errands always ended at the sacrosanct hour of four o'clock, when my uncle met his great (and pretty much only) friend Rubin Carson, who was Falstaff to Irving's Prince Hal.

Ruby was shorter than my uncle and at times nearly twice as large, overall a rather unhealthy-looking physical specimen with a big pockmarked nose, a strangely high voice, and a mad-scientist halo of hair that flew out in all directions. He called my uncle Bub. My uncle called him Bub. The mutual nickname was a verbal embrace, but even without it you could feel how much they reveled in each other's company.

Until 1969, Coffee Hour happened at Schwab's on Sunset; following the completion of the maison, when my aunt and uncle became more oriented to the Valley, it happened at Du-par's just east of Laurel Canyon on Ventura Boulevard in Studio City, where the two men always turned up punctually, always took a large booth in either the middle or the back of the restaurant, and always drank two cups of black coffee apiece. A slice of (fruit) pie was sometimes shared between them, sometimes eaten by my uncle alone.

Being invited to Coffee Hour was like being admitted to a Lewis Carroll world where coffee was a potion with transformative properties and a slice of pie could change grown men. I often wondered what my aunt would make of the way my uncle and his friend spoke. Ruby would lower himself into the booth and, as though resuming a conversation left off just minutes earlier, begin with a remark like, "Do you know what I think man's greatest problem is? He spends all his life trying to get back into a tiny hole." (It took me a while to work out its particular location.) He said, "Make no mistake about it, women like a funny guy only as long as he has lots of dough."

In Ruby's company my uncle spoke in a way that he did with nobody else. "Talent can get you laid too, Bub," he would say . . . which intimated what, exactly? A different aperçu began, "You know how it is when you're newly married, and you can't stop fucking your wife all the time . . ." Here, too, I had to pause to ponder: Had my uncle just emitted a forbidden *fuck*? Had he said that word in conjunction with my *aunt*? My eyes grew so wide I was certain they were going to bump up against my hairline.

For nearly a year Ruby and my uncle *and* my aunt had lived together, when Ruby was between marriages. During this time, which was before my time, he joined my aunt and uncle in their old house on Wonderland Park Avenue, where they had converted a freestanding garage into a studio apartment that they referred to ever after as the governess's house. I found this domicile to be one of the most unsettling interiors I knew. A space that had been devised and built for someone who never lived in it yet left her ghostly mark on it nevertheless, it looked sturdy but felt conditional, smelled odd, and was so indifferently cleaned that the water in the toilet was covered in a beige crust. Unthinkable as this was in my aunt's world, it was also filled with furniture that had never been logically arranged but was jammed in any which way.

The governess's house was haunted by the ghost of a child who (speaking of James, Henry . . . or Albee, Edward) had been planned and hoped for—conceived of, though never successfully conceived. The idea was that my aunt and uncle would have a child, likely just one, timed to arrive in sync with my parents' firstborn, meaning me— even though my aunt was ten years my mother's senior—so that the children could grow up together "almost like siblings." As a working woman, my aunt would require the services of a governess, much as she herself had when she was young (the lady being German, severe, and enormously fat) in the years before the Depression ruined my grandfather's fortune. The governess was to live in this room and take care of this baby, this cousin who would have been doubly my cousin as my aunt and uncle were doubly my aunt and uncle—more so, even, since these doubly shared genes would be located in a single person.

But this ghost cousin never came into being, because my aunt was diagnosed with endometriosis, for which in those days there was no treatment, and so she and my uncle remained childless.

My aunt often spoke about this unborn child, who interestingly was expected to be a she and whose name was to have been Agatha.

The *she* part somewhat lessened—somewhat—the competition between Agatha and me. It was already hard enough being the surrogate child, the alternate child who served as a substitute to a ghost and for many years, until the fantasy petered out, heard such pointed remarks as—

Agatha would have read The Mill on the Floss *by the time she was seven—but of course girls are always ahead of boys.*

Agatha would have been a wonderful mamma's helper, don't you think? I can just imagine us baking brownies on a gloomy Sunday afternoon, lifting our blue moods together.

Agatha sounds like a writer's name, don't you agree? Agatha Frank Ravetch. No. Better: Agatha Ravetch-Frank. Hyphenated, of course!

I expect Agatha would have started composing poetry as soon as she could hold a pen. Good poetry too.

Agatha would have been a very artistic *child. She might very well have illustrated her own writing, like the Brontë sisters. I don't think Agatha would have bothered with stamp or rock collecting or Simon and what-funkel.*

Agatha would have married a gentleman and a scholar, probably a Rhodes scholar. Why, she was likely to have been one herself!

Dear Agatha, how I would have adored you so . . .

Ruby was a writer, like my uncle. Unlike my uncle, he also had a day job as an upholsterer. He helped manage the business of his immigrant father, who had left his Glendale workshop to his two sons when he died. Ruby's finesse with draping and skirting and piping and tufting and welting and slipcovering earned him a special corner in my aunt's heart. As long as her chairs and sofas were expertly reupholstered, *quick-quick* and at cost too, she didn't mind Coffee Hour so much. She didn't mind when the two men began to go out to dinner once a week, religiously, on Wednesday (later Thursday) nights, always to Musso & Frank's, "the oldest restaurant in Hollywood," as it still declares itself, where my uncle liked to point out the bar where Faulkner drank himself numb after putting in frustrating days writing for the studios and where Irving had a special relationship with the maître d', whom he slipped one of his crisp twenties so that he and Ruby could always be assured of having the same large booth by the front door, where they dined on chiffonade salad followed by fried sand dabs, potatoes Lyonnaise, and heavily buttered peas. Ruby drank; my uncle never did. Between them the two men invariably knew several people at other booths in the room, among them old Hollywood luminaries like Billy Wilder and Pandro Berman, and part of the evening ritual was offering polite salutations to these diminished lions before settling into their usual booth.

Even rarer than an invitation to Coffee Hour was an invitation to Musso's followed by an hour at the cherished Pickwick bookstore farther west along Hollywood Boulevard: two floors jammed with pure reading gold from which I would always be invited to select a volume or two to take home.

Everything about these evenings contributed to their celebratory feeling, from my uncle's special relationship with the maître d' (learned how, and when?), to the old-school red-jacketed waiters, to the menus that were freshly printed every day, to the sighting of these Hollywood elders. "In the old days he was a kind of *god*," my uncle said the night he ran into "Mr." Berman. "He made it possible for Astaire and Rogers to dance their dance. He used to come to your grandmother for story advice. *Now* look at him. He's frail as a chicken bone. I wonder if that will happen to me. *Will* it happen to me? What do you think, Mike? Will I make it to his age? Will anyone stop by my booth if I do?"

Quite remarkably Coffee Hour and the Musso's dinners went on for years, decades. They were the only example I had growing up of male friendship in action. Although my father remained friends with two men he met as boys in 1939 when he was thirteen and moved from Portland to Los Angeles, they saw one another mostly with their wives, in ritualized couple-y dinners that had nothing of the vigor or furtive daring of my uncle away from my aunt. Wry, gossiping, reveling in conversation, in Ruby's company my uncle seemed to step out of one role, or character, and into another. One thing was clear: my uncle was free, and his freedom was infectious, and plain fun.

Alas, over the years, a shadowy side gradually edged into these meetings between the two men. One large and complex theme was their careers: my uncle's took off, impressively; Ruby's was far more mixed. On the page or screen Ruby's writing could be acerbic and dexterous, but he didn't have either my uncle's talent or his luck. To get by, Ruby wrote anything and everything: columns, magazine pieces, how-to books, radio and TV scripts, movie treatments, what used to be called additional dialogue. "Low-rent stuff," my uncle sniffed, if always behind Ruby's back; but how can you hold such an opinion of your close friend's work without having it seep out somehow? Ruby knew what Irving thought, and began to speak caustically about my aunt and uncle's talent and success. "The Rav*riches*," he christened them; especially after a new movie opened well, it could be uncomfortable to listen to him erupt in a little flare of jealousy, offered however candidly and in however blackly comedic a spirit.

Far more complex still—inevitably—was my aunt.

I remember with great clarity the first time I heard my uncle's friend say to him across a plate of sand dabs, "Bub, that woman detests me, you know."

That woman? It was as if someone had shot off a cannon in Musso's; only why hadn't the windowpanes shattered? And why was nobody ducking but me?

"Hank has been giving me those dark looks of hers again, Bub," Ruby said another time. "Don't pretend you haven't noticed." "I don't know what I did to offend Hank, but it must have been something pretty lousy. She's been treating me like dirt." He made these remarks openly, sometimes unhappily, sometimes grinning as though he knew he was crossing a boundary or breaking a rule, but always with a kind of fuck-it-all insouciance that I found alluring. No one else I knew—*no one*—spoke like this about my aunt.

How did my uncle react? That was the curious thing. He chortled. He emitted one of his six-step sighs. He waved his hand. He said, "Bub, she does not." Or: "Bub, you're right, she does." Or: "What do we care, Bub, about her?"

We. Her.

Her?

They were made to care, eventually, because eventually it became Ruby's turn to become one of my aunt's targets. She had been laying the groundwork for a long time. The first indication was his change of name. He went from Ruby to Rubin. Such a turn toward the formal was never a good sign. Next came the commentary. "Rubin is not as funny as in days gone by." "Rubin is so full of himself, I don't know what you two find to talk about." She would send one of his columns flying across the room, whip off her reading glasses, and say, "Rubin should have stuck to upholstery, what a shame he sold his brother his share of the business." "Rubin's new lady friend is *pas du tout comme il faut*. A manufacturer of lingerie! I don't know *what* he sees in that woman, much less what she sees in him." "I happen to have no plans for Thursday night. Do you know what? I may very well join you two at Musso's. It's been years since I've had a good sand dab . . ."

It wasn't until my uncle was well into one of his first illnesses that my aunt took the actual arrow out of her quiver and loaded it into her bow. During Irving's open-heart surgery, Hank kept close track of who checked in and how quickly and often. Ruby had gone AWOL. In actuality, if I recall correctly, he was out of town visiting his troubled daughter, but the facts don't matter, since they were always so much the same: even if he had not done his best, had been scared or flawed or self-absorbed, he was yet another person who had come up short, broken the rules of friendship as they were written by my aunt, and had *showed his true colors, at last.*

This was one number my aunt did dial for herself while my uncle was still in the hospital, thumbing through their phone book until she reached the appropriate page. With icy calm she informed Ruby, my uncle's friend of more than forty years, that he was not welcome at my uncle's bedside, either at the present moment or at any point in the foreseeable future. "A true friend," she told him, "comes around *before* a man is wheeled into the operating room. He doesn't wait a day, an hour, a moment even. A true friend stands by and stays close." Ruby had not been a true friend at this moment in Irving's life; now that she was free to speak her mind, she might as well say that he had not been a true friend for several—many—years leading up to now. A true friend was made of different material entirely. A true friend had integrity, morality, ethics; a true friend put friendship ahead of all other matters. A true friend . . .

How my aunt relished recounting these diatribes and dismissals of hers. She reenacted this one *en famille*, at our dinner table one evening following a long day at my uncle's bedside. As she reproduced these stinging sentences, her fatigue retreated and her eyes sharpened, and you saw the Hank of the story conferences, the Hank of the writing sessions, the brilliant, inventing, energized Hank spliced onto the intimidating, criticizing, dismissing, destroying Hank. It was quite something to behold.

My father, from his place at the head of the table, listened silently, his face turning grayer and grayer the more she spoke. My mother busied herself in the kitchen as she increasingly did when my aunt came to dinner, pausing to listen in and shake her head in dismay. We children stared into our plates, afraid of the fire in her eyes, the fury in her voice, the pleasure (it seemed like pleasure, a twisted form of joy) she took in imparting this phone call in gruesome and meticulous detail.

After she left, my father said, "My sister has gone too far this time. She is going to end up a very lonely woman, I am afraid."

My mother from the kitchen said, "He wasn't even *her* friend."

And Ruby?

The rage and heartache he experienced following this unstitching of his lifelong friendship with my uncle nearly matched the betrayal he felt when his first wife ran off with his best friend. He tried to phone my uncle for days, weeks, then months—but for as long as she could, my aunt made sure that my uncle would not come to the phone. When they did finally speak, my uncle used his health as an excuse for needing to take a hiatus from Coffee Hour and Musso's. Which is to say, he gave in, yet again, to my aunt.

Time, a lot of hurting time, went by before Ruby turned this rejection into one of his extended tragicomic confessionals, although (unlike most every other event in his personal life) it was one he refrained from telling on television or putting into print; but he did make the rounds of their shared social circle, and he did come for years to see my mother and my father, to rant and to vent and to ask for help understanding (as if), and sometimes to sob big messy spilly man tears in our living room over coffee that my mother brewed in her trusty Melita filter system and served black of course, but with no accompanying pie, though now and then she managed to rustle up a cookie or two to accompany her patient commiseration.

Years later my uncle and his old friend ran into each other in Studio City and began to get together again, now and then for dinner, sometimes alone, more often coupled. Either my aunt had undergone one of her momentary softenings or else her social calendar had more gaps in it that season than she would have liked, or perhaps she had forgotten (her mind worked this way too) why she was so angry in the first place with Rubin, who reverted back to Ruby, *dear pathetic old Ruby, whose life really is a tale of almost Shakespearean woe.*

When I was much older and one day found my uncle alone and in just the right reflective mood (these had to be gauged carefully and appealed to judiciously), I asked him whether he missed his regular four o'clock meetings at Du-par's.

"Quite honestly, Mike, it was becoming rather tedious, Ruby and all his *shtick.*"

He sat back in his reading chair. "Besides, the doctors won't let me have caffeine anymore. And what's the point of Coffee Hour without coffee?"

——— ———

Ruby waned, but there was still that open slot in my uncle's afternoon, when he was compelled to get out of the house and off the hill. Whom did he turn to for company at that point of the day? Often—regularly—my mother. By an arrangement I never understood, on many afternoons around four o'clock she would come downstairs in her sandals and sunglasses and stand in the window, just as I used to when I was a small boy. My uncle's Mercedes would swing into the driveway, and he would wait for her, never impatiently, never honking, as she gathered her keys and purse and made her way outside.

And where did they go, this pair of adult siblings? Off the hill. Always that. To the city, the Valley. Sometimes for an actual cup of coffee (now strictly decaf), but more typically, I learned later, when my mother made sure I learned these things (it was as if she'd deposited all the details into a savings account, not knowing how or by whom or when they would be taken out again later in life, but realizing that it was critical to accrue them nevertheless), they would simply drive, around and around, past The Apartment; up to Beachwood, where my uncle had lived on his own before he married my aunt; out along Wilshire to Santa Monica, whose beach light and beach scent brought a sense of well-being to both of them, from having grown up, happily, by the water down in Long Beach.

During these drives my uncle didn't talk so much as unload. That was how my mother put it when she came to tell me about them later: "Your uncle unloaded." Or: "There was no stopping him; he was like a faucet." *Merona, did you notice that Danny didn't look up from the television screen when we came over the other night? Why is it that Steve never happens to be home when we visit? Why doesn't he come to visit us? Michael*—in a dark, troubled whisper—*Merona, Michael is not reading enough. We have concerns about his intellectual development.* Later on: *Merona, Michael is drifting away from us, from Hank. What's going on there? Do you have any insights to share with me? Hank is up nights worried that he is becoming too like his father—withdrawn and remote. Something just is not right. Can you help me to understand? Please, can you?*

My mother responded by laughing—how else? *Irving, you do realize that it's ridiculous to be offended by kids who unwind by watching a little TV after school, or prefer to spend time with other kids rather than their aunt and uncle, or who aren't so up on their George Eliot. Come on.*

But, Merona, you don't get it. Hank's feelings are hurt.

Oh, I get it, Irving. I just think it's silly. More than that—it's absurd. What about the rest of us? What about our *feelings?*

What about them?

——— ———

My uncle was probably at his absolute most appealing as a storyteller. He told stories when we were out in the world in that cherished roadster of his, or at Coffee Hour with Ruby, or when, after Ruby was banished, it was just the two of us. He told them much more sparingly when we were at the maison, because if my aunt was around, more often than not, especially as I grew older, she would pipe up—

Haven't you heard all this before? I have—a thousand times, easily. What are you doing—writing a book?

What is it you find so interesting about the past? We live in the present—the present is what matters. The past is nothing but dust.

Or: *Why don't you ask* me *about* my *life? Do you not find my personal history as captivating as your uncle's?*

I had asked her about her life, in great detail, and I did find her as captivating as my uncle, there could be no question about that— although other adjectives might have been more suitable in moments like these. But asking my uncle about the past, or listening closely as he volunteered certain stories, was a way of drawing the Irving of the closet into the outside world. It was a way of extending the separate, jocose, charismatic Irving, who during day-to-day life at the maison often remained obscured.

That was part of it, to be sure. But there was something else. Many of my uncle's stories were little puzzles that I heard one way when I was a child and another as I moved further into life. All stories are like that, to some degree; they change as the listener does. My uncle's stories were a special case, however: being so polished, so *written*, they seemed to ask more than most for distanced review. I collected them as if they were talismans, or koans, sensing somehow (but how?) that I would want to return to them later on, possibly to see whether they held a key to the central mystery at hand, which was how it was that two such different Irvings could dwell within the same man.

My uncle's most straightforward stories concerned my grand-father, Shalom Ravetch—*the finest human being I have ever known, Mike. Not many sons can say that about their fathers, you will find.*

He told me about Shalom's own father, David Leon Ravetch, a forceful and apparently loathsome figure who, when his sons were sluggish at studying their Talmud, slid the belt out of his pants and lashed the backs of their hands until they were red and swollen, and the Hebrew flowed out of them as readily as their tears.

This story was always juxtaposed with Shalom's own teaching style: when Irving and his brother, Herbert, opened their Talmuds a generation later, pennies would miraculously drop down onto the page.

"You see," Shalom would say, "God is so pleased that you are learning what he has to teach that he is sending you pennies from heaven."

Irving told me—several times—about the night Shalom and his family hid in the woods from the pogrom that destroyed their village near Zhitomir, and he told me about the grueling year that followed, while they prepared to leave Russia. David Leon had had a decent job, one of the few permitted to Jews: he was a forester with a fairly substantial swath of land under his management. After the pogrom he lost his job, and money was so scarce that for several months my great-grandparents could not keep all five children together. They sent one, Shalom, to live with his aunt and uncle in a separate village.

On market day nine-year-old Shalom accompanied his aunt into town and saw his mother buying potatoes. If she saw him, she pre-tended she didn't, or she looked away.

At this point in the story my uncle would always slow down to draw out the suspense. "Imagine this, Mike. Imagine this good woman as she climbs up into a cart and faces forward. She can't look at her son because to look at him would break her heart—and his. She looks ahead . . . the horses start off down the road . . . and your grandfather, do you know what he does? He runs after her, clamps his hands onto the back of the cart, and cries, 'Mamma! Mamma!' He falls and he is dragged through the unpaved streets until his knees are bloodied to the bone, and he has no choice but to let go. He lies in the street sobbing, bleeding, aching . . . and his mother, she never looks back, not once."

My uncle told this story as he told most stories, with the kind of equanimity that you can summon only when you know what followed: the family was reunited; they left the pogroms and the Jew-haters behind; they traveled to America; they reinvented themselves; the children were educated; they built new lives in a safe, new, and free country. They were clever, they got away, and they thrived. He knew all that, and I did too . . . but I could not take my inner eye off my grandfather, who, at my age when I first heard the story, was sent off to live with his aunt and uncle and ignored by his mother, his knees bloodied and his heart breaking.

A child consigned to an aunt and uncle, alternate parents, the *wrong* parents—was that what burned itself into my consciousness? Undoubtedly. But there was another reverberation. This story echoed, or foreshadowed, the central story of my uncle's own childhood, which he told (and retold), not, as his friend Ruby did, for the avenging properties such retellings appeared to confer, but because, I eventually believed, he was trying to figure out how he had come to be who he had come to be.

Irving would never have put it this way. He wasn't wired like that. He would have said that he told this story because it was so comical.

Well, tragicomical; even he might have added that.

The story always began with the train trip west he took with his aunt Rose. He was ten—about the same age at which his father had been sent to a neighboring village. Only Irving was being sent to a very faraway village known as Los Angeles, also, as it happened, to live with an aunt and uncle, an apparently *kind* aunt and uncle, and their five children, his cousins. Every winter since he'd turned three Irving had come down with double pneumonia brought on, his doctors believed, by a case of asthma so extreme that the only thing they could think to do was banish him from the severe eastern winters. Shalom was finishing his rabbinical degree while working at a (dreaded) job as a pharmacist, and since the family resources were far too limited to maintain two households, the decision was made to dispatch Irving to California. "The moment I saw the western sky, Mike, I could not take my eyes off it," he liked to say. "The big sky, the big flat desert, the cactus, the wildflowers—it was like we'd traveled to another planet. When the train stopped for an hour in Arizona, we got out, Aunt Rose and I, and I took one breath of that crisp air, and it was the deepest, clearest breath I had taken in years. That's when I realized that the asthma was not going to kill me."

In Los Angeles, every Sunday Irving would sit down at his desk at his aunt Rose's instruction and write a letter home while she stood over him making sure that he hit all the key points:

> Dear Folks,
> Hello and how are you? I am fine. I am great, actually.
> I am healthy, and I am doing well in school.
> I love living in California, and I love you.
> Your son (and brother),
> Irving (Dover) Ravetch

Now and then a photograph would accompany the weekly letter. In the early ones Irving would puff out his stomach as proof of his robust health.

Once a year Shalom would take the train out west by himself, to see his son. He stayed for a week. This was the sum total of Irving's experience of his nuclear family between the ages of ten and thirteen. Each time he visited, Shalom would make sure he saw Irving alone at least once, and during this one time alone together he would ask Irving the same questions, without knowing that his sister, Aunt Rose, had been coaching the boy beforehand:

"How are you, son?"

"I'm great, Father."

"That's what you write in your letters. But I want to know really and truly. Is Aunt Rose treating you well?"

"She treats me great, Father."

"Is that true?"

"Well, she makes me lie down after school while the other boys play ball."

"She wants you to stay healthy, you know. We all do."

"And she makes me eat all my supper."

"That's a good thing. You need your strength. Now what about your cousins?"

"They're great. They treat me like a brother."

"So you're all right, then?"

"I'm all right. I'm great, Father."

"And you think you can stick it out until I finish school?"

"I *know* I can stick it out until you finish school. Really, everything here is going just swell."

He was ten, then eleven, then twelve. Every year, the same conversation, preceded by the same well-intentioned coaching. Then came the summer Irving turned thirteen. Shalom conducted a family bar mitzvah for his eldest son, and Aunt Rose prepared a festive lunch. Afterward father and son went for a walk alone together.

"How are you, son?"

"I'm great, Father."

"Is that the truth?"

This time, a hesitation.

"Irvalah"—he brought his face down to his son's level and leaned in close—"is that the truth?"

Fifty, sixty, seventy years on, here my uncle would always pause, then straighten his back. A nice long dramatic pause accompanied by a significant shift in body language, a deepening in his voice (perhaps to protect against a catch?), and then . . . and then he would produce a wide grin and say, "And then I burst into sobs so loud and so deep that I thought I was going to hyperventilate."

"And what did Grandpa Shalom do?"

"Well, first he took me into his arms and calmed me down. Then he promised me everything would change. He went home; packed up Sylvia, Herbert, and Merona; and sent them out here within two weeks. He gave up their house and moved into a furnished room, and followed a year later. And that began our life in California."

It was all in the tone—and my uncle's face: the absurdity of a boy's tears changing the course of a family's fate. The comedy of it—his rote responses, rehearsed with his aunt, for once not sticking. His worried, remorseful father putting his family further into debt as he hastily revised their life plan.

How many times did my uncle tell me this story? A dozen? Two dozen?

"To think, if only I hadn't cried . . ."

"But you cried for a reason."

Irving shook his head. "I cried because, I guess, I was unhappy. That day."

"What about all the other days?"

He shrugged. "I was fine. Like I said when he came before and asked me how I was."

"Your answers were coached."

"I told him I was fine in the letters too."

"But the letters were coached. Your aunt sat next to you while you wrote them."

He paused, then shrugged again.

"Are you *sure* you weren't unhappy—deep down, somehow? I mean, from ten on you were away from your parents, your siblings. It can't matter how kind Aunt Rose was . . ."

Another shrug. A wry, maybe slightly forlorn, memory-soaked smile. Perhaps one of his six-step sighs.

That was Irving. You could ask these questions ten times or a hundred, and he would answer them with a shrug or a sigh or an elusive, noncommittal smile. He went for the levity, the comic relief; the folktale curiosity, the cinematic flair. Yet he did keep telling the story, almost as if it were a kind of compulsion that arose out of some deep chamber of his inner self.

Over time I began to wonder if Irving returned to this story because it was his own personal Rosetta stone. My uncle possessed a deep detachment, a human isolation accompanied by an ability to separate himself into different facets, different selves. There was Irving of the maison and Irving of the closet. There was Irving the emerging (and soon to be full-blown) hypochondriac and Irving the tennis player. There was Irving the nimble, accomplished screenwriter and Irving who scrubbed his own kitchen floor and loved to zip around town dropping sheets at the dry cleaners and buying paper towels in bulk. Irving the brother and Irving the uncle were so star-tlingly different from Irving the husband, who was uxorious to an almost self-abnegating degree, as to seem at times like a different man entirely.

Did it all begin in his childhood exile? Did the split man origi-nate in the sickly boy split off from his family when he was barely ten years of age? And did the child who was deprived of his mother grow into the man fated to pair up with the ever-present, never-abandoning über-woman, that formidable and fractured, ugly and beautiful, con-nective and destructive tidal force who was my aunt?

It was not my uncle's nature to ponder, and certainly not to answer, such questions. This was not how his mind worked. He told stories in-stead. He charmed; he mocked; he made light. He left clues; puzzles, not hypotheses. Hints that led you to believe, or to hope, that a separate, more reasonable Irving coexisted alongside the man who was begin-ning to disappear into the daunting, proudly symbiotic fortress that was his marriage to my aunt.

"Going off the hill" meant going away from the intertwined, the over-lapping, the claustrophobic. Twice a year, for the five of us in our nu-clear family, it meant breaking the rules. A number of rules. Once in the winter, once again in early spring, my mother sent us off in the morning with a note addressed to the school secretary. In it she ex-plained that her children would be absent the following week. She always gave the same reason: we would be missing school, she said, on account of "family business."

Our family business was skiing—never over holidays, never on weekends, because my father would not tolerate waiting in long lift lines that cut into his time on the slopes, but right smack-dab in the middle of the school semester. On Sunday morning we would load up the station wagon with our gear and our sandwiches, slotting the skis and poles into the rack mounted on the roof, and we would set off on the interminable ride into the Mojave Desert and up, up, up into the snow-frosted Sierra Nevadas, where, after six hours, we would pull into a rented condo at Mammoth Estates. The droopy shag carpet, knotty pine paneling, and burnt-orange upholstery were the kinds of things my aunt would deride—*did* deride the one time she and my uncle invited themselves along. (To find out, was it, what we got up to when we were without them? To include themselves where they felt excluded? Most certainly not to ski.) My aunt didn't think much of the way we lived there either, stumbling home after a long day on the slopes to eat hamburgers off paper plates or pizza out of the box, Neapolitan ice cream, and store-bought cookies. We built a fire and played poker and we watched television and laughed at nothing and everything—our own actual family in temporary giddy exile from the close-knit sevensome; it was dreamlike and out of character, a footnote to our regular extended family life.

On one unforgettable occasion my mother picked us up from school and announced buoyantly that we were not going home that afternoon; instead we were having an adventure, just Mom and the boys. She had packed us each a bag, and she'd made a reservation at a hotel in Palm Springs called The Spa. For a moment I wondered whether she and my father had had a fight, until she reminded me that he had left that morning for a business trip, and she had thought, Why not just pick up and go? Why not indeed.

The Spa was on the site of the hot springs that gave Palm Springs its name, she told us, and its land still belonged to the Agua Caliente Indians; she'd been there several times before, on girls' weekends or when she and my father went away on their own to *take the waters*. The whole place was just so exotic, with those waters to be taken and the Indian history and the red, rocky mountains that came crashing down practically right into the enormous swimming pool, the palm trees and cacti and the exceptionally clear air, dry and spiced with the scrub that my uncle loved . . . loved so much, in fact, that he did my mother one better in the surprise department: he turned up on our second day there, just like that, taking those long loping steps of his up the front colonnade, grinning in his trademark chinos, a plain white T-shirt, and a terry-cloth sun hat.

When she realized who it was standing over her in that bright clear light, my mother nearly spilled out of her chaise longue. "Why, it's just like Shalom," she said, jumping up with excitement and sending her newspaper and bottle of Sea & Ski flying.

She and my uncle fell into each other's arms as if they had not seen each other at Sunday dinner less than a week ago. But of course they had not seen each other like this: alone, or alone with us boys, and not just off the hill but out of the city.

"That's where I got the idea," Irving said.

"That time, in Yosemite——"

"Shalom went away by himself to work on a sermon," Irving explained to us, "but the place was so beautiful that he decided to turn right around and come back."

"A five-hour drive each way! Can you believe that man? We drove through an actual redwood tree. The trunk was so large someone had carved an arch into it . . ."

"He was the finest man I have ever known," my uncle said.

"I miss him so," said my mother.

It had taken her a moment to realize who was absent. She looked around now over my uncle's shoulder.

They were siblings; they could read each other's minds. "Trudy's sleeping over. She's spending the weekend with her. There's some antique fair in Pasadena." He took in a deep, full breath, delivered one of his six-step sighs, and then added, with an almost conspiratorial smile, "You know what she thinks of the desert."

Oh, my mother knew. We all did. *Men with paunches and white leather shoes—they come to Palm Springs either to golf or to die. Not that there's much difference between the two! And the women, they have no purpose other than to lie around in the sun and splash around in over-chlorinated swimming pools. All those* mo-derne *houses with flat roofs and concrete-block walls. There's not any decent shopping within miles. I know your uncle says he breathes better in the desert air, but it's a myth, if you ask me. Personally I'd rather do without.*

She did without. She stayed back home, antiquing and playing house with Trudy while Irving practically sprinted into the room he had booked, returning afterward outfitted in his mustard trunks and with a full *équipe*: a stripe of zinc oxide on his nose, two towels, three books, *The New York Review*, a Cuban cigar, and several packs of matches.

Off the hill, sprung from the canyon, sprung period: my mother and my uncle spent the weekend tossing stories and memories back and forth like two children playing ball. Floating side by side on rafts in the pool, over Mexican dinner, looking up from their reading . . .

When we moved into Stanley Avenue, the neighbor saw so many boxes of books being carried upstairs that she thought Shalom was opening a lending library. She called the police . . .

How many marriages did he perform during the war? All those soldiers in uniform, those trembling brides . . .

Syl baked her sponge . . .

How about when he finally joined us out west? You were two years old. There was a big welcome party, and he spent the whole time playing with you on the floor. Afterward you said, "Mister, it's time for you to go home now."

I didn't recognize my own father!

You told Shalom to leave!

It was as if they were watching—sharing—a private movie of their own. No: it was as if they had stepped out of the movie we were all confined to and had become different selves; their own selves.

He always kissed me on my lips, even after I was married.

Me too.

You know, he loved you more than anyone in the world.

I know.

We were very lucky in our parents, weren't we?

A look far off into the distance, then . . .

My biggest regret? Can you guess?

The boys.

If only he had lived, I have a feeling things, many things, would be different in this family.

My uncle was not the only one who breathed better in the desert air.

———— —————

It turned out that there were rooms other than his closet that captured something of my uncle: these were the pretend rooms that were built (and decorated, and lit, and inhabited—pretend inhabited) on movie sets.

The first time Irving took me to see how make-believe was actually made believable was when I was still very small. The movie was *The Reivers*, adapted from a novel by Faulkner, who, like my aunt and uncle, was working in a lighter, folkloric mode. It was one of the few movies they made with a director other than Marty Ritt, teaming up this time with a younger man named Mark Rydell.

Shortly after their return from Jackson, Mississippi, where they had done all the exterior filming, my uncle invited Danny and me onto the Paramount lot. The "baby" (Steve was still the baby, at six) couldn't be relied on to follow the rules: "You must be very still and very quiet; the camera picks up every shadow, every sneeze. You must sit where I tell you and speak only when everyone else does, do you understand, boys? Because if you comply, then you can see a movie being filmed before your very eyes."

We knew how to be quiet, how to follow rules. We did not know anything else, though. We did not know how a story that seemed so real and seamless when you watched it on the screen was a set of illusions and sleights of hand and tricks and trials (and errors). We did not know that in an entire day perhaps one scene, not even two pages' worth of words, would be repeated over and over and over. We did not know that rooms that were done up—as at the maison—with wallpaper and fabric and pictures and chandeliers were only one-sided; the other half was raw plywood. We did not know that windows that looked out into a leafy garden in truth looked out onto a branch with paper leaves that had been propped up in a bucket that was positioned in front of a canvas backdrop smeared with green paint and lit with an exaggerated white light. We did not know that staircases led to nonexistent second stories or that wineglasses actually held colored water or that a woman wearing a big full Edwardian dress would lift her skirt as she swept by to reveal the kind of tiny bikini underwear we had never seen on a real live woman before, except maybe at the beach in Santa Monica, outside and in full daylight, in which context it wasn't underwear at all but a bathing suit.

She was playing a prostitute, a fact unexplained by my uncle, and the scene was at dinner in Memphis in a whorehouse, also unexplained, where Boon Hogganbeck (Steve McQueen) had taken the impressionable young Lucius (Mitch Vogel) on a weekend lark, having "borrowed" the new Winton Flyer that belonged to Lucius's grandfather (Will Geer). Phoebe (Diane Ladd), the prostitute, had come late to the table and was being made to pay a fine by Mr. Binford (Michael Constantine), the head of the house.

By the end of the day, having watched the scene being repeated half a dozen, a dozen times, my brother and I knew every syllable of the dialogue by heart. We had shaken hands with the actress whose underwear we'd glimpsed, and we'd met Mitch Vogel, who was not so much older than I was, and we'd seen my uncle at work, nodding when he thought the moment "sang," remaining politely neutral when he thought it did not. Now and then he slipped over to Rydell, who sat in a tall director's chair, and whispered a word or two through a hand cupped to his ear.

When he came back, the scene changed. Was that all it took? An idea, a word or two from my uncle, and these people behaved differently, spoke differently, moved differently.

My uncle was the puppeteer, the wordmaster, and on this movie, as it happened, also the producer. He had a certain unforgettable confidence, almost a swagger that day: the swagger of a man who was inhabiting his life, who was making something he valued and enjoyed, and who was himself captivated by the transformation of words (themselves already transformed from Faulkner's words) into scenes.

He also, for the only time in his entire life, contributed to the interiors of the maison by asking the set designer, when shooting was complete, to sell him some of the patterned brown velvet that hung on a wall in the whorehouse and the elaborate brass bed in which McQueen slept with his girl.

The movie came home; the movie became part of home. Ruby upholstered the fabric onto my uncle's reading chair, and the brass bed was set up in the maid's room. It seemed perfectly logical to us that my aunt and uncle would live with tangible pieces of their movies, just as they spoke in dialogue-like speeches (especially when they were impassioned or she was angry—therefore often) or staged scenes that seemed to belong more to invented than to actual life. This was how they spent their days, this was how they experienced and navigated and imagined the world, shaping it as they went along to fit their take and their take only.

A later movie was differently magical, though the invitation—for a much longer visit this time: weeks on location instead of a day on the set—came at a much more complicated moment, following Sylvia's death. My aunt and uncle sent for us (pointedly all *three* of us) to visit them on the set of a movie they were shooting with Marty Ritt on Saint Simons Island off the coast of Georgia. Adapted from Pat Conroy's first book, *Conrack* was an account of his year teaching the poor children of Daufuskie Island off the coast of South Carolina. Jon Voight played Conroy, Georgia stood in for South Carolina, and local elementary school students played the children who had originally lived in such isolation that they spoke a dialect called Gullah and could not even pronounce Conroy's name, hence Conrack.

Here the dream world was leavened by the crisp intelligence of Ritt. This wasn't a place of cut velvet and brass beds and beautiful women flashing their thighs at prepubescent boys, but of worm-eaten clapboard shacks and a one-room schoolhouse that was meant to capture one of the poorest, grittiest, more remote precincts of the American South.

I was rounding into my adolescence that summer, and my hair had gone wild. The word *Jewfro* was not part of the language of the day, or at least our intimate family language, but the tower of frizz I carried around with me *was* ungainly and notable, the only part of my body, or my self, that at the time hinted that I might eventually stop being the mirrorlike, silently observing creature I had been to date. Ritt called it a fright wig and ribbed me about it endlessly. At fourteen, I found him scary and fascinating; authoritative, opinionated, a straight talker on politics, actors, movies . . . and sex. One afternoon on the set, while we were waiting for a scene to be lit, he reminisced about the first time he'd seen James Dean perform a scene at the Actors Studio. He said, "I don't know if you could call it acting, but everyone in that room, man and woman, wanted to fuck him, I'll tell you that."

My aunt covered her mouth with her hand before sputtering, in a curious mixture of Yiddish and French, "Marty, *red nisht devant l'enfant.*"

"*Quel enfant?*" Ritt shot back. "He could be fucking someone himself, Hank. I was at his age."

When I think back over the people, the experiences—the words—that helped wake me from the spell that was cast over me in my childhood, that *fucking* of Ritt's stands out among them. His whole demeanor did. A sharp reader of people and behavior, of outward suggestions of inward struggles, he must have had a sense that here was a human being who needed some help being ripped free from a noxious enthrallment.

He took a milder approach to my little brothers, "the kids." One day, when the filming had transferred to Brunswick, which stood in for the town of Beaufort, where on Halloween Conroy took his class for a taste of the "city" and to go trick-or-treating, he turned to Danny and Steve and said, "How would you like to be in the movie, boys?"

No one ever ran faster to the wardrobe trailer than my two younger brothers, who emerged soon afterward costumed in sheets with oval shapes cut in them for eyes. Then came the lone, meticulously delivered instruction from the Group Theater–trained director: "Run around now and act like you're having fun."

Marty Ritt was one of the only people—perhaps the only person?—in my aunt and uncle's universe who kept my aunt in check. Maybe, as with his guess at my still-nascent rebellion, his experience with actors had honed his ability to maintain control of wayward personalities. Rare was a director confident enough to invite his screenwriters to come on location so that he could have them on hand to make adjustments when scenes needed more, or less, or different dialogue. Ritt did this, faithfully in the case of my aunt and uncle, but there was never any question as to who was in control of the set, who was responsible for the ultimate vision, who was quite literally calling the shots—until very late in their collaboration. On a movie called *Murphy's Romance*, one of the last they made together, my aunt began to assert herself more and more vocally, especially with regard to the lead actress, Sally Field, whom she found deficient for not speaking the lines as she and my uncle had written them or as she would have said them if *she* were the actress or (this was closer to her skill set and onetime actual ambition) director. When Field complained to Ritt that it had become unclear where the direction was coming from and that she felt she was beginning to lose her way in her performance, his famously fierce temper was quickly activated and just as quickly brought under steely control, and he banished my aunt and uncle from the set that very day.

Some years later Marty sat down with me for an interview. The conversation was part of my quest to decode and dissect the peculiar world I had grown up in and the peculiarly troubled people who dominated it. What surprised me that day was that Marty seemed to have his own need for decoding, or catharsis. With a grizzled chin anchored in his palm he said to me, "I am still confounded by what happened on that picture. I have never seen someone transform so dramatically over the course of thirty years. Sending her—them—away was a low spot in my life. But your aunt gave me no choice."

Even at this point, when I was well into my twenties, I was still in such thrall to, and lingering fear of, my aunt and uncle that I turned off the tape recorder, which is a shame since Marty talked for hours about that mysteriously constructed person who was my aunt.

But this conversation belongs to later, to a time when I was driven to compare my experience of my aunt's imbalanced ways with other people's, just to make sure (and sure, and *sure*) that I wasn't the one out of my mind, as for years my aunt, and uncle, maintained I was.

For one last glance at the magic at the tail end of my childhood, how about the moment when it came to be my time on-screen with—who else?—my aunt?

We were invited to sit in the background of the diner in Brunswick-as-Beaufort, where Conrack and the children were being served milkshakes at the counter. Instead of "Act like you're having fun," I heard, "Pat down that fright wig," which was soon followed by the appearance of a hairdresser with a spray bottle and a wooden brush. "Off with the sunglasses, she looks too Hollywood" was the directive thundered toward my aunt, who not only obligingly tossed them into her lap but also dug in her pocketbook for a tissue to wipe away her Max Factor Salmon Ice lipstick and the beauty mark (still there, though in its death throes) from the upper corner of her right cheek.

"What are we supposed to *do*?" I asked tentatively, as a tepid hamburger and limp french fries were dropped in front of each of us.

"Eat," she said, "or pretend to eat. And talk. Just make sure you don't look at the camera."

"What happens if I do?"

"You break the illusion that we're just regular people having regular lunch in a regular diner, Lovey," she said. "And we most certainly cannot have that."

SEVEN

FIVE PLACES, SIX SCENES

Christmas at the Maison

It was the centerpiece of my aunt's year, therefore our family's year. *A holiday made for decorating*—and for giving, two of her life's delights.

On a high closet shelf she kept a box large enough for a child to play in; inside lived yards of green garlands and gold beads, wreaths and sparkles, holly, berries, red ribbons, pottery Santas, pinecones with their tips daubed with white paint, Scandinavian angels, tartan pillow covers, bayberry (later Rigaud) candles, cinnamon sticks, silk birds peeking out of twig nests. Every December, on the first Saturday of the month, my uncle wrestled this formidable kit into the living room, and I was invited to help make Christmas, meaning to hang and arrange and *k-nock-k-nock* until all this bounty and beauty were arrayed. And these were special days, happy days, when the city of smog and palm trees, the school dreariness and the school bullies, were forgotten and beloved *jaunty* Victorian (Dickensian) England was invoked as the house was decked out for the *hols*—because *there's no interior in the world that doesn't wake up with a swag of green and a splash of red* and because *everyone needs one time a year when she can kick back and simply play!*

In the weeks leading up to Christmas my aunt shopped and shopped. She set up a wrapping station in her guest bedroom, and she turned out dozens of elaborate packages, which afterward she arranged in the living room around a sober carved wooden angel, old, Flemish, and each year shedding more powdery dust. Did it matter that we were Jewish? *You'll never see a Christmas tree in my house— the daughter-in-law of a rabbi? Nevertheless we all know that Christmas is a holiday made for decorating!*

All these preparations culminated in my aunt's annual Christmas Eve dessert party, where the triple-butter brownies were joined by oranges in port wine, vanilla cake with chocolate frosting, almond cookies rolled in powdered sugar, strawberries paired with an enormous bowl of whipped cream, and much more. The word *Lucullan* was pronounced, and often. Christmas was my aunt at her happiest and most heightened: doing things up; shopping and giving; baking and delighting; enticing us with limitless treats; bringing together (as she and my uncle otherwise seldom did) their friends and their family; and leading. Leading was central. Leading might have been, deep down, the whole point. No one else contributed. No one else collaborated. Certainly no one else was allowed to make a suggestion—the idea, floated at one point by my mother, that we begin by eating something wholesome to offset all the sugar was dismissed as *pedestrian* and *the notion of a spoilsport.* Any proposal to limit the children's gifts, to rein them back into sensible proportion, received an emphatic (and conversation-stopping) *Don't be a Scrooge! Christmas is a time to loosen the purse strings and give, give, give.*

My aunt, distributing her packages at the appointed hour, dressed in a red sweater and half a dozen sparkling gold chains, with a tartan tam completing the ensemble, stood in for Santa . . . though he, too, made a memorable appearance one year when we were very small, because of course Hankie was so powerful she had a direct line to Santa himself.

Another time—on a later Christmas—at the moment when the entire room was called to attention so that the presents could be handed around, Ruby's by then not-so-new new wife, who had been at the Harvey's Bristol Cream, said boozily, "And now once again in the role of Lady Bountiful, our very own Harriet Frank Ravetch." It was as though some underground seismic activity had set all the bibelots in the maison a-rattling. Everyone fell silent and watched my aunt as her eyes darkened. She hesitated for a moment; then, after a glance at us children, she went on bestowing the packages.

We didn't have to wait to see if this wife of Ruby's would be invited back the following Christmas; she was banished before New Year's with a scathing epistle. But *Lady Bountiful* was like Ritt's fright wig and the ambidextrously fuckable James Dean—it punctured the spell, ever so slightly, the way any reasonable, questioning, perplexed outsider might, merely by introducing an independent take on the goings-on at the maison and its purlieus.

And then, suddenly, there I was, on the cusp of adolescence. I was beginning to wake up; beginning. Waking up meant going beyond knowing and noting; it meant putting things together differently. It meant taking in these outside points of view and seeing if they fit. It did not mean breaking rules or doing drugs or getting into more conventional kinds of trouble. It meant—just once, and hesitantly—saying no to my aunt.

In the first December that followed Sylvia's death, the annual call came to help dress up the maison . . . and I told her that I was busy.

"Too busy for Christmas?"

"Just too busy to come help today."

"How about tomorrow, then?"

"I think I'll just—just skip it this year if you don't mind."

A beat.

"You'll do *what?*"

"Take—take a break. I'm just not so much in the mood. I—I have a plan with Barrie and Wendy."

My aunt snorted.

I could feel her *thinking* at the other end of the line. "I just want to understand this correctly, Michael. All of a sudden you're not in the mood for the *hols?* All of a sudden those *girls* take precedence over *me?*"

The frostiness in her voice caused me to backtrack. "Maybe you could start, and—and in a few days I'll come over, and we can—"

"Don't bother," she said, and the phone went dead with an emphatic click.

•

Not much more than an hour later the Riviera pulled into our drive-way, announced by a series of loud, urgent Riviera honks.

My mother glanced out the window. "It's your aunt and uncle. It looks like they have something to drop off," she said. "I have a feeling they're looking for you."

The horn sounded again.

My mother looked at me and shook her head. "There's no way I'm going out there," she said. "You don't have to either, you know."

Again the horn. Louder, sharper.

"They—*she*—can stop honking and come inside like civilized human beings."

There was still more honking.

I sucked in a breath and went outside. The car was idling along-side our driveway. My uncle was driving, though my aunt's hand, reaching over, was activating the horn.

A tall stack of packages was piled up in her lap. The darkest of her dark glasses were pushed up high on her nose.

She rolled down the window.

"As you have no Christmas spirit, Michael," she declared. "I have decided to cancel the holiday this year."

She handed the boxes through the window. I received them, dumbfounded.

"But you can't *cancel* Christmas," I said.

She tilted her head so that I could see over her glasses and into her eyes. They were livid. "Watch me."

"What about the party?"

"Your uncle has been on the phone all morning. We've disinvited every last guest."

"What about the brownies? The *angel*?" I sounded like a con-fused child; suddenly that was also how I felt.

"You should have thought of that when you refused to come help."

"I didn't mean you shouldn't *have* Christmas. All I meant—"

"I know perfectly well what you meant." She gestured to my uncle to start the car.

"Uncle Irving," I said, "can't you talk to her? Can't you *reason* with her?"

My uncle stared ahead through the windshield. He didn't even look in my direction. This was as bad as my aunt canceling Christmas. Maybe, in a way, worse.

"Be sure to tell your parents and your brothers," my aunt said. "We can't have them showing up at a dark house on the twenty-fourth."

"But what am I supposed to say?"

"The truth."

"But what's the truth?"

"I think you know all too well."

The holiday came and went, I wish I could say pleasantly, with all of us on Greenvalley eating sensible food and watching old movies on TV, but a palpable air of gloominess, and suspense, hung over the canyon, as if the hills themselves were expecting the phone to ring, the edict to be withdrawn, the tradition reinstated. Instead there was nothing but silence and a dreary concatenation of short, gray, late-December days and early nights. I felt miserable and guilty, too power-ful and yet weirdly not nearly powerful enough, since apparently I was capable of stirring the waters to the degree that I could cause a holiday to be canceled, but I was unable to make my aunt see reason or, rather, be reasonable. My aunt *and* my uncle, who was after all her coat-holding, car-driving, call-making partner in this as in so many of their *folies à deux*.

Between Christmas and New Year's my father took it upon him-self one afternoon to go to the maison to speak to his sister. That was how things worked in the family—how things got worked out. Sooner or later one strand of the brother-sister-sister-brother-grandmother-grandmother interleaving was tweaked this way or that, until peace, or more precisely the appearance of peace, was once again restored.

He was away a long time. Even my mother now and then looked out the window, the very same window I used to look out, waiting for my aunt to come visit when I was a child.

Eventually we heard the garage door open and close. My father came into the house, his skin gray and his eyes tired and distant. He dropped into his chair, and we gathered around him.

He said, "These are very illogical people. Honestly I cannot say I know what to do about them."

My father, it had always seemed, knew what to do about most everything—everything *else*.

"But what did they say?" I asked, my heart racing.

"They say . . ." He hesitated. "They say that they have been injured. By you, Michael. But not just you. They see a plot—a cabal. That was the word they used. *Cabal*. Us against them. Greenvalley against Skyline. Apparently your mother and I—your mother in particular—resent their presence, their generosity. Their *love*. They have given and given, and in return we have seeded all this, plotted all this . . . this resistance." He paused. "There were a lot of histrionics involved."

"Histrionics?"

"Yelling. Banging of fists. A cigarette."

"But she doesn't smoke unless she's in a story conference."

"Well, it was a kind of story," my father said. "A ridiculous story. A fiction—a scene. One of the most absurd scenes my sister has ever written."

"I just didn't feel like playing house, Dad. That was it. I—"

"It's not your fault. And putting out her holiday tchotchkes is not the real issue. You're fourteen. You're growing up. It's normal. Your aunt cannot let go, and your uncle does not understand why she needs to." He shook his head. "I'm glad my mother is not alive to see any of this."

It wasn't the first time these words were said, and it wouldn't be the last.

July at the Boulevard Court

Time passed; anger receded. That was how the family worked. One day a call was made, and we were invited to Sunday dinner at the maison, where we gathered around one of my aunt's intricately set tables as usual. No one said anything. No one mentioned the canceled Christmas. And of course no one, least of all my aunt, apologized. Not then; not ever.

It was as though we all agreed to succumb to a tacit collective amnesia. We sat down at the dinner table, ate the salad with the sugared dressing and the triple-butter brownies, and pretended that this evening was no different from all the other evenings that preceded it.

The following summer we traveled, all of us together, to the Pacific Northwest, to the same peninsula at the mouth of the Columbia River in Washington State where my father and my aunt had summered as children. My aunt had had the idea, after Huffy's death, that we should return to the beach, and this was now the fifth consecutive year that the two families had rented a pair of bungalows, spending sometimes as many as four weeks virtually living together, in far closer proximity even than in Laurel Canyon.

In the early years these, too, were joyful, inspired times—times inspired by my aunt's perspicacity in having organized our reconnection to the beach and made joyful by her teeming verve and curiosity, hers and my uncle's together. These were not people who packed a picnic basket and parked themselves with a book under an umbrella; they were people who investigated and adventured and explored, teaching us, by example and practice, how to give ourselves to the experience of new places.

Most every day there would be an excursion. We visited tiny museums of local history and faraway coves where ships had gone ashore. We ventured along the coast to pioneer towns and old Indian settlements, and we hiked up to see the still-working lighthouses nearby. We toured a re-creation of the fort where Lewis and Clark, who had first "discovered" the area, spent part of the miserable winter of 1805–1806, and we drove up to Oysterville to see the faded, elegant remains of that boomtown at the tip of the peninsula. Many times we had lunch at the marina in Ilwaco, where fishermen brought in salmon that were nearly the size of Jessie, the short, fierce fishmonger who cleaned and filleted and sliced them up (or canned or froze or smoked them) in a red shack around which seagulls circled and honked, sweeping down for the entrails she tossed out the window.

The bungalows we rented were very simple shingled structures, mirror images of each other that shared a common wall and a common front porch. They were small, two bedrooms apiece, with a single bath, a living room, and a kitchen. Because each cabin slept only four people, every year either Danny or Steve always went to lodge with our aunt and uncle.

"This is how we give your brothers a chance to feel singled out," my aunt once said to me in a conspiratorial voice. "Though you *know* who I would like to have for a roomie, if only they would let me."

Even if *they* allowed it, I would never have agreed to stay with my aunt and uncle. The idea of sharing an actual house with them, having one thin wall between their bedroom and mine, felt altogether too close.

At the beach my aunt did all the cooking for both families. For these weeks each summer she managed to take command of our shared domestic life, thereby (the reasoning went) giving my mother a break from the demands of feeding three hungry boys. She was a better cook than my mother, but the food wasn't the point; being in charge was. Being in charge somehow, I never quite understood how, made her feel whole, at ease; almost at peace.

She took charge of the interiors too, at least of her bungalow, since she was utterly incapable of spending a single night in an environment she had not first altered in some way. In London she decorated the Dorch with her Portobello and Bermondsey market finds, in Paris the Plaza Athénée was made even more *raffiné* with the help of the *marché aux puces* . . . and in Long Beach the humble Boulevard Court bungalows were transformed following her copious visits to the peninsula's various junk shops.

Our summer visits always began with my aunt diving into the crates she stored locally from summer to summer. She never unpacked so much as a toothbrush until she had first redecorated—or, rather, decorated, which meant that we boys were enlisted to heave and to haul until all her boxes were moved in and unloaded. Then she (we) got to work. Rag rugs were laid down on the floor; slipcovers or quilts were draped on the sofa. Pictures were either *k-nocked* or (if they were unframed) tacked up on the knotty-pine walls. The kitchen cupboards were jammed with dishes upon dishes. Sheets, comforters, shams went on the beds. Flowers were brought in and changed frequently, while outside on the porch a veritable Petit Trianon of urns, cachepots, baskets, and flower boxes proliferated.

All this was what we did, what was done. All this proceeded, as long as we complied. Complied meant accompanying Hank on her junking excursions as she filled her bottomless need for more stuff. It meant running to the hardware store when she needed more nails or thumbtacks or string or glue. It meant helping her cook. It meant eating what she wanted when she wanted us to. It meant praising what she prepared. It meant washing (and washing) the piles of pots and pans and dishes and bowls and platters and glasses and cutlery and utensils that were left in the wake of every meal.

Since there was no phone to answer, no canyon to hurry across, it meant being perpetually on call; perpetually at her beck and call. When she said "Jump," we jumped.

We were such good little boys.

Until we weren't.

Every year the town put on a lavish display of fireworks for the Fourth of July, and we often missed them because our dinners, and ensuing dish duty, ran late. Finally the summer came when, as we were washing up after dinner on July 3, I found myself looking ahead to the next day and dared to float what was, in the context of this particularly organized family, a revolutionary idea.

"What does everyone think," I ventured, "if we eat off paper plates tomorrow? We can just throw them away and head down to the beach early."

It was seldom the *what*. The *what* always seems trivial in retrospect—circumstantial. Stupid even: the cigarette butt tossed out of a passing car that just happened to land in a very dry, very dense forest.

"I do *not* dine off of paper plates, Michael," my aunt said sharply. "You of all people should know better than that."

"But why not—just this once?"

"*Why not?*" Her eyes widened; her voice went up. "Because they are inelegant. Because it is not what I do. Because it is not what *we* do in this family."

A year before, a month before—who knows, maybe even an hour before—I would have demurred. Instead now I persisted.

"Can't we, just this one time, make an exception?"

"A what?"

"An exception."

"We cannot, no. And we *will* not."

I continued. "Why is it your decision alone? Why don't we take a vote? We're all one family, aren't we?"

I looked around at the others. My uncle, predictably, was sitting impassively across the room. My mother's arms were crossed in front of her chest, but her eyes met mine, and her whole face and body conveyed a steady if silent encouragement.

My father said matter-of-factly, "The boy has a point, Hankie."

"Oh, don't you *dare* 'Hankie' me, Martin. You know perfectly we—"

Danny piped up. "I vote for."

Slowly she pivoted in Danny's direction. "I don't give two hoots whether you're for or against, young man. This is not a democracy. *I* am the person who decides how we are to dine in this house! *I* am the one who sets and maintains the standards around here!"

Emboldened by my brother's support, emboldened by my own boldness, I tossed down my dish towel and said, "Then you can be the person who does the dishes afterward."

Danny tossed his towel down too. "Ditto to that."

Philip Roth somewhere mocks Henry James for describing moments in which characters are said to rear up. Who, he wonders, rears up in actual life?

Roth never laid eyes on my aunt.

She pulled herself up to her full five feet ten inches, sucked in a big breath to lubricate her sharp tongue, and let rip a full-throttle, all-caps harangue:

"DO YOU KNOW WHAT YOU BOYS ARE? I'LL TELL YOU. YOU'RE INGRATES. ALL I DO, ALL YOUR UNCLE AND I DO, IS GIVE, SUMMER AFTER SUMMER, YEAR AFTER YEAR, AND ALL YOU DO IS TAKE AND TAKE AND *TAKE*. I PROVIDE, AND YOU REJECT. I LOVE, AND YOU DEFY THAT LOVE.

WHY, YOU WOULD NEVER HAVE COME TO THIS PLACE IF I HADN'T BROUGHT YOU. DO YOU THINK YOUR MOTHER OR YOUR FATHER WOULD HAVE THOUGHT TO BRING US BACK TO THE BEACH? TO GIVE YOU THESE SUMMERS? TO TAKE YOU TO SEE MOVIES BEING MADE? TO GIVE YOU BOOKS, *OBJETS*, IDEAS? WAKE YOU UP OUT OF THE TORPOR THAT IS YOUR DAILY LIFE? I DO NOT UNDERSTAND WHAT IS GOING ON WITH ANY OF YOU, MICHAEL IN PARTICULAR. FIRST IT WAS CHRISTMAS . . . NOW THIS. WHEN WILL IT STOP? I REQUIRE IT TO STOP! THIS IS MADNESS, CORKY, THIS ATTACK ON WHO AND WHAT WE ARE. MADNESS, I TELL YOU!"

The effort of mounting this tirade caused her to drop down into a chair. She placed a palm on each cheek and in a softer voice said, "It's a good thing that Mamma is not alive to see what we have all come to. Imagine finding solace in the notion of my mother being dead!" Then she burst into tears.

Danny touched me on the shoulder. "Let's get out of here," he said.

We left the cabins and headed for the approach road that led down to the beach. It was a day early, but already people were setting off fireworks. They echoed like gunshots over all those open dunes.

"You understand you didn't do anything wrong back there?" my brother said after a moment.

I nodded, but I didn't understand, not really. I kept hearing my aunt's voice, her tirade, playing over and over in my head.

"There's something *wrong* with her—not with you, not with us. With her. You get that?"

I nodded again, but halfheartedly.

"This is so fucked-up."

In via della Vigna Vecchia

A pattern began to emerge.

My aunt would erupt, and for a time the two families would stop speaking. These breaks would sometimes last days, sometimes weeks.

Months, too, on occasion. Eventually there would be a back-channel communication. A dinner invitation would follow, and we would gather together again. The episode would never, ever be addressed head-on. There was a lot of stepping around the elephant in the room or, since the room belonged to the maison, hiding it behind a Zuber or Coromandel screen. You simply did not *undo* a family this closely knit because one of the kids hit adolescence and found his voice and one of the adults ceased being able to manage her rage, or had maybe begun to go out of her mind, or . . . who knows what. It was a puzzle. An immense, unwieldy, exhausting puzzle.

The change in my aunt's personality was widely remarked on and studied, sometimes obsessively, by nearly everyone in her orbit other than my uncle. We spent many charged, compulsively appalled hours huddled together as a nuclear family, trying to figure out what had happened to the magician of our youth—and not just of our youth but our father's and our mother's before us. We were regularly joined by other relatives or ex-friends of my aunt's and uncle's, Ruby being just one of more than a dozen people whom my mother took to calling the "walking wounded," people who had been cast out from the enchanted kingdom and had nowhere to go to disburden themselves of their stories except my parents' living room on Greenvalley Road, where the walls soaked up so much sadness and frustration that it seemed remarkable that the plaster had not begun to sponge and crumble right before our eyes.

It was not entirely true that the change in my aunt went unnoted by my uncle, however. It was noted by his body, more and more acutely as time passed. Irving the sickly asthmatic child had grown into a robust youth and adult; at midlife, however, he began to develop what would become a decades-long hypochondria. He was convinced he had cancer ten times over. Emphysema. Heart troubles. Stomach ulcers. Sometimes the auto-diagnosis was not so grave; he was simply— simply!—suffering from what he called depletion, a lack of energy so profound and unshakable that he would spend entire days in his reading chair, or even in bed.

For a period of more than a year he kept what amounted to a standing weekly appointment with our family physician. When

Dr. Derwin, upon reviewing the latest set of negative test results, at one point threw up his hands and suggested that my uncle consider consulting a psychiatrist, my aunt flew into a rage. *There will be no psychiatrists in this family, do you hear me?* She threatened to *sue the pants right off that horrid man.* Surely the whole world knew that her husband possessed *simply the most sane, rational, healthy mind I have ever in my life had a chance to know!*

As my aunt became less stable, my uncle became more fearful about his health. There were scans, scopes, biopsies, angiograms, and Holter monitors; he accrued a chart, in the aggregate, as thick as the L.A. County phone book. He gave up tennis, then swimming. He worked less and less, which meant she worked less and less, which meant they had more time to sit and stew and write dramas into life instead of onto the page. He weakened and shrank, literally, by inches from his original six feet, and figuratively into himself. She lashed out and wounded, and he mopped up the mess as dutifully as he did the kitchen floor. Afterward he retreated to his chair, or his bed, or hurried over to Dr. Derwin's office in Century City to allow his body to voice what the rest of him could not.

Meanwhile my aunt went on reeling people in and then casting them out, a rhythm that had come to seem as natural, if as variable, as the weather. My aunt Trudy was treated like an on-again, off-again lover, regularly broken with and (when no substitute could be found for Saturday antiquing excursions) summoned back again with kisses and *cadeaux.* Everyone, simply everyone, was judged, relentlessly. Trudy, when on the outs, was cold and miserly. Her husband, Pete, my aunt and my father's older brother, was an insensitive and remote father. His children, my cousins Dee Dee, John, and Lisa, did not live up to their early promise. Their boyfriends or girlfriends, later their spouses, inevitably failed to meet The Standard. The cousins on the Ravetch side were earnest, literal-minded, *not really our cuppa.* Old friends had suddenly turned, like milk; new ones were captivating, until suddenly they were not.

It was both maddening and strangely magnetic. Attention stuck to my aunt the way it did to stage figures like Mary Tyrone and Amanda

Wingfield and Albee's volatile Martha. You might cover your eyes at times, but you always ended up watching; watching and waiting for the good Hankie to resurface, as now and then, remarkably, she continued to do—because what rational person would go back for more Sturm und Drang if it weren't interleaved with relatively benign episodes? She was like some kind of unpredictable contrapuntal piece of modernist music; you never knew where on the scale the next note would sound. She beguiled and she eviscerated; she gave generously and she took arrogantly; she celebrated and she excoriated; she was an angel, a devil; she was a mystery and a burden, everlasting.

It became clear to me that my parents, despite their various strengths and fundamental sanity, were not going to be able to free me, let alone themselves, from the strange power that my aunt held over our family. My mother had come a long way since she had first met and been dazzled by my aunt at age thirteen, but it was simply not in her nature to confront or challenge or disrupt; instead she slowly pulled back and showed my aunt an increasingly blank side of herself. She was there and not there at the same time. On family outings, she would often be late (*It's a sickness with the Franks*, Hank regularly announced to anyone who would listen—though what she meant was that it was a sickness with Merona); at family dinners, which my mother continued to attend and even to host, she would find all kinds of reasons to avoid sitting down at the table until the meal was nearly over. In the moment I used to think she was either very busy or very bad at managing in the kitchen; now I see those absences of hers as a strategy that was as unconscious as it was unsuccessful, because they only turned her into a ready-made target for my aunt's invective. The less visible my mother was, the easier it was for my aunt to finger her as the rabidly jealous driving force flaming both my rebelliousness and the disintegration of the closeness between the two families: two profound misreadings of human character braided together by a narrator with a dexterous tongue.

My father's situation was even more difficult. He and his sister had been each other's greatest loves when they were young. There was a photograph of the two of them that I used to pore over. It radiated a feeling that seemed to me as remote in time as the clothes they were wearing or my aunt's bobbed hair: their two child selves were lying face-to-face on a sloping lawn in Portland in the summer of 1929 or so, looking at each other; in the position of their bodies, the way their heads were propped up on their hands and their elbows planted in the grass, and in their locked gaze, I could feel the powerful love between these two children.

During long stretches of their childhood Marty and Hank had been inseparable. They shared a bedroom in winter, a sleeping porch in summer. They rode the one family bicycle together, one sitting behind the other, and on Saturdays spent the entire day at the Irvington movie theater, where they watched two serials and the latest Mickey Rooney or Laurel and Hardy, sometimes three times over. At the height of the Depression, when my grandmother in a panic took just the two of them to live with her in a boardinghouse in Longview, where she hoped to find a job with the help of her older sister, Marcia, they bonded under the adversity of those grim circumstances, just as they bonded during the change in fortune that came not so long afterward, when Huffy went to work in Hollywood and they moved to a land of sunshine and promise and virtually overnight went from being the woebegone Goldsteins to the Mighty Franks. Their friendship survived their parents' troubled and unconventional marriage, Marty's two years away in the Navy, and his marrying his older sister's husband's younger sister. But it did not survive my aunt's downward mental gyrations, since, in my father's eyes, his sister never managed to recover from her fall from the particular kind of protected grace known as sibling love, with its attendant shared history of times both awful and wonderful and its intense, encoded, often wordless ease of communication and assumptions of understanding and agreement. I think it's correct to say that the experience presented my father with the single knottiest, most extended problem in his life, the only one of any significance, with the exception of his mother's fatal illness, for which this man who was used to working out all problems failed to come up with an even moderately successful solution.

•

Since my parents were not going to free me, I would have to free myself—but how? Adjusting the amount of time, or the kind of time, I spent in my aunt's company clearly didn't work, since limiting my engagement with her only made her more grasping and barbed, and staking out my few little postage stamps of turf provoked eruptions that affected not just me but all seven of us. The obvious choice, it seemed clear, was to go away.

Go + away: such beautiful, unattainable words those were, representing such a beautiful, inspired, and also downright terrifying idea . . . not to mention an experience for which I was utterly unequipped.

I made some early attempts. The first was a summer trip that a sympathetic, in a way almost clairvoyant, English teacher had told me about in junior high school: a bus tour of the East Coast sponsored by the YMCA. I can still remember the combination of joy and fear—it was a feeling I could *taste*—I felt when I saw the itinerary, which was to take a group of kids my age all through New England. When I excitedly showed my aunt the (entirely secular) brochure, as of course I did, she said, "You do know what the *C* in *YMCA* stands for, don't you? The *C* is for *Christian*"—which she pronounced the same way she did *mo-derne* and *not our cuppa*. And that was the end of that.

Why was that the end of that? One effect of being told what a magnificent prince you are, then being told what an insensitive piece of shit you are, is that you don't always know *who* you are. Or what you need. Or where you might unearth the courage or the confidence to step outside the powerful story you've been born into.

By the time I was eighteen I had become more determined. For several summers I worked in my father's office from the day school let out until it resumed again in the fall, so that I might earn enough money to go to Europe as soon as I graduated from high school. Against the wishes of my parents, who suspected I was not ready to be so much on my own in the world, I traveled by myself, with no companion, no contacts, no structure, and no firm plan other than to enact some sort of version of the grand tour my aunt and uncle (and all my reading) had been preparing me for my whole life. The expe-

rience was—what else?—a humiliating disaster. Unskilled at planning my time, making friends, and navigating unknown places,
I succumbed to homesickness and a loneliness so distressing that I
had to be rescued by an impromptu trip to Europe by—who else?

It's only in the reconstituted version of your own lived experience
that you can allow yourself the momentary fantasy of being able to
reach or call (or scream) back at the younger, duller (dullard) version
of yourself and bellow *no!* No—stop—don't—don't forsake the lessons that loneliness still has to teach you; don't so quickly leave that
grimy B&B in Belgravia, even if the shower is full of bugs and you
have to drop a coin into a slot to turn on the heat; don't climb into that
cab and feel such relief as you instruct the driver to deliver you to the
Dorch (*don't* call it the Dorch); don't step out of the cab and be so se-
duced by the discovery that, despite the pouring rain, you are standing in an oasis of impossibly unwet air made all too possible by the
liveried doorman who holds over your head the largest, blackest, most
enveloping umbrella you have ever seen and continues to hold it over
you as he escorts you from the taxi along the red carpet to the revolv-
ing doors whose polished brass handles he uses to send the doors
spinning and you along with them, right out of one world and into
another.

      During the two weeks my aunt and I spent together in London
that summer, Hank was in her fullest, most buoyant Auntie Mame
mode, and my loneliness and, worse, the grinding humiliation I felt
upon finding myself so inept at coping on my own in a faraway place
had softened me up into an agreeable and compliant Patrick—and for
the first time in years we had some fun. It was like a set of parenthe-
ses had been dropped into the ever-undulating arc of our experience
of each other; like that and unlike it at the same time, since of course,
unsurprisingly, there was a set of unspoken rules to be followed under
these circumstances too. They were a variation on the rules I had
learned from very early on and knew how to follow, or how to fall back
into following, as easily and automatically as I knew how to breathe.
The price of this respite was my reverting to the compliant nephew
who trailed after his aunt through museums and to the theater and

through the markets at Portobello and Bermondsey, activating that great eye of mine and affirming or enthusing, validating or encouraging, as my aunt gathered up so many paintings and porcelains and pieces of furniture that when the shippers came to collect them from the Dorchester they thought she had been installed there for years, like some sort of crazy American lady out of the movies, which in a way was what she was.

In those two weeks there was one moment that tore into me and planted itself so deeply that I returned to it several times in the subsequent years, a what-might-have-been interlude if during that trip I had been someone else, or some*where* else in my own grindingly slow trajectory. When my aunt, who was fighting a cold, decided to take a rare morning in, I ventured out for a walk. I walked for hours in the milky London sunlight, without map or plan or purpose, until just before eleven, in Kensington, on a street that ran along the perimeter of a green square, I glanced over at one of those immaculate, gleaming white row houses and saw a girl leaning out a window on the third floor, a pre-Raphaelite, Julia Margaret Cameron sort of girl wearing a white nightshirt and shaking out her long golden hair. We looked at each other and joined in a mutual fixed gaze. It lasted for an undefinable length of time. As we stood there looking at each other, I was suddenly not the enthralled (the in-thrall-to) nephew, I was not the escort, the mirror, the companion, or the shadow of my aunt, meaning also the shadow of myself, but a young man looking at a young woman with interest, curiosity, and longing—that above all. Compressed into my gaze was a dangerous quantity of yearning that shot up to the third floor of that white building with a searing, almost electric crackle. The gaze was reciprocated too, as unexplained to me as mine was to her.

It was as if in that gaze the world—a world of possibility—had opened itself up to me and in me. Without having the faintest idea, at that point, how I might avail myself of that possibility, I had at least recognized it, felt it, in my guts, my groin, my soul.

After a few minutes the girl was joined in the window by a little boy—blond, yawning, then smiling. Her brother, I surmised. Or decided. He tugged on her sleeve; she reached over and set her hand on his shoulder as she must have done hundreds of times before. Together they looked down at the street, at the square, the trees, the horizon. Then they turned away from the window and stepped into their day, leaving me to turn away and step back into mine.

For a long time after that trip, I loathed myself for being trapped in myself; yet in the end the only way I could live with this experience was to transform it into a comic (tragicomic?) episode in which I was a young naïf abroad, so floundering and inept that I had no choice other than to be "rescued" by my so colorful, so eccentric aunt. And I didn't merely live by this version; I made a record of it too. For several weeks I sat alone in my room and transformed the diary entries that, heeding Huffy with true discipline finally, I had accumulated during my time away. I had put down many impressions of the buildings and paintings and places I had seen or visited and the people I had observed, and I had tracked all the details of that B&B-to-Dorch metamorphosis, none of them, I venture to say now, filtered through a terribly self-knowing eye. A document of thirty, forty pages emerged, patiently typed and retyped. I bound it with brass brads between blue covers and delivered it to—of course—the maison.

This happened on a Friday afternoon. Not an hour later, I received a phone call from my aunt. "Michael, I must speak to you now," she said in a high, animated voice. "I cannot wait for you to come over. I am just going to tell you on the telephone—I am utterly *bedazzled* by what you have written. This is the most delightful travel narrative imaginable. So refined and specific and perceptive. And expressed with such evocative, restrained language. And of course, hee hee, with a certain familiar person brightening matters up at the midpoint. I have to say, I had no idea that you had this kind of talent. You are a *writer*. The real thing. Goodness me, that you are."

A pod of pure pleasure opened itself within me and began to diffuse its contents all through my brain and body.

"Now listen to me. You must quick-quick promise me," she continued, "that tomorrow morning, first thing, you will sit yourself down at your desk and write more. More and more and *more*. The only way to become a writer, you know, is to write. Everything and anything, let it come *pour*ing out of you, and then bring it to me and we will go from there."

Where we would go I did not stop to think. I was so stunned by her reaction to my pages that I went upstairs that very afternoon and, flooded with excitement, put away my sketchbook, my colored pencils, and my pastels, and reorganized my desk. No. 2 pencils only; a little box of pink erasers; tablets of yellow-lined paper. (Because hadn't all "real" writers always written a draft by hand first? Didn't that keep you closer to the language? Hadn't I read somewhere that Virginia Woolf derived physical pleasure from the very act of putting that violet ink of hers down on cream-colored sheets?) On its own small table alongside, following my uncle's example, I repositioned the Adler electric typewriter that had been a high school graduation present from my parents, ostensibly portable but in fact a bulky humming monster of an object that all of a sudden seemed to have acquired a sorcerer's properties of its own.

You are a writer. Was it true? I had been reading forever (even if not, when I was younger, as profusely as my aunt and uncle would have wished); I had been listening to every morsel and insight and tip that they had tossed off in conversation, sometimes between themselves, sometimes explicitly for my benefit, for as long as I could remember. And, since I did not live in a complete and utter *larky sevensome* vacuum after all, I had had two significant mentors in high school who had taught me the rudiments, and more than the rudiments, of constructing a sentence, a paragraph, then an essay. As a Mighty Frank in training, I was disinclined to acknowledge that I needed to be taught—*You have born writers and made writers,* my aunt liked to say, *and I can always sniff the difference*—but I nevertheless recognized that I owed something to these two men. Bald, deep-voiced, and stern, George Schoenman (tenth-grade composition) was a Dodgers-obsessed, Sartre-citing, Hemingway-loving existentialist who drilled into me the rules of the expository essay. His rigid, brick-upon-brick, mortar-tight-in-between way of constructing the famous inverted pyramid laid down an organizing infrastructure to my language and thinking that I never afterward completely shook. Richard Battaglia (eleventh- and twelfth-grade literature), with his long hair, swaggering mustache, low-riding bell bottoms, colorful shirts, and panther-like way of moving around the classroom, always had a blonde, dreamy-eyed waif of a student teacher sitting to one side inhaling his every word as if it were ambrosia, even as she had competition from most of the girls and some of the boys in the class. But what mattered to me, what riveted me, was his love of literature, which poured out of him with a visceral heat. Battaglia had his lodestars and got us to read and love them as much as he did: the Brontës, the Romantics, John Donne, Gerard Manley Hopkins, Hardy. Every summer he traveled to England, visited the Sacred Sites (the parsonage at Haworth, the Lake District, Carlyle's House in Cheyne Row), and brought back postcards, pamphlets, and photographs, which once installed on his bulletin boards were like holy relics fitting out the temple of his classroom. And he, too, got us to think and to write, to talk about character, story, plot, subtext; biography, interiority, language—language above all.

The day I received that call from my aunt I sat down as instructed and for the next several months I wrote short stories. After all, that was how my aunt had begun, producing scores of them in the early days of her writing career, when with that bottomless energy of hers she would come home from a day at the studio, prepare and eat dinner, then sit down at an ordinary card table and produce a story, sometimes two, a week. The choice of genre was a no-brainer for me. The content? What was an un-self-aware eighteen-year-old to put in these stories? I had never been in love; I had proven myself incapable of exploring the world on my own; I was haunted, you might say psychically imprisoned, by a family I had not yet broken away from. I had lost two grandmothers I adored, I had read a lot, and I had observed a lot; I had some ideas, and maybe I had a decent ear—I did the best I could with the material at hand. I plotted and invented and wrote, worked and reworked, six stories over the next few months. Then, once again, I typed them up, bound them, and delivered them to my aunt.

This time there was no immediate call. Nor was there one within an hour, or two, or six. I stared so hard at the telephone in our kitchen that I thought I might go blind. Once, then twice, then ten times I picked up the receiver just to make sure that there was still a dial tone. I never felt time move so slowly in my entire life. In the kitchen I waited; in my room, unable to concentrate on anything, I waited; I waited sitting listlessly in our backyard, watching the sun go down behind the Japanese elm.

My mother, seeing me standing out in the garden, came outside to ask me if something was wrong. I shook my head, making sure she could not see my face.

My aunt did not phone until the following afternoon. "Michael," she said, "I think you should come over so that we can have a little talk."

Her voice was not quite angry, but it was colorless and solemn; it revealed nothing—nothing good, anyway. I left immediately, walking up Greenvalley and across Crest View to Skyline with both a racing heart and feet that were so heavy that they might have been dipped in concrete. Up—across—along the driveway of the maison—up the brick steps—under the canvas awning with its chic black tassels bobbing in the breeze—and to the door.

I rang and heard my aunt approach. How many times had I stood there on that doorstep, listening for her footsteps to grow louder, come closer? With (often) what pleasure; with (sometimes) what dread? This time I waited with neither. All I was aware of was a heartbeat so loud that I could feel it in my throat.

She opened the door and lowered her cheek, as usual, for me to kiss. Her face was cold. Her posture was stiff, and her shoulders curled inward.

She told me to come and sit down by the fireplace in the living room. By the fireplace in the living room was for serious conversations, for tea parties and sips of sherry in winter. No one else was at home that day, not even my uncle; there was no tea trolley, nothing but my pages, dog-eared, stacked up sloppily on the low table between the settees that faced each other.

"Sit," she said.

I sat. She sat on the settee opposite me.

"Well," she said, planting her palms on her knees and taking in a long deep breath. "I am going to be honest with you, Michael. There's no other way. Especially since that first installment of work you presented to me after your travels showed such promise. This, instead . . ." She gestured at the pages. "This instead is not good. It is not good in the least. It is worse than that. What you have done here is false. You have described emotions you do not have, you cannot possibly, at your age, begin to have. Or understand. Your language is strained, sometimes even incorrect. The images are hackneyed. The rhythm is clumsy." She paused. "Quite frankly, what you've produced here is not art but artifice."

My brothers and I used to play a game at the beach as children in which we dipped a magnet into the sand and drew out an adhering clump of fine black iron filings. That was what my brain did to that phrase; it sucked it up and discarded all the rest: *not art but artifice.*

"I—I did my best," I said, tried to say, over a racing heart. "They're only a first draft," I added anxiously. "What did you . . . you didn't care for . . . the story about the young painter and his grandmother, when he realizes she is dying . . . you didn't feel—"

She looked at me with sharp eyes. "That one is the most egregious of all. The boy, guessing what he had been forbidden from knowing? No child would deduce that. No child *reasons* like that. I did not believe it one bit. Nor, I'm sorry to say, any of the others." Was she really sorry to say? Why was her voice so full of vigor? "No, the only thing to do here is set everything aside and start over from scratch. This time, I want you to come to me with a paragraph at a time, a page at most—no more. We will discuss, we will correct, I will help you to see the difference between what is true and false, what is clear and what obscure. Yes, that is what I will do for you."

I began to feel weak. How had I gone so wrong? *Had* I gone so wrong? Three months earlier I had been refined and specific and perceptive; now I had produced not art but artifice.

She reached for the pages. For a moment I thought she was going to toss them into the fireplace, even though there was no fire burning in it at that moment. Instead, she handed them back to me. "Read these stories over again, Michael. You will see that I am correct. And remember that every writer, each and every one, has to serve an apprenticeship. Sometimes quite a long one."

I started home—how I could not say. One concrete foot after the other.

At the midpoint between the two houses, the maison and Green-valley, I came to a trash can. I lifted up its lid, tore the pages in half and then in half again, and threw them away.

At home I went to bed and crawled under the covers. My mother found me there an hour later, when after she had repeatedly called me, I had not come down to dinner.

"Michael," she said. "Is something wrong?"

I took one look at her and burst into tears.

"Are you sick?"

Deep, uncontrollable, unstoppable sobs.

"Please, darling, tell me what it is."

No words could come out between those convulsive, hiccuping tears. I didn't even begin to understand what they were about. Three months ago I was going to be an artist. I had never thought of being a writer. In the interim I had come to realize that the desire was always there, burning from way back and deep, deep down. It wasn't even a choice; it was who I was, I understood that with perfect if fearful clarity. But I had been pronounced an abject failure by the family tastemaker, the family talent. Now what was I? Who was I?

My mother took me into her arms and calmed me down as best she could. Then she got me to tell her what had happened.

As she listened a shadow passed across her face, a very dark and angry and long, ages long, sort of shadow. "It doesn't sound like your aunt did the best job of encouraging you to try again," she said.

"I'll never try again," I said.

"That would be wrong in so many ways, Michael. You're eighteen. You can't expect to produce finished work on your first try. What do you think your aunt was writing at eighteen? Or twenty? I'll tell you what she was writing at twenty-three: a novel. She gave it to me to read once. It was terrible."

Something shifted in me when she told me that.

"What was it about?" I asked, wiping my eyes.

"Portland. Your grandmother and her—her boyfriend, the rabbi. The whole thing was a fantasy, cleaned up of every real . . . every real complication. Like so much in your aunt's life."

She thought for a moment, then added, "You can't allow her, or anyone else, to do this to you. If you have something to say, and I have a feeling you do, and will more and more as you grow up, then figure out how to say it. Patiently and calmly. You can't let one person's opinion have this kind of effect on you, least of all your aunt's."

——— ———

Slowly, too slowly, I began to realize that I had to find a way to take myself very far away physically and mentally—it was the only chance I would have to grow up, to figure out who I was. Although during college I spent two semesters as a transfer student in the East, essentially four years went by before I again ventured into the wider world. But I set a goal for myself: I put away every dollar I saved from a variety of summer jobs, and as soon as I graduated I went to live— not travel—for a year in Europe; not to the sanctioned merry England of Shakespeare and Dickens and Trollope and Bloomsbury and *dear amusing* E. F. Benson, not even *la belle France* of Proust and Balzac and *our own* Colette, but to the more exotic terra incognita of Italy. Despite my aunt's fondness for rows of cypress trees and painted Venetian furniture, no one in my family had any significant connection to the country. No one spoke a syllable of the language. No one understood, myself included, that by going to Italy I was joining a long tradition of young people who traveled there to be awakened and altered; to shake off one constraint or another (or a hundred others); to be set, or set themselves, free.

This time I was determined to do everything differently, more intelligently—or with as much intelligence as I could summon within myself. In Florence I made sure to enroll in a language school so that I would have structure and routine and would meet some sympathetic peers, which I did. When I became proficient enough in Italian, a language in which I came to feel open and expansive, at moments almost a differently (more calmly and comfortably) wired me, I presented myself at an American language school and I obtained a job teaching English. Eventually I took on private students and fell into teaching English to students of diplomacy at the university. For the first time in four years, remembering what my mother had said about persistence, I began to write again. I made a number of friends, and I moved into my first-ever apartment on the top floor of a Renaissance palazzo in via della Vigna Vecchia, by far the most beautiful in a long line of temporary habitations that I would drift through for years and years, the maison and its suffocations putting me off from committing to a domicile of my own.

I also had my first adult relationship, with an older woman who was involved with another man and was set to leave Florence well ahead of me. A tortured challenge at the beginning paired with an escape hatch at the other end: this inaugurated a pattern that would bedevil me for years, and would impede my capacity for intimacy just as those many borrowed or subletted apartments would impede my connection to a fixed place. For a long time, too long, I lived in dread of being trapped, an obvious legacy of my childhood, though it took me ages to come to see it in this way.

While it lasted, though, this relationship felt uncomplicated and liberating. The first time we went to bed was curiously close, in feeling, to the time I vanquished Alfred with the garden hose; here, though, I was triumphing over something even more daunting: my fear that my experience of my aunt would forever prevent me from making a physical or an emotional connection to another human being, any other human being.

At many moments during that year an almost-audible *ping* went off in my head that caused me to stand outside myself and wonder whether I actually recognized the person who was living this independent other life. These thoughts often came to me while I was lying in the loft bed that overlooked the large square living room in via della Vigna Vecchia, and the more doubtful I felt, the more determinedly I examined my surroundings; it was as though I were trying to burn them into my consciousness, make them real, make myself real in them. In the opposite of the house games I used to play when I was a child, I was decidedly inside the room, and it was right-side up. No wandering on the ceiling here, no drifting out into the garden to change perspective. I absorbed the small corner fireplace, with its frieze of Greco-Roman goddesses picked out in gold against an aqua ground . . . the ceiling with its daub of a fresco depicting a basket of fruit and a bottle of wine . . . the old, cold, deep dark orange terra-cotta floor with its chips and fissures . . . the uncomfortable flowered linen sofa and chair . . . the table at which I ate, taught, drew, and wrote.

In this setting I placed myself and I watched myself the way I would a character in a movie or a play. Sometimes I concluded that this freer, more easygoing me had been waiting inside me all along, a different bird in a protected shell that needed only to land in the appropriate nest in order to hatch; at other times I thought, Who are you kidding? This is merely a respite. A pretend life in a pretend house in a city to which you are pretending to belong. Wait until you wake up in that other story again; wait until you're tested, buddy, and then we'll see how free you really are.

The test came soon enough.

At the Hôtel d'Angleterre

Because I was following the academic calendar, my Italian year ended in June. In early July I planned to travel with my brother Danny before returning home. Our first stop was to be in Paris. As it happened (and how was it, I wonder now in retrospect, that it just happened?), my aunt was in Europe herself that July, and she herself was going to be leaving London for Paris at about the time my brother and I were to arrive there. She was not traveling with my uncle, who had been feeling too ill to take such an ambitious trip; instead she was traveling in the company of her on-again, off-again friend (and sister-in-law) Aunt Trudy and Trudy's daughter, my oldest cousin, Diane, whom we called Dee Dee.

Even before my brother came to Florence, the letters from my uncle started arriving, always by special delivery:

Just thought I'd give you a heads-up, Mike, but it seems like your aunt's travels are not going quite as we had hoped.

Another began:

Let me ask you a question. How would you and your brother feel about moving up your arrival in Paris? I'll make it up to you both.

Another:

I am sorry to have to do this, Mike. But I am going to have to call upon you to help out your aunt. Something is just not right between her and Trudy and Diane. She reports being ill-treated by the ladies. Abused is what it sounds like. I must confess I am not entirely surprised. I warned your aunt before she agreed to travel with them. We in our inner group all know what they're like, do we not? We have for years. It would mean the world to me if you and Dan could arrive in Paris by the weekend of the 18th. I'm happy to pick up any extra cost involved in changing your flights. I'd be in your debt. Really I would.

As we came closer to leaving for Paris, my uncle's letters were replaced by telegrams asking me to set an appointment to speak to him from the call center, which in those days was the only economical way to place calls abroad. I went, and phoned, and listened. The situation, as my uncle reported it, was this: The three women had set off together on an adventure. Because Trudy and Dee Dee, who were both schoolteachers, had more limited resources than Hank did, she had agreed to travel on a moderate budget; however, she did not find the London accommodations they had chosen to be at all *copacetic* and it was with great reluctance that she had compromised on the Angleterre in Paris. The same went for the restaurants her traveling companions favored. And as for sitting up in the mezzanine of the theater, what was the point, really, of going to a play if you couldn't see the actors sweat? So she had stepped in and paid the difference in the tab. Out of the goodness of her heart she had done this. She gave, as she always had, without strings. Only instead of being appreciative, the ladies had bristled; there had been arguments; they were stubborn, resistant, and clannish. They inevitably shared the double room while leaving her to lodge by herself. There were even days when one of them insisted on going off on her own, but to do what, and why? Wasn't the whole point of traveling together *being* together? "It's just not larky, the way it is with the *Martin* Franks," she had told my uncle. "Not larky in the least."

The day we arrived in Paris—on our original schedule—my brother and I checked into our hotel. Then Danny turned to me and said, "I'm going for a walk. I'll see you back here before dinner."

Just like that, for the moment anyway, Danny went off. I watched him go with a flash of anger undercut by a pang of admiration. After he left, I began to think about how each of my brothers had had their own complex trajectories with our aunt and uncle.

Steve's was the least burdensome for sure—a by-product, or blessing, of birth order, perhaps. He was the third born, the least colonized, the most unfazed. He had little trouble dipping in and out of life at the maison, making casual talk about literature, movies, politics, people. An emerging writer himself, he even brought my aunt and uncle his work to read (neither art *nor* artifice for him: even-keeled encouragement instead), which after my second experience I never once did again. When they were sick, he visited; when they were in a panic (something that happened more and more as they grew older), he popped over and sat with them until whatever crisis that had erupted had ebbed or been resolved. My little brother was gifted with an uncommon mixture of a darkly ironic sense of humor and deep reserves of patience, and he was generous with his time . . . but unsurprisingly none of this allowed him to escape my aunt's withering remarks.

One in particular became a refrain of hers and a secret wry shorthand among us three brothers. Steve would drive my aunt and uncle to dinner and hear, "If all else fails, you'd make a splendid chauffeur." A gifted cook, he would invite them to congenial family dinners and hear, "If all else fails, you'd make an excellent chef." *If all else fails*: it was a more stinging iteration of, earlier in life, pegging him as the family athlete. As it happened, all else did not fail—far from it—but why embed a razor blade in praise? Why distrust small, or large, acts of kindness? "You do realize that your brother Steve only comes over when he *wants* something," Hank memorably, and absurdly, whispered to me one day when he was just out of earshot. What did Steve want? To try to sustain this exceedingly difficult connection? Imagine being suspicious of that.

Danny, in Paris, was still recovering from a particularly mortifying experience with our aunt and uncle that had taken place the year before, when he was a junior at UCLA and had a serious girlfriend named Kathy. As the temperature rose toward summer, he began bringing Kathy to the maison for afternoon swims. Trays of refreshments were produced; conversation percolated; my aunt and uncle were engaged (and engaging), available and curious, so slyly curious, in fact, that they took studious note of Kathy, from top to bottom, inside and—notably—out.

The screenwriters had come to a point in their careers where they were trying to shake things up creatively; instead of adapting books and plays, as they had done since they'd begun collaborating, they had started experimenting with "originals," as they called them, a misnomer if there ever was one with regard to the script they sat down to write that fall and promptly, way too promptly, managed to sell: *Beginners*, it was called, and it told the story of a first love between a thin, bookish young photographer (Danny had his own darkroom in this period) and his sharp-witted and charming girlfriend, who just so happened, like Kathy, to be fat.

The day my brother Danny read this script was, I think it's fair to say, one of the darkest of his twenty years. Almost as if they anticipated how incendiary it would be, my aunt and uncle explained to Danny that he and Kathy had "loosely" inspired the screenplay, and they gave it to him, insisting, however, that he read it at their house, which he did, sitting—where else?—by the pool. As the ice cubes dissolved in the pink lemonade and the Weby's Florentines melted in the heat, he turned the pages rapidly and with mounting disgust.

Finally he came to the end. He went inside. Hank was stretched out on Field Marshal Montgomery's daybed, and Irving was sunk into his reading chair as usual. In a voice blistering with anger my brother asked my aunt and uncle what on earth they had in mind by taking this one aspect of his girlfriend's features and making it so prominent in their script. Did they have no idea, he asked, how wounded she would be? And by her boyfriend's own family?

My aunt, quickly backtracking, denied that the inspiration behind the story was actually what it was. "A writer never knows where she gets things," she said archly, her head tilted back.

"Kathy's greatest fear is that people will look at her and not notice all of her accomplishments or her character or anything other than her size," Danny said. "What if I ask you to change just that—just that one detail?"

My aunt and uncle, in unison, both shook their heads at him. "I'm afraid we can't do that, Dan," said my aunt. "The whole script is built around this idea, as you see."

"What if I *told* you to change it?" said my brother, his voice rising.

"Told us?" said my uncle. "Why, that would be censorship."

"Yes, that's exactly what it would be," agreed my aunt.

On that day my brother went into a rage—not a fiery, Bergman Temper sort of rage, but an icy-cold, deep-down rage that in fact went beyond rage to nothingness, as our aunt and uncle became, effectively, nothing to him. It was as if molten iron had been poured into a mold of my brother and, in their company anyway, he was forever after hard, metallic; impenetrable. He made sure that he was unavailable to my aunt and uncle in any meaningful way. He never shared with them, or showed them, anything personal about his life. No wonder he could go off to tour Paris while I, seeking to comply with my uncle's request that I take the temperature of the situation, went to see my aunt.

I approached my aunt's hotel in the rue Jacob with some apprehension. It was the first time in a year that we were to come together.

I saw her before she saw me. She was standing in front of a tall mirror in the lobby, looking around a lavish arrangement of flowers and tucking a few stray hairs back under the brim of her tam. She had on one of her more maximal collections of jewelry, half a dozen gold chains at least, each with a cluster of medallions or charms or Georgian seals hanging off them that I had never seen before. She had on more makeup than usual too, a thick pink glazing on her cheeks and a bright blue pigment on her eyelids, below which two unnaturally bright eyes were set in a field of especially electric white.

Now, I had observed and studied my aunt as closely as I had observed and studied any human being anywhere, and I knew, even before she said a word to me, that something was not right with her; this not-rightness was pulsing through her eyes, her body, and her more-is-more (-is-more) maquillage and ornamentation. But even beyond that, it was communicated in the way she was regarding her own image in that spotted French mirror: she had the same pleased look in her eye that she had when she pulled together a new arrangement in the maison; it was as if she had become one of her own *mises en scène*, and it was downright weird. Weird and alarming and . . .

"Lovey!" she said into the mirror, where she had glimpsed me. With an abrupt change of focus she turned around, took a few rapid steps forward, and drew me into an embrace. "I am so desperately happy to see you that I could almost *weep*. Thank God you're finally here. Come, let's sit down."

We moved into the lobby and sat. She was holding a bag. She handed it to me. "I have prezzies. I'll tell you what they are. A cashmere sweater from Berk's—they're the best in London. I know red is your color—and not to worry, you don't have to save it for the hols. The other is the newest Virginia Woolf biography. I started it on the plane. If I've said it once, I'll say it a million times: Leonard was a perfect *saint* to our Virginia. That woman, she would never have written a *stitch* without him. The rudiments of the story are gripping, inevitably, but the book is just so-so; it's taking one of those knock-the-statue-off-its-pedestal approaches that I find so deplorable. It's a far cry from Boswell and Mr. Edel, let me tell you; but of course I'll let you make up your own mind. First, though, we've simply *got* to talk. I want to hear your plans, *our* plans."

My heart began to beat anxiously. "Our plans?" I asked. "What . . . what do you mean?"

"Obviously I mean what are we going to *do*, where are we going to *go*. Your unc assur—"

"But Danny and I've only just arrived in Paris this afternoon," I said as evenly as I could.

"Paris! I'll tell you about Paris. I expect you'll find it as tired as I do. I mean, after you've seen a few paintings, and paid homage to Colette at the Palais Royale, which is still very beautiful I will admit, you'll see it's no longer really *comme il faut*. The antiquing is an absolute disaster, the food is too rich and overpriced, and the French, oh, they are just as dislikable as ever—*méchant* is I believe the appropriate local word. You'll see how they are, how they stare at you in the streets and turn their nose up at you when you try to speak French. They are just unrepentant snobs, always have been and always will be." Several strands of hair had again loosened themselves from her tam; she shoved them back up into the pile before resuming, "Lovey, your unc has spoken to our fellas at the Dorch, and they can take us on twenty-four hours' notice. If we arrive by Thursday we can hit the markets—Bermondsey is Friday, you have to go at dawn and bring a flashlight so you don't make any terrible mistakes. We can try to scare up some decent theater, although from what I determined the season was grim, grim, grim. Maybe we'll even hire a car and driver and do a little damage in the country. I think you would just *adore* Bath, and you've never been to Oxford, and you just never know what's next, do you? A nice little graduate degree in eighteenth-century literature might be just the thing. Think of all that delicious reading: the birth of the novel . . . Dr. Johnson . . . cunning old Jane . . ."

A rocklike object had formed in my chest. "Well, you know," I said, "this is Danny's first time in Paris and—"

"But he'll find London so much more congenial—just as you and I did." She paused pointedly. "You recall that trip, Michael, do you not?"

I inhaled deeply. "What about Trudy and Dee Dee? You can't just abandon them."

"Oh, I can't, can't I?"

"But it's not . . . it's not what you worked out, is it?"

"Darling, *nothing* is what I worked out, nothing is what I expected of this trip. What can I say? They are not *bad* women, exactly it's not that. It's just that we don't see eye to eye on many things, more things than I ever would have guessed. The truth is, being with them is just not larky the way it is with us. There's a lack of *esprit*, or understanding—you know what I mean, because you and I have shared it from the very beginning." She made a slicing gesture with her hand. "But anyway, now that you're here, we'll put all that behind us. We won't bother about them so much. Of course we don't want them to feel *ex*cluded, so tonight I've had the man here book a table for all of us at La Coupole at seven. La Coupole is your unc's favorite brasserie. How I wish he were here," she added, her eyes misting. "And how I do."

At La Coupole, as at the Angleterre, I had a chance to observe before I was observed. From far across the crowded room I saw my two aunts and my cousin sitting stiffly and silently at a round table. Trudy and Dee Dee were reading their menus; Hank's was closed, and she was tapping on hers with her glasses. It was always striking to be reminded how much my cousin resembled my aunt physically; they looked far more like mother and daughter than Trudy and Dee Dee did. My cousin shared with Hank the same small round face, high cheekbones, and receding chin, though Dee Dee put herself together very differently—no makeup, hair down, blue jeans, a single ring on a single finger.

My cousin and my aunt Trudy greeted Danny and me coldly. Or warily. Warily was probably more like it. Every sentence they spoke was short and clipped at first, and eye contact hovered around zero.

Hank ordered before anyone else, ate her food before anyone else, asked for dessert ahead of everyone else. She had always been a fast eater, but she gobbled her *steak frites* at a rate that seemed almost dangerous. I had never seen anything quite like this before. She was still chewing when she waved at the waiter and called loudly for *l'addition*.

"Hank," Trudy said calmly. "Why are we rushing? Is there somewhere we need to be? Michael is just telling us about his year in Florence—"

"Yes, yes, and it's all very exciting," she said. "But tomorrow's Saturday, and we need to be up early for the *marché aux puces.*"

The waiter brought the check. Hank tossed down a wad of francs.

My cousin said, "Will you please let us know what our share is?"

"We can keep our calculators in our pocketbooks tonight, *mesdames,*" she said acerbically. "This is a welcome dinner for my nephews." She patted my brother's hand. "Shall we?"

My brother removed his hand to his lap. "Shall we what?"

"Be on our way."

"Hank," Danny said, "maybe you didn't notice, but we're still eating."

She looked around the table. "So you are," she said. She crossed her arms in front of her chest. "Quick-quick, then. There's no point in lingering with all these dreadful Frenchmen." She leaned forward and added, not exactly sotto voce, "Don't tell me you don't feel it. The way they stare at us with such hostility and venom."

I looked around our table. No one was staring at us. No one was even looking at us. I poured myself a second glass of wine.

My aunt's eyes keenly followed the wine bottle to my glass. "A *second* glass? Really? Is *that* what you've learned from your year in Florence?"

"Yes," I said. "I've learned that it's nice to drink a glass of wine with dinner."

"Or two."

"Or two."

The waiter brought her change. She stood up. "Ladies, our taxi awaits."

When neither of them responded, she said, "Is no one joining me?"

"You know what, Hank," Trudy said evenly. "I think we'll just sit here and keep the boys company for a bit."

"But Corky said he would make his nightly call at eight-thirty. It's nearly eight now."

Trudy glanced at her watch. "It is, yes."

Hank hesitated for a moment. "Go ahead and suit yourselves," she said icily.

And with this she left.

•

None of us had much appetite. We picked at our food for a few minutes and sat in silence. The restaurant was loud, busy, full of other people having other dinners; normal dinners, they would likely have been. Eventually we agreed to go.

Out on boulevard Montparnasse I asked Trudy and Dee Dee if they would like to stop somewhere to have a drink.

"Or two," my cousin said drily.

As soon as we sat down in the closest café I said, "So what's going on here?"

Now, I had known these two women all my life, but not with great intimacy. Like so much in our world, this, too, was my aunt's—my aunt and uncle's—doing. They preferred to keep people separate: their friends from their family, different family pockets from other family pockets. They saw everyone individually and spoke negatively of one group to another. It did not help that, for years, almost everything we had heard about these relatives of ours was pretty much relentlessly critical; but I had no choice. I felt I had at least to *ask* what had been happening.

The words just came pouring out of my cousin. She said that this had been a lifelong dream of hers, to travel with her mother to Europe. She had been planning and saving up for it for years. When Hank asked if she could join them, neither of them could figure out how to say no. Trudy assured her that Hank was in a stable phase. She believed that Hank would be good fun to romp around Europe with and that, as long as they were clear with her about the economic parameters, everything would work out. Well, it hadn't worked out. Not one bit. Almost from the moment they landed in London, Hank was unhappy with every single arrangement that had been made. She bullied them into spending more money than they had budgeted, and when she picked up the difference, as she insisted on doing, she would expect them to do what she wanted all day long, which basically meant shopping. Like an addict, she was not happy until she had had a fix. Actually two fixes: one antique in the morning, another in the afternoon. Or if not an antique, a piece of jewelry or an article of clothing. At the Tate or the National Gallery, she lasted half an hour tops. She insisted on choosing the plays they saw, and then more often than not she walked out at intermission. She wouldn't dream of wandering through a neighborhood simply to explore it or setting out without a plan to allow the day to unfold. She never once, as we had seen, lingered over a meal. Everything was rushed and ill-at-ease . . .

All this, my cousin went on, was minor compared with the way Hank dedicated her conversation to the relentless excoriation of *every*one they knew in common or were related to. My parents. Her parents. Her sister, Lisa; her brother, John; her husband. When at one point Dee Dee made a mistake—"a stupid, naive, terrible mistake; I still have no idea what I was thinking"—of telling Hank that she had been having a rough moment in her marriage, Hank told her that she should follow her grandmother's example by tossing her hat to the wind and taking a lover. "I said that I did not think that was the best solution for me and I wondered if it had been the best solution for Huffy, and Hank said, 'What was good enough for your grandmother is good enough for you. She was twice the woman you are, and don't think I'm ever going to forget the way you have just spoken about Mamma; in fact, I think I have half a mind to put the story of your failing marriage into my next screenplay . . .'"

At dinner in London, the women told us, she would hold up her necklaces and say, "To whom shall I leave all of my jewels?" Ever since they had arrived in Paris she was convinced that Gypsy children were trying to rip these very same jewels off her neck, but even after they asked her not to wear so much jewelry when she went out, she insisted on layering it on as soon as she got dressed, more and more day by day, almost as if she were inviting some kind of trouble.

At night they had heard her talking to herself in her room, muttering incoherently for hours at a time. And that very morning, around the time I turned up at the Angleterre, where they'd deposited her in the lobby before going out for a walk, Hank was adjusting her hair in the mirror when she said to Dee Dee, "I am afraid Michael will find me very aged. Will he find me very aged, do you think? Will he think I am no longer beautiful? Will he no longer love me?"

I took this in—I wasn't sure how to take this in. With some incredulity, at first. Was it possible that my cousin, out of her own frustrations with my aunt, was exaggerating or dramatizing or (even) fabricating?

The little-boy part of me actually hoped that this was the case. The detective part asked, "Did she *really* say those last things—the ones in front of the mirror?"

Dee Dee took in a deep breath, but it was Trudy who answered, "Those precise words, Michael, I regret to say."

The rock in my chest dropped down into my stomach and lodged itself in an all-too-familiar groove. Only then did I realize I had been without stomach pain for the entire past year.

Later as we walked back to our respective hotels, my cousin went on to offer as incisive a reading as I had yet heard of my aunt's character, or one aspect of my aunt's character at least. All her life, she said, Hank's approach to people who were born into or came into her orbit was to divide and conquer them. It was how she kept herself central, in a place of (illusory) power. She would come between mothers and daughters, fathers and sons, husbands and wives, one friend and another. There was Irving and Ruby, Irving and Merona, and Irving and his mother too—because hadn't Hank been just dreadful about Sylvia, especially after Huffy died, when she seemed to resent Sylvia for nothing more than the fact that she had gone on living? She said horrible things about Merona to Trudy and doubtless the other way around. Even as she had been longing for us boys to come to Paris, she had been telling Dee Dee some pretty hateful things about us and probably we had heard some pretty harsh things about her too over the years. Only on this trip, for the first time, it wasn't working. Much as Hank had tried to drive a wedge between mother and daughter, she was failing, and she was not able to find her ground, her place. Hence the muttering, the way she used her money, the need to shop, her wish to decide their movements every moment of every day, her deep, constant dissatisfaction and constant communication thereof.

This made sense, as far as it went. A lot fell into place—except maybe the why of it. The why eluded us all then, as it did afterward too. Though now that I am well along in my own life, I see what I missed, what my frustration and my own anger made me miss, all those years ago: I see my aunt's fear; I see how she was consumed by fear. Because surely it was dark, stinky, oily, pulsating fear that drove her to divide and conquer, and to fill herself up with more and more things; surely it was fear that fed her anger, because isn't fear what is always lying, snakelike, at the bottom of every basketful of rage? Fear at being out of control—of the decoration, the food, the moment, the conversation, the connections between other people, the story; always the story, which had to be as she saw (or invented, or interpreted) it and told it, or else. Then there was her fear of change. Her fear of losing what was precious to her. Her fear of being unloved, and possibly unlovable. Her fear of being childless (one of the deepest, most ancient, ongoing fears of them all). Her fear of being friendless, brotherless, motherless, nephew- and nieceless, and surely somewhere also husbandless. There was her fear of being alone with that fearful, unstable, ever unstitching self of hers. Fear of death? Was that part of it too? Because why else would a human being work so hard to kill off her connection to all the people in her life unless she was so afraid of being consumed by hurt and grief, as she had been when her beloved mother died, that she had to demolish them herself first, while they were still breathing?

None of this occurred to me, to any of us, then. Even if it had, even if we'd identified the scared little girl buried inside that angry, troubled, and irrational older woman, we still had the angry, troubled, and irrational older woman on our hands in Paris, far, far away from home.

My cousin asked the obvious question as soon as we left the café: "The issue now is, what are we going to do about her?"

How was I supposed to know? I had traveled six thousand miles away from home because I did not know what to do about my aunt.

The next morning we all regrouped to make a plan for the day ahead and, after taking a vote, unsurprisingly settled on the Manet retrospective at the Jeu de Paume instead of the flea market.

I had studied some art history in college and knew a bit about the period, which may have helped bring some energy to the conversation Trudy, Dee Dee, my brother, and I had about the paintings, though it may have derived its vigor as much from the simple fact that we had been freed, for the morning, from the topic of Hank.

My aunt hurried through the show as she had hurried through dinner the night before, and she made it clear by the way she stood in the doorway adjusting all her rings that she wished we were not lingering so long in front of the paintings.

At one point Trudy said, "Isn't this just one of the loveliest mornings we've had? Michael is really making all these pictures come alive for me."

"So he's read a few books," my aunt said tartly. "Big deal."

"But, Hank," Trudy persisted. "Is it not possible for him to have learned something, and to have something to share? He just seems so grown-up after his year away . . ."

"Quite honestly, I wish he would stop all this chatter and take me antiquing," Hank said. "Paintings you can see any day of the week."

When it came time for lunch, we fell into a nearby brasserie, where as soon as we sat down, and before we had even opened our menus, my aunt said, "All this fumphering around is becoming a major obstacle for me. Right here and right now, fellas, I think we need to talk about our plans."

Our plans, my brother explained to her calmly, remained unchanged. He and I were spending the next week in Paris, as she knew.

"We should have worked this out better ahead of time. I need you to accompany me to London."

"We can't do that," I said. "I'm sorry."

"But you *must*."

"Michael and I organized this trip a long time ago, Auntie Hankie," my brother said as gently as he could, "way before we knew you were even going to *be* in Europe."

"And you boys cannot be flexible? Really? Your uncle—"

"Was speaking for us," I said, "if he told you that we would come with you to London."

She sat back in her chair as if she had been slapped.

"I see," she said as she looked off into the distance. These visual asides of hers, which evoked a habit of my grandmother's, had become increasingly frequent. It was as though she were checking in with an invisible something just offstage, like a camera, or someone, such as my absent uncle, or perhaps my dead grandmother herself.

"Well, I, personally, have had enough of Paris—and the French." Her voice was loud, carrying; excruciating. "Let's not forget how they behaved during the war, welcoming the Nazis at Maxim's—why, I would have sooner set fire to the place. I would now, if someone gave me a match! They are just, all of them, so icy and rude. They stare at me, I don't know why, either, everywhere I go. And as for all of you—" She looked around the table at the four of us. "I find *you*—" Her eyes grew wider. "Every last one of you—" Wider still. "A great and enormous disappointment. You are a blot upon the word *family*, all of you. Goneril and Regan—and Edmund—are charmers by comparison."

With blazing eyes, she went on: "But I do not see how I can *get* to London on my own. I have several very large bags, suitcases of clothes, new acquisitions for the maison. The only solution is for you to take these bags *for* me, boys. Yes, that's the solution right there."

Even as I felt my entire body tense up, in as calm a voice as possible, which was not in the end very calm at all, I said, "Hank, I wish I could help, but I've been away almost a year. As maybe you can imagine, I have so many bags, myself. Two alone just of books . . ."

"It's not really a question, Michael. You *will* do it, or else."

My heart had begun to pick up speed. "Or else what?"

"I will simply abandon them and bill your parents."

"I'm sorry?"

"You will be," she said. "You have the *nerve* to hesitate? You *dare* not comply when I ask you this one favor? After *all* I have done for you?"

"I—I have not asked you to do *any*thing for me," I said, "except maybe be kind."

"Well, I'm not kind. There you have it. I'm tough. And I'm mean. And plain-speaking, and truth-telling like my mamma before me. That's who I am, pure and simple." Her hands gripped the side of the table. "And, yes, in case you're curious, and even if you're not, I *am* going to tell you what's on my mind, you bet I am. The truth is this, Michael. For years and years you have taken from me, taken and taken. Yes, I know. I've said it before. I will say it again. And I don't mean only financially either. I hate to embarrass you in front of our relations, but when you went to Europe the first time and could not hack it on your own? Who came and rescued you, and invited you to see something of the world, in comfort and in style? And when you were away at college, who wrote to you every week, devoted, chatty letters to cheer you up out of your misery and homesickness? And who sent you care packages? Biscuits and books and *objets* to brighten your dreary room? And sweaters and gloves? And during this year in Florence," she added acidly, "which has *grown you up so*, who sent money every single month? Two hundred dollars in care of American Express in via dei something-or-other-ini, on the twentieth by airmail from L.A. to arrive on the first? 'Ingratitude, thou marble-hearted fiend'!"

She was quoting Lear to Goneril—to *me?*

"I've always been grateful for the help," I said. "But I would never have accepted any of this if I'd known you expected something in return. Other than love," I added. "Or friendship."

"Love!" she said with a snort. "Is it love to leave an aunt high and dry in a foreign land? Is it love to treat me as an antagonist, a ghoul—a monster? Is that your definition of *friend*ship?"

"I have tried to be your friend. I have never called you a monster."

"You don't have to. It's written all over your face. It's suggested in every last bit of your behavior," she said. "And you are no *friend*. A *friend*, when he is called upon, simply does what he is *asked*."

"Even when it's unreasonable?"

"It's so unreasonable, it's so *awful*, to come have a few larky days with your aunt in London town—all expenses paid?"

"I appreciate the invitation," I said, "but I'm afraid I have to say no."

She studied me. "You know what, Michael? I am actually very sorry for you. I understand you better now—now that I know more about your year. You cannot maintain your relationship with me, or your uncle, that much is clear, and has been for a while; now it's also evident that you cannot maintain a relationship with anyone else. We have proof finally of what we've suspected for *years*. Proof clear as day. The woman you wrote your uncle about? The poet, wasn't she? And teacher there in Florence, like you getting by on a few lire here a few lire there? Where is that relationship now, what happened to her?"

She looked theatrically around the restaurant. "I don't see her here with us? Do you, ladies?"

The ladies, my cousin and my aunt, were staring into their laps, mortified.

When they failed to respond to Hank, she turned to me. "I have to ask you, what is it about *you*, Michael, that is so broken and wounded? Hmm? What about *you* drives people away? You keep telling me how unreasonable *I* am, how irrational *my* behavior is, how demanding or whatever. Why not take a good hard look at yourself? In your place I know I would."

She pushed her chair back from the table triumphantly. Without ordering, without hurrying through her meal, without hurrying the rest of us through our meal, she stood up and she walked out. She left Paris the next day, by herself. She went to London, by herself. And then she went home to Los Angeles. All by herself.

Back at the Boulevard

That July, strange though it may seem in retrospect, we all convened again at the beach. It would be the last such summer, because in the fall my father would bring an end to these conjoined vacations by buying a small piece of land farther down the peninsula in Seaview, where we would build a summer house of our own the following year, while my aunt and uncle would buy a cottage farther up the peninsula north of Long Beach, where my aunt could play house unimpeded by her insubordinate nephews, or any other dissenting voices.

But first there was that summer. To travel all those miles around the globe after the year I had had, and the days in Paris that my brother and I had had with our aunt, felt like reading far ahead into a long and complicated book only to lose your place and have to begin all over again in one of the earlier chapters.

It was like that . . . and it was not quite like that. When we arrived at the beach, my aunt and uncle were already there. My aunt had managed to heave and wrest her bungalow into place with the help of a hired hand from the local hardware store, but that year's decoration had a sketchy feel to it. The pictures had been tacked up haphazardly and hung askew on the paneled walls, and she had resorted to using silk flowers to fill in here and there—this was not the great decorator at her most aesthetically deft. The offness of the setting extended to the offness of the general atmosphere, where the mealtime conversation had all the ease of a state lunch organized during the short-lived detente of two warring nations. What could we talk about, anyway? Florence? Paris? Merry old London town? All those cities, and what had happened in them, were strictly verboten. My uncle's health? His time apart from my aunt had appeared to have put him back in the pink. My brother Danny's fall plans were good for five minutes or so, since he was going off to medical school that September and into a faraway and different future. As for my own uncertain future, after Paris I was disinclined to tell my aunt anything of my intentions, anything about *me*, since I had learned that it was impossible to predict what fact or circumstance, what mere occurrence in my life, might become fodder for one of her vituperations, and so I decided to keep the facts, all the facts, to myself.

We were only two days into our strange, stilted time together when my uncle asked if I would like to have coffee with him that afternoon. This was not an invitation in the old sense of joining him at Coffee Hour. It felt more like a summons.

We met at Milton York's, one of the oldest continuing enterprises from my father and my aunt's childhood. In their day York's had been the town's candy maker, specializing in saltwater taffy and hand-dipped mints; over the years it had expanded to add a small restaurant whose walls were hung with enlarged vintage photographs of the peninsula in its heyday. Among these images was one of the narrow-gauge railroad where my father used to leave pennies to be flattened on the tracks, and another of the saltwater baths where my great-grandmother went religiously every afternoon to take a plunge with her friend Mrs. Robbins. These associative pictures made for a curiously apt setting against which to have the conversation that unfolded between my uncle and me.

As soon as the waitress delivered our coffee Irving produced an envelope from his pocket. He stared at the bright red *exprès* label for a moment, then slid it across the table.

Inside was the letter that, after much upsetting conversation with my brother, I had written to my uncle from Paris the night after my aunt stormed out of the restaurant. I had described, in great detail, the situation as I had found it, and lived it, in the previous few days. I'd given him what I felt was an accurate reading of the difficulties between Hank and Trudy and Dee Dee, and then I'd added:

> I realize, Irv, that you will probably receive my perception of this predicament with some skepticism. In addition, you will soon start hearing that Danny and I (though I primarily) have mistreated Hank as Trudy and Dee Dee have—that we have not rescued her as she imagined us doing; but I want to appeal to the vestiges of your clarity and impartiality in dealing with your wife's complaints and eventual rage. If her behavior this week is any indication, there has been an alarming decline in Auntie Hankie's contact with reality this past year, and unless you are completely oblivious, I appeal to you to try to lead her to a more humane understanding of human beings.

A more humane understanding of human beings? My eye landed on that phrase, and I felt my skin begin to redden.

"Did you read it?" I asked.

"Don't be ridiculous. Of course I read it. More than once."

He sat back in his chair. Irving looked old to me all of a sudden. His eyes had a dusty remoteness to them; an unfamiliar remoteness.

When he didn't say anything else, I said, "And what did you think?"

"Well, since you ask, Mike, I thought it was a work of surrealism. A Salvador Dalí, René Magritte kind of letter."

"Because it made no sense to you?"

"Because everything in it was backward. Because I did not recognize the person who wrote it, and I *certainly* did not recognize the person it was written about."

An incipient queasiness began to form itself into my stomach. It was like the early stages of food poisoning, before you run to the bathroom with an exploding mouth or bowel. All my life I had thought, even despite a great deal of evidence to the contrary, that if matters with my aunt turned truly extreme, my uncle would see what was going on, step in, and help out. Matters had now turned incontrovertibly extreme, and Irving was not only not helping out; he was denying that they existed. Utterly.

"But that *was* Hank," I said urgently. "And it was also very much me."

"I am sorry to hear that," he said.

"You are sorry to hear the truth?"

"Whose truth? What truth?"

"The truth of what I saw in Paris. Of what your wife, my aunt, was doing, saying—how she was behaving, treating us, the terrible things—"

"That's your truth. Hers is different."

"Really?" I said, shaking my head—at her, at him.

"She says she was nothing but generous, to all of you. Kind and considerate, as she is, unfailingly. Open. Patient. Loving."

It was not easy to remain even-tempered. I heard my voice go up as I said, "And the rest of us?"

"The rest of you ganged up on her. Went after her, flat-out."

"But, Uncle Irving, that is simply not the case."

He shrugged. "I wasn't there."

The shrug got to me: denial by gesture. "*I* was," I said, with still more intensity coming into my voice, "and let me assure you, she was very—*extreme.*"

"Maybe she was just impassioned. Have you thought of that? She is a passionate woman, your aunt. Full of vigor, of ideas. She has a point of view on most things, as we know."

"Yes, she does. A very mistaken one. An appalling, misguided, sometimes vicious point of view."

"Who's to say, Mike, what's mistaken or appalling? As for vicious—the things you wrote here, the things you said to your aunt. Couldn't those be described as vicious? Wouldn't any reasonable person say that?"

"Me, vicious? You know me better than that."

He put up his hand. "Your aunt is a good woman. A great woman."

"In Paris," I said, "this good, great woman was not in her right mind."

He winced, but I did not care that he winced. I didn't care what he thought, what he felt. I wanted to be *heard*. I wanted to be *acknowledged*. Just this once.

"You can't make these assertions, Mike," he said, "without giving me specifics."

"How about if we just start with the way she treated Trudy and Dee Dee—"

He swept his hand through the air. "They don't *count*. They don't *mean* anything. Not to our inner group."

That again. "What does count, Irving? Do I count?"

"You count, yes. But you also disappoint."

"I disappoint?"

"You did not come through for your aunt when she was in need. That is a disappointment. A huge one to me personally."

"But her behavior—it was not rational. It was not sane. The way she thought she was being stared at and treated, by complete strangers. The harsh things she said about, well, *everyone* in our families, and about me, my year, the girl I—what I'm capable of, or not capable of. When she knows nothing, when it was all in her head, a fantasy—a script, another script. Dialogue, lines, mean awful lines. I just don't understand how you can support—"

"She is my wife," he said simply.

"Which means what?"

"That I believe her. I believe *in* her."

"Your wife lives in a fantasy world. She always has. But something has changed—gotten worse. She spins endless fantasies about herself, about me. About her mother."

He sat back. "Your grandmother? How does she enter into it?"

"Hank makes Grandma Huffy out to be more perfect, more brilliant than any of the rest of us could ever hope to be. She's even turned her parents' marriage into a model. Really? What kind of model is that? All those affairs—all that unhappiness? She compares everyone to Huffy and finds us all wanting. She makes *you* out to be perfect like that too. If we're not like Huffy, or like you, we're lesser, we're flawed, we fail. Where is the reality? The honesty? Do you know what she said to Dee Dee about taking a lov—"

"There's no harm in her maintaining a positive view of her mother. She was not perfect, but she was a remarkable person. I knew her. You did not."

"I *did* know her. As a child."

He shrugged. "Children," he said disdainfully.

"Children don't know things, perceive things?"

"You know very well that I always skip the childhood chapters when I read a biography," he said.

I felt my frustration building and building. "For many years now I have seen Hank behave—problematically. And do things to—hurt people, many people. Me among them. And to bully and to attack and to lash out—" I sucked in a breath. "But you don't see any of this?"

He shook his head gravely.

"And you don't plan to *do* anything?"

He pushed the letter farther across the table. "I think it's best if we put all this behind us now, Mike."

"That's not possible," I said. "I cannot go on as if nothing happened."

"But what has happened, really? How do you know that all this isn't in your head? Or a mood, a phase? That's what your aunt and I believe. That it's a phase. Some kind of delayed adolescent rebellion, probably very normal but to us also rather trying."

In my head. A phase. *Trying.* "You're wrong," I said, my voice cracking. "It's not just me alone. Do I have to name names, Irving? Honestly, I just don't get it—I don't get *you*." I stood up. "You've always been a different person away from Hank. Reasonable—logical. Another Irv. Now I don't know who you are anymore. Your whole life—it's just fake. It's a *lie*."

He was very still for a moment. "My life is a lie," he said.

My stomach began to burn. It had been one of my greatest worries in life, that I would become a lacerater like my aunt. Or some crossbreed of my aunt and my father, the Hank irrationality fanned into greater flame by the Bergman Temper.

"Yes," I said. "It is."

He lifted his coffee cup and looked beyond it into the distance.

"As I say, it's best that we put all this aside, Mike. Yes, that really is for the best."

It was hard to know where to go from there, in every sense. The idea of returning to the side-by-side cottages, to tell my parents and siblings about this conversation, to whisper (since my aunt would likely be next door) and hash over, rehash, yet again, the permutations of my aunt and uncle's thinking and behavior, felt as withering as the conversation itself had been.

I went down to the beach instead. The ocean on the peninsula was very deceptive to look at. It appeared flat and easygoing, with low, gentle waves that were like poor relations to the big, dramatic tide that struck the shore closer to home in Santa Monica or Malibu, a surf we had learned to swim in and make friends with when we were very young. But this northern Pacific was not that southern Pacific; these waves kept all their grit and tug hidden below the surface, where sneaky malevolent riptides every summer, year after year, sucked down one or two innocent or stupidly undaunted bathers. In our first years a very explicit sign had been posted on the approach road: SURF BATHING DEATH TOLL TO DATE, it read, with the number 456 crossed out and replaced with 457, then 458. Later on, the sign was replaced with one that had more circumspect wording, but the message remained the same.

You had to be in the right frame of mind to seek solace from this particular surf. At least the beach that ran alongside it was almost always empty, since even on the hottest, clearest days only a few intrepid or desperate sunbathers would set up camp with a wind-flapped umbrella, a six-pack, and a plastic chair that was carried off like tumbleweed the minute someone got up out of it. Here and there the pristine, unpeopled white sand was punctuated with enormous driftwood logs that had floated down the Columbia and out to sea before being smoothed and silvered and redelivered to solid ground. On some days there would be a scattering of Dungeness crab shells without the crab in them and salmon reduced to head, tail, and bone, the in-between flesh having been breakfasted upon by vigilant seagulls; occasionally you would come upon a dead sea lion, alternately puppy-like in its eternal rest and moldering as it reverted back to elemental goo before being snatched up again by the tide that had spat it onto the beach in the first place.

I had a back-of-the-hand familiarity with this beach, and I walked it in all moods, seeking relief from many of them. This time I took myself there to try to walk off the frustration and fatigue brought on again, yet again, by my aunt and uncle; but no matter how far or how hard I walked, there simply appeared to be no end to this story, to these people. None, anyway, that I could see on the immediate, or distant, horizon.

Later that evening I did speak to my parents and brothers, and they did listen and nod and commiserate, but the situation yet again felt bigger than all of us, with the burden of it falling on me, for reasons that at the same time seemed clear and unclear, just and unjust. At times it felt like I was expressing not only my own individual defiance but also my family's bundled up with it. After all, I had been the favored nephew, the golden substitute son who, at my brothers' expense, had been cultivated from very early on to read and think and form and articulate his opinions, our own Laurel Canyon Philip Pirrip; but when the opinions deviated too far from the prevailing gestalt, I was quickly recharacterized as vicious, disappointing, angry-beyond-adolescence, a general all-around bad seed. High/low, black/white, period/*mo-derne*, love/hate: none of us had been able to map out a safe middle path through this thicket of polarized judgments, least of all me.

The next day my mother came up with the idea to take us boys to Portland for a few days to outfit my brother for his first year in medical school, and that felt just like the right thing, a brief escape from the charged juju at the Boulevard Court. We booked a hotel downtown, and while my mother and brothers went shopping, I put in several hours at the local historical society, reading about Portland in the twenties and thirties, the time and place that formed these people, my father and my aunt and my grandparents. I had always been interested in our origins, and now began a phase during which I looked to facts, to history and setting, and to every family document I could get my hands on licitly or illicitly, for clues to help decipher these particular psyches that haunted and troubled me like some kind of fire-breathing household deities I was born trying to appease——or be done in by.

Steve, the newest driver in the family, took the last shift as we made our way back to the peninsula two evenings later, and the instant we pulled into the driveway at the Boulevard Court I knew that something was amiss. The windows of my aunt and uncle's cottage were black sockets, curtains drawn and lights off, and out on the porch in front of our side there was a mini-orchard of houseplants (silk iterations included) that had my aunt's touch, now her untouch, written all over them.

Inside we found my father sitting in front of the television, pallid and unshaven, not even dressed really, unless you considered "dressed" a white undershirt and some battered khaki shorts. Surrounding him in the living room were more of my aunt's and uncle's goods and chattels, the decorative stuff along with their blankets, their electric water pick, their sun hats and canned goods and the books they had been reading, with the bookmarks still marking their places midway. As so often with my aunt, or my aunt and uncle, the objects communicated before or (like captions in a comic strip, or subtitles in a foreign movie) in consort with their actions. The actions were described soon enough, though, by my ashen-faced father, who waited for us all to come in and find a chair before he told us what had gone down in our absence. In the hours after we left for Portland my uncle had begun to have a severe bout of chest pain brought on, he maintained, by the "stressful conversation he had with Michael," which gave him "a lot of ugly material to stew over," specifically the his-life-is-a-lie part and other accompaniments he described as toxic. He had taken one, then two, then three nitroglycerin tablets to try to alleviate the pain, and when they didn't work, he and my aunt decided they had better hurry back to Los Angeles to be seen by the same battery of doctors who had performed an angiogram on him scarcely a month before and had sent him off into his calm, steady, in-the-pink summer that had suddenly turned uncalm, unsteady, in the black-black-*black*. "If it hadn't been for Michael's sharp tongue," my uncle declared, he might have remained a well man; but he was well no more.

"You realize, of course, that this is not the thinking of rational people," my father added—perhaps superfluously.

My mother said, "Irving's heart irregularities have nothing at all to do with you, Michael." She looked at my father. "They are turning out to be a much bigger problem than any of us thought."

"Actually," said my father, "I think I've had the size right for several years now."

I nodded appreciatively at both my parents—but these were words, and words didn't feel very helpful just then, as my aunt and uncle clearly had understood. They were real pros: for all their polished purposing of talk, they worked in a primarily visual medium and recognized when the negative space, the image or setting alone, could pierce more powerfully still.

At Café Madeleine

That day at Milton York's was one of the last times that my uncle and I ever addressed the subject of my aunt head-on. I realized that there was no use in going *at* the subject, at her, or them, or us. Instead I learned to circumvent. I found it impossible to break off with them completely, because to break off with them completely was to cut out too much of my past, too much of my life as I knew it and the love that had once, early on, coursed through it. It was—I came to understand— to give up the stubborn hope that I might again somehow, against all probability, manage to retrieve a grain or two of that almost drug-like excitement that I experienced so often in her company, their company, when I was a child.

Instead, I sized down; the young man, and later the less-young man, who visited the maison was a shadow of me, restricted and highly edited. I was polite but superficial, engaged but only to a safe degree. Like Danny, I never spoke to my aunt and uncle about my private life or my interior self. I never asked them for any kind of help. Often when I visited I became very logy or addle-headed, since to me the very atmosphere in the maison had a lotus-eater gelatinousness about it that I had to fight against to retain any vividness of mind. Much of the time I reverted to how I had been when I was small: someone who observed and absorbed, a collector, not of *objets* like my aunt but of impressions, signs, stories, facts; evidence. I hoarded them, because I believed (or hoped?) that in them one day I would find the key to the enormous puzzle of how a world that seemed so bright and dazzling and full of possibility had become so shadowed, suffocating, and sad. Tragically sad, you might almost say; I do say.

I lived in New York, then in Florence again, then New York. I spent a lot of time in Italy.

I was often haunted by this childhood, and these people gone awry. I did not know who I was. I thought I might learn by working my story out on the page. I tried to capture my aunt in fiction. People like this do not exist in real life, my readers said. This character is not credible. She is too extreme. Who would stay friends with her, who would stay *married* to her? How could she possibly endure?

She endured.

For many years in the fall my aunt and uncle would come to New York—not to visit me, they were always very clear to say, but to "take in" the theater, visit museums, and see the one or two friends who might happen to be in town when they were, and to shop. Of course they could arrange to be free and available—usually six out of seven nights a week. What a mixture of grandiosity and loneliness they expressed, and how pitiful all this was, when seen in a certain sympathetic light.

I anticipated their visits with a mixture of curiosity and dread, worry and, oddly, hope. Inevitably they were deeply mixed experiences. I sent a side of myself out to dinner and to the theater with them, an old false-self Cliff's Notes version of me. I almost never introduced them to my friends. Conversation was superficial, limited, what my mother sardonically called safe sex—and we often ran out of it by the middle of the second evening we spent in one another's company. Now and then I would concede and go shopping or antiquing with my aunt, ever trying to recapture the delicious feeling I had when I went out with her as a child; instead I tended to feel oppressed by all the dead people's stuff, all those shipwrecked chattels from all those (I was convinced) unhappy and now forgotten lives.

My aunt's stamina and conviction, in matters aesthetic as most everywhere else, remained entirely undiminished. She would visit whatever sublet I was living in and, because she was never impressed with the surroundings I had found or made for myself, dive into a whirlwind of doing-up. I would hear

> *I won't take no for an answer—*
> *Please for once be gracious—*
> *Michael, you're spoiling my pleasure—*

And rather than disturb the delicate waters, I would wait patiently until she had Hankified my place to her satisfaction; when she left town I would weed out everything she contributed and return it or give it away. One year when I was between apartments she persuaded me to rent and furnish, *quick-quick*, an alcove studio in Murray Hill that I despised from the moment I spent the first night there, but still it took me two miserable years to move on. When I did, I sold off its entire contents except for two lamps, my grandmother's cutlery, and my books. It was a great and symbolic liberation but nevertheless a colossal waste of energy and time.

Finally there came the evening that our *pax familias* could not hold, probably because there was only so much self-editing, self-squelching, self-abnegating, and self-unselfing a human being—three human beings—could do.

We were going to the theater and had arranged to eat first at Café Madeleine, a French-style bistro far west on Forty-Third Street that had only fair food and fair ambience but was for some reason a favorite of my aunt and uncle's. Was it the name of the restaurant that attracted them? Probably not, since my aunt and uncle, as they aged, were the least memory-abiding people I ever knew; but, oh, did it resonate with me, every time we met at the Madeleine and tried to coax out of all that lost time the feeling that had once existed so strongly among the three of us but was now, except in my own unrelenting memory, so decidedly changed.

As soon as we sat down my aunt, as she often did, slipped one of her traveler's checks, her preferred form of currency, across the table.

She saw only generosity in the gesture, I do not doubt; I saw Lady Bountiful trying to ease whatever tension there was in the atmosphere by treating (buying, bribing, subsuming) her boy/man nephew yet again, and as gently as I could (knowing that I would soon hear *Please for once be gracious*, or something akin), I told her I was doing all right, asked her to save the check for my birthday or the upcoming holidays, and slid it back in her direction.

Before going to bed that evening I meticulously recorded the scene that followed in my journal, which—in part thanks to that long-ago prodding from my grandmother—I have kept for much of my adult life.

Among the many things that surprise and sadden me now, looking back across that serious accumulation of pages, is how ever-primed my aunt was to go to battle—and how ever-ready my uncle was to back her up. All it took was that one, to my mind, prudent piece of boundary setting for her eyes to start flashing as she made an elaborate display of putting the check back into her wallet.

Irving, registering her upset, said tersely, "What kind of evening are we going to have here?"

"A pleasant one, I hope," I said.

"Oh, I somehow doubt that, Michael," my aunt said sharply. "You have not been interested in having a pleasant evening with me or your uncle for years now. For years you've condescended to us, patronized us on every subject and at every turn. I can take it for me—but your uncle!"

Zero to sixty in less than a second.

"Patronized?" I asked.

"The other night in the theater, telling us not to talk!"

"During the play, was all I meant. I meant that it was rude to talk about the playwright's bad choices while the curtain was still up."

"You are so cold and distant. So rude."

I deliberately forced myself to take a breath before answering. "Distant, maybe," I said. "But all I've been trying to do is protect myself—"

"Protect yourself from what?" said my uncle. "We're not monsters."

"From all this," I said, gesturing.

"This what?" Irving said.

"This scene right here. Hank's eruptions. Her criticisms and attacks."

She leaned forward over the table, the way I imagined she leaned forward in one of her story conferences. "But, Michael, *you* are the one who has attacked. You have had no feeling for us for the last ten years. You have thought only of yourself, you have been selfish, you have maintained the barest forms of civility. You have had no compassion, no human affection."

Again a breath, a pause. They were only half, less than half, successful. My voice wobbled as I said, "That's very harsh."

"But true," said my aunt.

"Even you must see," I said, "that we have had a great deal of trouble making the transition from child-adult to adult-adult relationships. You have not been able to withstand the distancing that is a natural part of growing up. You could never listen to my point of view on *any*thing. All you could ever do was lash out at me . . . at me and so many other people."

"We've simply been confused, Mike," said my uncle, in that cool, even-tempered voice of his. "All we've ever done is love you and been devoted to you. Next to Hank you were the only person I loved so intensely, that I found so clever, thought so special in the whole world. And you returned this love by saying that we hated you, that we poisoned you. I don't get it."

It was like being caught in some kind of hall of mirrors, to have my experience recast and my language distorted like this. I hardly knew where to begin. "I never said 'hate,' Irv. I said, and felt, stifled. Obliterated."

"Obliterated!" said Hank. "Honestly, you turned us into villains. We have been the villains of your life."

"Do you know what I feel, Mike?" said my uncle. "I feel betrayed. It is the chief betrayal of my life, to have loved so deeply and to be treated in this way for ten years."

Hank nodded vigorously. "Yes, betrayed is *exactly* how I feel! After all the love we gave you, what did you do? You betrayed it. You betrayed our love."

You betrayed our love. Where was I to go, what was I to do, with that?

"I think it's very sad, if you feel that way," I said. "But it's not the whole story. You're just not looking at your own participa—"

"How is it," my aunt interjected, "that you are the only person in my life that this has happened to, the only relationship that has ended up this way?"

I had known my aunt to rewrite history before, but this was one of the most flagrant, perhaps absurdly flagrant, instances ever. "Do you really think that's true?" I asked. "If you look at your past honestly? I am the *only* one?"

"Absolutely."

I nodded. "Without even trying very hard, I can get to eleven, twelve people. Fourteen." I stopped myself. "But I won't make a list. That's your way of doing things, not mine."

"Well, life is certainly full of conflicts. Look at *your* life, Michael. Look at *your* failures."

I put up my hand. "I know where this goes from here. I don't want to hear the laundry list of everything you've given, or done, or everything that I've failed to give, or do. We've had that already. Too many times."

"*I* have no memory of any such thing. Of speaking like that."

"Nor do I," said my uncle.

I shook my head incredulously. "You have so little memory. Both of you. I think that's been your salvation." I paused. "But surely, even you must remember Paris . . . and leaving the beach . . . and saying that I caused Irving's heart troubles that summer, and before that, when I was younger, Christmas, and—"

My aunt began shaking her head. My uncle the same.

"Nothing. Not a moment."

Irving looked at Hank, then back at me. "Is it possible that the thing you could come to, Michael, is that there's some neurosis at work here, that you're neurotic? Troubled? Somehow broken. Deeply broken. And that you need help fixing it—fixing *you*?"

I crossed my arms in front of my chest. "I have had help," I said. "A good deal of it."

My aunt turned to my uncle and in a voice that I could describe only as gloating said, "I told you."

"Told him what?" I asked.

"Never you mind."

I looked at the two of them, locked, forever locked, in their own private, hermetic—symbiotic, claustrophobic this (or that) side of deranged—world, and as calmly as I could said, "You must realize that 'fixing it' is not the point."

"What is the point then, Michael?" asked Irving.

"The point . . . the point is to make some peace with what you've been dealt in life. Where you come from, and the people who have formed you, and . . . and challenged you."

"Well, aren't you lucky to have been born into such a dramatic family!" said my aunt.

"Lucky?"

"Think of the material, my dear. The best writer always writes what he knows best."

How we managed to eat after this, my journal does not reveal. But we did, at my end with an abundance of wine and even more indigestion. My aunt ate, as usual, speedily and with appetite; my uncle, who was always very careful when it came to food, more sparingly.

After dinner Irving said, "Well, are we going to the theater as planned?"

"Sure," I said.

The play was by A. R. Gurney, *Later Life*—first the madeleine and then later life! There was a speech about psychiatry and the younger generation ("It may work for them . . . they strum on their own psyches like guitars") at which my aunt chortled, loudly arranging and rearranging her bracelets as usual all the while.

"What an insipid mess of a play," she said before the actors had even had a chance to take their bows.

Afterward out on the sidewalk she turned to me and in a voice that was a combination of wounded and melodramatic said, "Well, this is the last we will see of each other. We leave on Friday."

That was three days away. "I'm sure we'll speak tomorrow," I said.

As I put them into a cab, there seemed to be a moment when my uncle was about to offer me a hug. Instead he extended his hand, which was very strange because we never shook hands, but I took it anyway. As I did he said, "I'm just a failure, that's it, isn't it?"

He said this, remarkably, with a grin. Was the grin a way to ease the awkwardness of the goodbye? Or was he using his usual irony as a way of saying, Come on, Mike, it's not so awful as that? Or did he think he was repeating back to me, in exaggerated form, what he thought he'd heard me say at dinner? Or did he simply need to disguise the fact that he felt bad? I had no idea, but as I stood there watching their cab merge into traffic I suddenly felt beaten, beaten down, and probably as tired as I'd ever been in my life.

The next morning I called their hotel to check in on them. "Mr. Ravetch is no longer with us," the operator said. One more disappearing act: this was how they dealt, or didn't deal, yet again.

EIGHT

LAST ROOM

My aunt and uncle grew old, but in very different ways.

For many years, time was very gentle on my aunt physically. Only a scattering of lines disturbed her immaculate complexion. She remained tall and unstooped. Her energy was undiminished. The one ailment she suffered was an intermittent bad back. She went on enticing and then dismissing people, adoring them and then devouring them. The pattern was so familiar that whenever I turned up to Sunday dinner and found a new arrival sitting to her right, which in childhood was my fixed spot at the table, I could predict almost to the month how long she would last. She was nearly always a she, typically a she with a large personality and an amount of fame (wattage being drawn to wattage) and not slight in build. She would be accomplished, verbal, and troubled. She would love, or learn to love, all things house-related, and would in any event soon find her own home transmogrified by the Hank touch and filled, often to brimming, with deaccessions from the maison. She would be certain to have few other close women friends, because my aunt did not like to compete in her category. And having heard about how horrible we had all been over the years, she would tend to regard us with a combination of suspicion and disdain—there was simply no other way.

Eventually my aunt ran out of new faces and—how to put this kindly?—resorted to circling back to whoever needed her as much as she needed them. Meaning, for the most part, people who needed her money. These were often family people; distant, formerly maligned relatives who were now reeled in because their need of her put her need of them into a kind of workable if always fragile balance. They were her yes-men and yes-women, and not a one among them, I think it's safe to say, ever called my aunt on a single thing she did or said.

As my aunt aged, the maison grew more and more dense with *objets* and darker and darker in its palette. When my future wife laid eyes on it for the first time, she christened it the Death Barge. Until then I hadn't quite realized that not only had the woodwork and the trim on the exterior doors and windows been painted black, but so too had every single flowerpot and piece of statuary—so much for the bright, buoyant spirit of Palladio. Inside, my aunt had had a Sunday painter, the mother of a friend (who, in time, unfailingly, was dispatched like everyone else), darken the clothes on the gentlemen and ladies in the eighteenth-century portraits acquired over the years, which in moments of levity we had humorously referred to as our ancestors. This same painter stained any remaining trace of light wood dark; meanwhile the upholsterer who succeeded Ruby was kept busy with ever deeper, richer, and darker velvets and linens and silks. There were new and lasting obsessions: with obelisks, Napoleon, and the Grand Tour, whose bronze souvenirs (fluted columns, models of the Arch of Constantine, mini Pantheons, and the like) were grouped on ever-more-crowded tabletops. *I cannot jam another object into this house*, she declared over and over, *but I simply cannot stop acquiring. I simply cannot.*

There was so much she could not stop herself from doing. There always had been.

My uncle, by contrast, finally became really, truly sick and really, truly old, in nearly all parts of his body except for his mind. His imaginary illnesses were replaced by a smorgasbord of actual ones. He had that open-heart surgery, followed years later by angioplasty and stents. His nascent emphysema blossomed. The years he had spent out in the Southern California sun produced dozens of small skin cancers on his face, neck, and arms, which were periodically burned or frozen away. He had his hip replaced (an experience he called more arduous and painful than open-heart surgery) and later, when he entered the falling phase of life, fractured the bones in his legs and back and had various procedures or surgeries to have them mended. His world got smaller and smaller, more medicalized and interior. Our family doctor retired, and my aunt and uncle found a substitute who was enamored of their career and their charisma. This physician had something of a Hollywood clientele, which placed them in his, or he in their, catchment; but mainly—and for a substantial annual fee—he was available day and night for their often-panicked calls, which made him truly indispensable.

Now and then people would come to speak to my aunt and uncle about their Hollywood past. For years they had refused most interviews, public relations being far too grubby and beneath them, but now they began to admit an occasional journalist or film scholar to the maison, and these encounters would be good for a fleeting sort of *Sunset Boulevard*–ish lift, but a fleeting one only. They grew lonelier and lonelier. When one of the few remaining peers with whom they had managed to sustain a friendship would die, they would never attend the funeral and never again mention his or her name. Until very late neither of them ever acknowledged the inevitability of their own deaths.

There was a decided shift among the three of us when I introduced them to the woman who would become my wife, although I had no inkling of that turn of events on the April afternoon I took her up to Skyline, a day that was both so illogical and unprecedented in my life as to be downright dreamlike. Jo Anne and I happened to be neighbors and, I thought, just friends on West Eleventh Street . . . she happened to be on a work trip to Los Angeles, where I was attending my nephew's baby-naming . . . we happened to go for a hike together up through Runyon Canyon . . . and I happened to take her to meet first my beloved niece, then my aunt and uncle, then my parents. Happened? When I had never before taken any of my friends to the maison? It was a day out of context, out of sync, during which I seemed to be acting on a kind of autopilot that was alien or new (new on account of Jo Anne, I recognized later) to me. My aunt and uncle, by contrast, could not have been more *in* context and *in* sync, a certain sync anyway.

Within minutes the tea trolley materialized as if summoned by fast-working kitchen elves and all systems were go—actually in overdrive—on the sparkle and charm fronts.

Before any of us had even sat down my uncle took one look at Jo Anne and said, "You know, my dear, we are Jewish people." This was one of those provocative opening sallies he sometimes produced, and it meant something like *We are one of you, you are one of us, let's come to an understanding right from the start.* The remark, intended to zip through the air like a cleverly aimed dart, instead just hovered in place while Jo Anne, blinking at him in confusion, tried to figure out what on earth he meant.

"Well, thank you for telling me that, Irving," she said evenly.

She hadn't seen anything yet. My aunt soon pronounced her, to her face, *charmante* and *so very attractive and well-spoken.* "Are you a house person, by chance? You must come for a tour and you must tell me what you like. Chinese porcelain perhaps?"

I felt my stomach knot. Before Jo Anne could even respond, my aunt continued, "I *knew* it. Let's see what kind of treasure we can find for you to take back home to New York."

Bestowing an opening gift, on that afternoon an eighteenth-century Ch'ien Lung foo dog, was a classic gesture of my aunt's and was meant, in part, to win over the unknown (and, in this case, not so easily knowable) other; in larger part it served to draw the age-old hierarchy by which my aunt, as the giver, felt she exerted a certain control over the recipient.

Jo Anne, whom I'd elected not to prep in any way for this encounter, later told me she had to revise her first take (Death Barge; Miss, and Mr., Havisham) against the seemingly embracing welcome and silken charisma that were on such extravagant display. Nevertheless, as soon as the door closed on this inaugural visit, she turned to me and said, "Jewish people?"

"It's his way of trying to make friends," I said.

"And this?" she asked, indicating the foo dog. "Does everyone get a Chinese antique?"

"Not exactly *every*one."

•

That day initiated a moderate lightening in the strained atmosphere the three of us inhabited. Was it possible that, seeing me paired, as afterward I soon became, relieved my aunt and uncle of a certain guilt that deep down, in some obscure part of themselves, had haunted them for many years? They watched me embrace a woman who was quickly deemed to be endowed with a suitable portion of intellect, beauty, and panache to allow her to be admitted to the ranks of the Mighty Franks. *Things with Michael haven't turned out so very dreadfully, after all, have they, Corky?*

In December of the following year my aunt and uncle made a rare—and as it turned out, final—trip to New York to attend our at-home marriage. Despite a huge, paralyzing white blizzard, they managed to reach my apartment and summon up, for nearly the last time ever, their best-behaved, most-polished public selves as I cried my way through my vows.

With the passage of time, between my uncle and me there was an easing. It helped, I'm sure, that we lived on opposite sides of the country; when we came together, it was at a very special, highly curated juncture where, by tacit agreement, the best of the past was allowed to show itself to the best of the present. We talked a lot about Irving's far-off childhood, his father's childhood in Russia, his mother's in Palestine. Nearly each time I visited, he gave me one of the few pieces of his sartorial finery that still hung in the closet, the odd Liberty shirt or pair of DAKS pants, and he went on setting aside books for me on the shelf where he used to set aside shirt cardboards when I was a boy. In this way we wound down where we began, by entering his closet and finding each other there, on that safe, neutral, now essentially nostalgic ground.

In a less troubled configuration with a less troubled past there would have been more spaciousness in every sense, you might say a whole house's worth of connection rather than only a single room's—but at least we had that one small, defined, *con*fined room, and all it meant. It stood apart from the rest of the maison as it always had, and remained largely unobserved and unvisited by my aunt; within it there was, I came to see, an undeniable goodness and nearly half a century of accumulated feeling that I was finally able to allow my-self, in small pockets, to find again, to feel again, without being dis-mayed or vexed by all the rest.

It had not been easy, but I had learned to accept the fact that my uncle's entire life had been built around an intractable blind spot. Of course it helped that nothing of importance was tested or challenged any longer and that Irving was too frail to sustain, as I knew, any such test or challenge. All this had been a lesson, one of many from him, from them: I had learned to live with paradox, to sift out the good from the bad, and to continue on under very imperfect circumstances. In a way I think that may be the essential lesson sustained family life has to impart: you learn to carry on, no matter what, and not to wait for people to become what they are incapable of becoming. Either that or you go to live somewhere very far removed from the place you began, and you never, ever go back.

─── ───

Just before the Jewish holidays in September 2010 I received a phone call from Steve telling me that the situation with our eighty-nine-year-old uncle, who had been admitted to the hospital a week earlier, had begun to look even more worrisome. For several days I followed his condition from New York, uncertain whether to fly out, as I had on several previous occasions. I spoke to my brother the doctor, my mother and father. No one could say definitively whether my uncle was near-ing the end of his life. Because who can ever say that definitively? He had had some bad, actually some quite dire, physical patches in recent years, and rebounded. He had had some dicey mental moments too, but they had passed so conclusively that my uncle himself had been able to tell me afterward, "That last time I was in the hospital, Mike? I was out of my mind, you know. I thought Napoleon, your aunt's pal, was knocking at the door. I thought your aunt and all the doctors were conspiring against me. I even, if you can believe it, called Hank a *bitch*. A *fucking* bitch." He let these words float there for a moment before adding, "And the strangest thing is that I remember it all per-fectly clearly, yet I couldn't do anything about it. It was like there was a different me in there. A secret me."

A year earlier, following an unrelated episode, my uncle told me he had looked over a precipice and seen a blast of light with people beckoning, "Just like they say." My uncle was not a just-like-they-say sort of thinker (or speaker), but he *was* by profession and nature a dramatist who didn't shy away from a theatrical effect; with him, as with my aunt, it was critical to listen for clues, confirmations that had the air, or the texture, of the actual. "I wasn't ready yet," he said that time, making his one and only reference to his own death. "I told them to go away."

This time I could scarcely call him up to ask if he was ready. So I called Roger, his private nurse, instead.

"Something feels different," Roger said. "I can't tell you what it is exactly, just a sense I have." Then he added, "Mr. Irving will know you if you come."

I flew to Los Angeles and arrived at the hospital that afternoon. I had seen my uncle at the end of August, just a month earlier, but he looked different to me now. The bones were standing out in his face like the folds in a sheet of paper; his eyes were wreathed in ink-dark shadows; and his breathing, even with the help of the oxygen mask that was clamped to his face, was raspy, effortful, and weak.

I was not even sure he noticed me, or recognized me if he did. My aunt, by contrast, turned abruptly toward the door when I walked in, though all she said, in a flat, faraway voice, was "Oh, Michael, you came all this way? Really?"

Did it matter to her that I'd come, or was she indifferent? I didn't care. I hadn't come for her; I'd come for my uncle—and for myself.

There was busyness in the hospital room. One staff nurse was sorting out my uncle's tubes and leads; another was adding notes to his chart. Roger was packing up his bathrobe and slippers. My aunt began pacing back and forth on a small patch of scratched linoleum, her gold bracelets producing a tinkling, faintly musical sound.

All of a sudden my uncle curled his hand into a fist. He raised it and made a circling motion in front of his cheeks.

"Is it the oxygen mask, darling?" my aunt said. "Your face? Is something bothering you?"

He repeated the gesture.

"Darling, I don't know what you're trying to tell me."

Again.

"I'm sorry."

His hand floated back down to the bed in frustrated defeat.

"That's good. Just rest. Everything will be better if you do."

She was speaking to him in a voice I had heard her use before when Irving was sick or hospitalized. Compassionate but artificial, it was the kind of babying voice you use with people who show signs of not being in their right minds, a voice stretched beyond fear and beginning to edge, it seemed to me, toward detachment.

My aunt resumed her pacing, and I stood there, mute, leaning on the handle of my suitcase. Again my uncle's hand rose to his face. And as it did, an unbidden movie began to screen itself in my mind. It was made up of scenes I had witnessed and remembered and others I had only heard about. It was scrambled as to time and place, a cross-cut nickelodeon summary of the physical being my uncle had been. I saw him in his tennis whites, wiping his forehead with a hand towel as he came off the courts after a match against my father. I saw him before I was born, playing baseball on a Monday night at the park near Gilmore Field. I saw him at the beach, in the early years, marching us boys along the approach road to watch the sun go down, a little ritual he liked to enact most every evening because the sun set so late in the Northwest and because the sky was sprayed with such spectacularly different colors every night. I saw him, again at the beach, as ever in that hideous mustard-colored bathing suit, braving the icy surf with us children, though of course prudently, meaning only up to our knees, and I saw him at the tiny local Ilwaco airport nearby, striding onto the runway and standing right there in the middle of the landing strip, looking up at the sky as if to dare it to produce an airplane to interfere with the nervous, giddy laughter that was pouring out of us boys. I saw *him* as a boy, tented under a towel in New Jersey, his head swallowed up by a cloud of steam as he gasped for air, and I saw him lying in bed at Aunt Rose's house in Los Angeles, forced to take naps while the kids in the neighborhood played ball out in the street. I saw him getting himself up, up, up, out of hospital beds and wheelchairs and off walkers and commodes, post-surgeries, post-illnesses real and imagined, post-"depletions," as he used to call those long periods of puzzling lethargy that seized him more and more in later life. And I saw him diving naked into the pool at Skyline, swimming underwater from one end to the other in a single breath, which to me as a child had seemed superhero-like, an inimitable arc of lung power and physical prowess.

I saw all this and then I saw him, in real time, use all his energy to raise his hand, once again.

"Are you worried about where you're going, darling?" my aunt said. "Is that it? To a new room—that's all. On a different floor. Just for a little bit longer."

My uncle shook his head. Yet again the hand, again the pantomimed circles, though more flummoxed this time, then more urgent.

"He wants his razor," I said.

"His *razor*?" My aunt's tone, and face, suggested that I might as well have said, He wants to go tap dancing. "Darling, that can't be it. *Is* that it?"

He nodded.

"Yes, of course. Your razor." She emitted a dry, hoarse laugh—at the absurdity? The inconsequentiality?—of being concerned about one's whiskers at such a moment.

"It's already packed, Mr. Irving," Roger said.

Mr. Irving closed his eyes and breathed.

"Just a few more days, darling," my aunt said. "Before you know it, we'll be having soup and watching *Jeopardy* from bed. Soon, darling, we'll be *chez nous*. We'll be home."

——— ———

The room at Cedars that my uncle was transferred to was on the third floor of the south tower. As with all the rooms in that big impersonal complex, number 3829 was one of a cluster of four private rooms that faced an alcove off a common corridor; in this alcove there was a desk, a computer, and a comfortable office chair where doctors or nurses sometimes sat to update charts, or where tired family members could take a break while remaining within earshot of the patient. Inside, beneath a dirty tinted window, there was just enough space for a cot to be squeezed in every night for my aunt, who insisted on remaining by my uncle's side twenty-four hours a day.

As the nurses settled my uncle into his new room and information was exchanged among them, I learned precisely how worrying his condition was. He had pneumonia in an early stage, and he had developed bedsores and picked up a strain of MRSA from being so weakened and in the hospital for so long. Because he had had trouble swallowing, he was being fed by a tube inserted into his nose, through which a ghastly yellow liquid was flowing—an apparatus he clearly loathed. He was on constant oxygen. His heart rate was being monitored. The circulation in his hands was so poor, and his fingertips were so blue, that each hand had been set on top of a hot-water bottle. He was catheterized, and there were pressure socks on his legs that emitted a *whooshing* sound every time they inflated; but that was downright mellifluous compared with the various beeps and alarms that went off when he moved an arm and accidentally bent an IV line or when his oxygen level went down or when an antibiotic was finished or when his heart threw off an irregular rhythm. A restful ambience this was not, but since by the end of the day my uncle was barely conscious, I agreed to go to dinner with my mother and brother, who had met me at the hospital, and promised to return to see him early the next morning.

Before I left, I heard him say five soft, hoarse words: "I . . . want . . . to . . . go . . . home."

The effort of expressing this thought made his head bob forward in exhaustion.

"Soon, darling," my aunt said brightly. "Soup and *Jeopardy*, I promise."

The next morning I found another Irving sitting upright in the bed. Roger had just finished giving him the shave he had been so desperate for, and was wiping his face with a warm cloth, which my uncle was enjoying.

"I almost died last night, Mike," he said when I walked in. His voice, while still hoarse and faint, was vastly clearer than it had been the day before.

"But you didn't."

"They did awful things to me. I thought I was gone. Here I am."

"Here you are, Irv, yes."

In a whisper Roger clarified that he was confused. He was speaking of two nights before, not this last night.

"I'm hungry too. Ready to eat. Maybe I should get up and sit at the edge of the bed."

He started to push himself up, and several of those alarms went off at once.

Roger and I convinced him that he should wait for the physical therapist to come to give him a hand.

"Okay," he said. "I'll cooperate. I guess I can do that."

He sat back in his bed. My aunt reappeared. She had been downstairs in the cafeteria with my cousin Josh, my uncle Herbert's middle son and someone on whom she had become particularly reliant in recent years. Despite spending the night (actually by now more like seven nights) in a cot next to my uncle's bed, she was remarkably well put together, made-up, hatted, bejeweled, and ready—for what, of course, was the abiding question. She was carrying a hot meal, and it gave off a strong smell. My uncle said that he wanted to eat what she was having, but again we advised him that it would be better to wait, because he was scheduled for an endoscopy that morning, a test by which they were hoping to discover why he was having a hard time swallowing.

My aunt and my cousin went off to eat in the waiting area down the hall. I pulled a chair up to my uncle's side and sat down to look at him once again. His spotted, scabbed, and oddly yellow skin was draped over an infrastructure of prominent bones—I was aware of the shape of his skull, so close, too close, to the surface. His eyes had become very tiny and dim. Fungus covered several of his fingernails, and the tips of his fingers were blue again, apparently beyond the help of the two hot-water bottles that gurgled under his absent grasp.

After a long silence and out of nowhere, or what felt like nowhere to me, he said, "You have been a great person in our lives, a son, like a son."

For a moment I wondered if I imagined these words. Dreamed or invented them—willed them into being.

From love to disappointment, then back to love . . . from love to betrayal, then back to love again: what was it about time, that it could so easily fold in on itself, smooth away all the parts of our shared experience that didn't fit this version, the good version, the bright version; the version to die by?

And then there was that *our*. Did he mean *our*, really? Or was *my* simply too hard, or too uncomfortable, to say?

Even as my mind worked through these thoughts, the tears came up in me surprisingly fast. They soon began shooting out onto my shirtsleeve.

My uncle did not seem to notice. He seemed to be there and not there at the same time. He said, "I don't think we are going to make it to the bat mitzvah." He meant my niece's bat mitzvah, which was scheduled for the following weekend.

I said, "Probably not, Irv. But we'll take lots of pictures and bring them to show you."

"That will be good."

A few moments went by in silence.

I reminded him that my daughter had started kindergarten at her new school earlier in the week. He nodded, mentioned her by name, and my niece too, and he said, "They carry on our spirit. They go forward, the life goes forward."

He actually said these things; the things you think you want to hear at such a moment.

"Your daughter's smile. It is an amazing thing. Such a life force."

"Yes," I said as my eyes began to produce more tears. "Yes, that is what it is. What she is."

I sat there holding his hand, feeling him, his life—what was left of his life—and his presence next to me; with, maybe even with*in*, me. The tears continued to dribble down my cheeks and he continued to breathe his shallow breaths and then he drifted off to sleep.

The following morning I returned to the hospital early, and I found still another Irving in that bed. His eyes were pink, and he was wheezing and coughing miserably, trying to bring up something, some phlegm or mucus, that was lodged in his chest. He was agitated, and his speech was intermittently garbled, its content less and less coherent.

I sat down next to his bed and I did not get up, except to go to the bathroom and to inhale a sandwich, for the next eight hours, and for many of those eight hours my uncle sat rigidly upright, his head held stiffly away from the pillow, his hand clasped around a Styrofoam cup into which he kept trying, and failing, to expel whatever it was he felt in his throat or chest.

Hour after hour after hour this went on. I had never in my life seen a human body in such unrelenting distress.

Every now and then he closed his eyes. When he did, I opened the small black sketchbook that had replaced my Académie sketch pad, and I drew his portrait.

"I wish you wouldn't do that," my aunt said when she saw me.

I closed my sketchbook, but as soon as she left the room, I opened it again.

Sometimes his eyes popped open and he spoke.

"I am a citizen of two countries," he said more than once.

And: "Has the ambassador arrived yet?"

And: "What is my job here?"

"Your job, Irv," I said, "is to rest and to sleep. That's all."

"To rest. To sleep."

Sometimes he did sleep, but always briefly and never with ease.

At one point my uncle gestured to me, and I moved in even closer. With great difficulty he pushed a sentence out of his occluded windpipe: "I'm ready to go."

"Irv," I asked hopefully—because by that point I was hopeful that he was asking to go where I was beginning to feel he belonged, and wanted, deep down, to be—"you're ready to go *where*, exactly?"

With irritation he said, "You know where."

"I don't, Irv. Tell me?"

"Out of here."

"Out of here—home?" I asked.

He nodded; I sighed. I found myself wishing, for his sake, that he had said, *Don't be ridiculous, Mike. I mean out of here, die!*

But as he didn't, I explained, not for the first time that day, that he had to stay a bit longer in the hospital, rest a bit more.

He nodded again. We sat together in silence.

Late in the afternoon he opened his eyes and in them I saw, or thought I saw, a clarity, a sudden vividness.

"Passive," he said. "I have been too passive in my life."

At first I wasn't sure if he had said these words to the air or to the heavens or to me. As with "like a son" the day before, I wasn't even sure he had *said* them. I thought maybe I had imagined them too, manufactured them. But no; they had come from this tired, weakened body; my uncle's tired, weakened body. They had been formed in his throat and spoken in his voice. To me they had been spoken—given.

Passive.

I have been too passive in my life.

I didn't hear these words so much as receive them, in my stomach, my soul. He had said these words so softly, the very words, or a variation on the very words, that I had been waiting to hear from him for much of my adult life. Were they—weren't they—*it?* The truth, finally: acknowledgment finally, validation finally, of all that I had said and struggled over and anguished over; and not just I, but so many of us, rooms full of us, a family—a world—full of us, with him, with them?

But he didn't say them to a room or a family. He said them to me, alone, as I sat by his bed, grasping his hand and feeling it grasp mine back with unexpected firmness.

Passive.

I have been too passive in my life.

Maybe he didn't mean what I thought he meant, what I wanted him to mean. Maybe he meant, I have been too passive in the hospital and during this long illness. In allowing them to catheterize me and scope me and suction me and hook me up to that hateful feeding tube. Or tie me into this vile spotted gown. Or—

But no; that didn't seem right, or feel right. There was in that

room, and between the two of us, a strange, intensely charged stillness. It was as if everything outside that room simply turned into a
powdery dust and drifted away. The long corridor, the other patients,
the mass of bleak tinted windows. It had the time-warp quality of a
dream where you cannot be sure whether a minute has passed or an
hour. Or a lifetime. Where, actually, time did not seem to move at all
but came as close to stopping as I have ever known it to do except in
the minutes after my daughter was born. There, too, trickster time
seized me and held me in its grasp. Held me, period. Now it was holding us. My uncle and me together.

———— ————

Time started up again when I next saw my aunt. She rejoined us after
my uncle had managed to fall asleep. I asked her if she had eaten
anything since breakfast, and she shook her head. So I convinced her
to come down to the cafeteria, and I put a cheese-and-tomato sandwich in front of her.

Once she had taken a few bites I asked her if they knew what was
causing the problem with Irving's lungs, if it was the pneumonia or
congestive heart failure or something else. She said that they knew
but she wasn't prepared to go into details with me.

"So you mean there is a tumor," I said. "It has to be cancer, what
else?"

"They found a few cells," she said, without making eye contact.

"A 'few cells' are causing his lungs to fill up with fluid?" I said
dubiously. "That doesn't sound right. That doesn't explain this agony
that he is in—this struggle. I've been sitting with him all day. It's
terrible."

"I know it's terrible, Michael," she said, looking off into the
distance and crossing her arms. "I know that Irving is dying. I'm
not a fool, but I am determined to take him home, and I am determined to make this final period, however long it lasts, a peaceful
one."

"*If* you are able to take him home . . ."

"*Of course* I will be able take him home. That is where he wants to go. Where I want him to go. Home is everything to us. Home is where we have shared the most glorious life together. Your uncle, he was the most glorious man, he saw to my happiness always, he put it ahead of everything else. He was my life partner in every way. He put up with all my eccentricities." She paused. "He put me first, and if that is not the measure of a good husband, I do not know what is. You might want to keep that in mind, yourself."

I nodded. What else could I do?

A few moments went by in silence, and then I said, "I wonder . . . if you . . . if you and Irving had a chance, the two of you, to discuss what he might like, how he might like this to . . . go?"

She shook her head. "I see no reason to confront him with his own mortality. It's not as though, after all these years, he does not know how I feel."

It was simply astonishing. She even managed to make Irving's dying be about *her*.

"But don't you think it's less . . . less about what *you* feel for him than what he feels about himself . . . about his fate . . . about how, and when, he might want to die?"

She shook her head. "We never talk about such matters. We never have, and I'm certainly not going to start now."

——— ———

The next morning when I arrived at the hospital my aunt was standing in the doorway to my uncle's room, staring off into the distance. As on every other day I had seen her, she had managed to put herself together, but her voice was somewhat less dogmatic as she filled me in on the night. My uncle had slept, which was good. He had stopped coughing, which was not really good, because it suggested he was not fighting so hard to breathe. He had a different new infection in his lungs, and possibly another from the catheter . . .

I took all this in and then stepped into the room and asked my uncle how he was doing.

"Great!" he said, his thick Irving sarcasm in perfect calibration.

The respiratory therapist had just finished trying to suction more phlegm out of his lungs. "It's too deep," the therapist said to me as he came out of the room with a defeated look on his face.

Both my uncle's private nurse, Roger, and the hospital nurse, an English fellow I had met the day before, were trying to make him comfortable. It was not an easy job. My uncle looked mauled. There was no other word for it. His face was not the face I knew him to wear, either by color or pallor or shape. His eyes were thick with crust, which the hospital nurse was trying to wipe away, and which was causing Irving to moan. There seemed to be even less flesh separating skin from bone. When the English nurse finished, I asked him if the pneumonia had progressed, and he answered that I would have to speak to the doctor. Hospital policy, as I knew, but not a good sign. When there was a good sign, or a clear test, or a bit of bright news, I had noticed, people were unafraid to bend the rules; when it was the opposite, they hid behind them.

I asked my aunt if she had eaten, and again she said no. She said she did not feel like leaving, however, but would appreciate a sandwich. I went downstairs to the cafeteria to have one prepared for her. It seemed to take forever to put two slices of cheese and a piece of lettuce between bread.

When I returned I saw a man sitting at the desk outside my uncle's room. I recognized him as the post-Derwin physician.

I gave my aunt her sandwich and looked back into the hall. The man was paging through a thick medical chart. On the computer screen in front of him was an image of a lung, my uncle's lung. Now and then he looked up at it, then back to the documents on the desk.

"The doctor is here now," my aunt said. "He is looking at test results."

After a moment he got up and came into the room. He barely glanced at me before launching into rapid-fire doctor-speak. He explained that Irving had a new infection that was resistant to the drugs. He said that his right lung was not functioning at all. He said there were signs of pneumonia in the left lung too. He said he was going to prescribe a new round of antibiotics, but not until he had called for a consultation with an infectious-disease specialist, because he was worried about interactions among the drugs and their efficacy.

Then he turned to my uncle. "Are you in any discomfort, Irving?" he asked. When my uncle indicated no, the doctor started to walk out of the room.

I could not believe that was it. I said, "Irv, do you have any questions for the doctor?"

Again my uncle indicated no.

The doctor returned to the alcove desk. He began to pack up his things, ready to move on to the next patient, the next task. The next death? I touched my aunt lightly on the shoulder and said, "Maybe we could have a word outside?"

She followed me out the door. I introduced myself to the doctor, or reintroduced myself since we had met some years before, and then I said, "What's the story here? What's going on?"

With supreme matter-of-factness this man turned to me and said, "Irving has end-stage cancer. His right lung is shut down. He is not absorbing the oxygen. The big picture is not positive."

I took in this information as quickly as possible. "Then why are you starting with a specialist and new drugs? Why are you prolonging his suffering?"

Quick to anger as ever, my aunt erupted. "I will *not* have his life ended just like that. I will *not* play Solomon. I simply will *not*."

I said, "Maybe you should consider how Irving is feeling."

"*I* will know when he is ready. *I* am the only person who will know that. The rest is *no one's* business, Michael."

It had taken me nearly half a century, but I was no longer afraid of this woman—of her anger, her vitriol, her tirades; none of it. I saw her, quite simply and clearly, as someone who was terrified and not doing her best thinking. Not really thinking at all, at least in a way that I could respect.

I said, "I think you should ask Irving what he wants."

Her voice went up higher still. "I will *not* do that. I will *not* confront him with the fact of his mortality. I *refuse*, point-blank."

I turned to the doctor and said, "If it were your father lying there, what would you do?"

He looked at my aunt, then at me. "Well, I would have to ask my mother, I would consult her first. Just as here, it is Hank's decision.

Even if Irving responded now, I would not be able to listen to him—legally or ethically. He is in effect *non compos mentis*. It is all your aunt's, his wife's, decision now."

"He did just answer two questions he was asked," I pointed out.

"With a gesture," said the doctor, making a dismissive gesture of his own.

I stared at him with a combination of disgust and dismay.

He went on: "I see, I sense, that you might not do it this way, and I, myself, might not do it this way, but . . ." He glanced through the door at my uncle, then back at my aunt. "But you must understand, I am treating the couple here. What I am doing might be ten percent against Irv's best interest and thirty percent in Hank's. So I figure when you do the math, it's not so bad, and I come out on the positive side."

I felt myself, my consciousness, split in two. Inside, in a private inner me, I thought: Doctor, you have fallen into the trap, like a long line of people before you. The trap—the lure—of my aunt; my aunt and uncle. Here is yet another variation on the *folie à deux—à trois*. Don't you see how you have been blinded by this woman and her baroque—to certain people, still-magnetic—personality? You are not treating her—you are treating *him*. They are two people. Two *separate* people. Two separate *bodies*. You are willing to let my uncle's body go on struggling and suffering because you want to protect my aunt. That is patently absurd to me, just as your arithmetic is specious.

The outside me nodded at him and said, "Yes, I see what you're saying."

He smiled. How I despised that smile of his. Yet I met it in kind.

Before he left he said that, if the situation changed, he could be paged anytime, day or night, of course.

"Of course," I said.

I took my aunt to the waiting area. We sat down as far away from the television as possible, and I encouraged her to eat her sandwich. Which she did. When she had finished, I said to her, "I really think it would be a good idea if you asked Irving what he wanted to do, what he wanted to have done to him. I also really think it would be important for you to tell him that, if he wants to, and is ready, it's okay for him to die."

I said all this very calmly and clearly.

She—unsurprisingly—began to scream. She began to scream at me in the waiting room of Cedars, at the top of that big, undiminished voice of hers. Solomon again. Confronting him with his death again. Her refusal again . . . and again and *again*.

For good measure, she added that none of this was my affair, that I was speaking up out of turn, that I had no business, and so on.

I waited until she took a breath, because even the formidable Harriet Frank, Jr., had to pause to breathe, and then I said, "Irv of all people is not someone who wants to be in pain. Look at what he went through yesterday. Look at him today. And I don't happen to agree with your doctor—I think he is still mentally present enough to be able to answer you, or at least *hear* you, which may be as important. *More* important. If you don't ask him, you cannot know what he is thinking. And on top of that," I added, "I feel pretty sure that he is still here because of *you*, he is holding on for your sake, he has to hear you say that it's okay for him to go."

"It is *not* okay," she screamed. "I want to keep that man for every possible moment, I want him to die with me holding his hand, I want to float into eternity with him, I do *not* accept this, I will *not* do what you say! The poet had it right: 'Rage, rage against the dying of the light.' I am *raging*, and I will *not* do this, I will *not*. Do you hear me, Michael? *I WILL NOT LET THAT LIGHT GO OUT OF MY LIFE*."

She went on and on in this vein. It could have been for two minutes, it could have been for twenty.

When she finished she crumpled up the bag in which I had brought her the sandwich and said, "I'm done here." Then she stood up.

As I walked her back to my uncle's room I saw that she was crying. I put my arm around her. It was like embracing a log.

When we reached his room, she walked straight inside and sat down by the bed. I stayed behind at the outer desk a few feet away.

And then the most amazing thing happened.

My aunt leaned in close to my uncle, and she said, "Darling, I want you to know that if you want to keep on fighting, I will back you up a hundred percent, and we will do everything to keep on fighting. But if you are . . . if you are through, if you are . . . if you are tired now and want to rest, I will be here too, everything will be calm and serene and I will be by your side. No one, you know, has ever been happier than I have, you have loved me all my life, I have loved you all your life . . ."

She was clear-voiced, steady, giving, tender—and rational. She had done precisely what I'd asked—begged—her to do, for the first time ever. It felt like we'd all, all three of us, been released from some kind of lifelong spell.

Though quite honestly whether she had been writing and delivering dialogue or speaking from the heart I could not be 100 percent sure. With her you simply never could tell. But no matter what, she had put Irving first, for once.

She sat for a few moments by my uncle's side. Then she came out, sat down heavily into the chair across from me, and declared, "Well, I had the talk."

"I'm proud of you," I said.

"I'm not," she said flatly.

I waited a moment before asking: "And what did he say?"

"He didn't answer."

"Nothing? No gesture?"

"Nothing."

Soon my cousin Josh came and asked if my aunt would like to sit in the waiting area, and she nodded. They left, and I returned to my uncle's room, where I saw something quite striking: for the first time in days he had actually settled his head against the pillow. For the first time in days he seemed to be resting at peace.

I stepped outside his room to phone my mother and my brother, who said they would come to the hospital at once. Then I resumed my place by my uncle's side. His head sank with more weight into the pillow. Under his oxygen mask he was breathing shallowly but calmly.

The English nurse whispered to me that it looked like it was starting. *It.* He printed out a pamphlet on what to expect at the end and brought it to me.

"Does she understand what's happening?" he asked.

"I think she may, finally," I said.

When he left I took my uncle's hand again, and I said, "It's all right, Irv. It's okay to go."

I sat there in silence for a long time, watching my uncle. His breaths were long and quiet and calm. Finally I asked Roger to find my aunt and bring her back.

My aunt came in with Josh and sat down. The room became very silent. Irving's head was beginning to tilt to one side against the pillow.

The printout the nurse had brought me was sitting untouched in my lap. I glanced at it now. Earlier I had noticed my uncle's neck becoming mottled, and there it was, in print. A sign. The skin, this pamphlet said, could change color at the end. His fingers were even more blue than they had been—another sign. Not cold (not to my touch, anyway), but that was because Roger still kept them on top of those hot-water bottles. The pamphlet pretty much made my uncle's dying feel like a textbook case: it spoke about how important it was to tell the "loved one" that it was okay to go, how there could be remarks made in the last days that seemed disconnected but profound, or others that didn't make sense, but that really the most important thing to do was not to correct or introduce reality but to listen, to comfort, to make everything as easy and peaceful as possible.

Is that what we all come down to, I wondered, a pamphlet with these few universal truths, printed from the hospital computer?

The door opened, and my mother and Steve joined us. My mother sat down next to her brother. She was well into her seventies, but this was the first death she had witnessed. She had arrived at The Apartment as her mother was being hurried away in an ambulance; her father had not wanted her to come up to his hospital room after his second, and eventually fatal, heart attack, and she had regretted consenting to that forever after. Now she was facing her brother full-on, taking his hand and looking unblinkingly at what little was left of his life.

I was sitting on my aunt's sleeping cot, which had never managed to get folded up from the previous night. I asked Hank if she wanted to sit where I was, in line with my uncle's face rather than behind his head, and she said no. I asked if she wanted to be alone with him, and she said, "I need you all here, I want him to be surrounded by people who love him."

That he was. And she told him that he was, over and over.

Irving kept breathing. Long peaceful breaths, with long pauses. I watched the pulse in his neck throbbing, persisting. I watched the color of his skin change, turn blotchy, then gray. All the while his left eye remained half open, as he had always maintained it did in sleep.

I thought of all those sleep masks stockpiled in the top left drawer in his closet, which he wore to cover up that perpetually open eye.

I watched drool seep out of the corner of his mouth and onto his pillow. Somehow even that was beautiful. It was all beautiful, to me at least, because it was peaceful, because finally my uncle seemed, after so many hard days—weeks, months—finally at rest.

He breathed again . . . again . . . and then it came: the last breath. One last breath after the millions, the hundreds of millions, that preceded it. Nearly ninety years' worth of breaths came to an end, and with them so did the body that had housed this man, my uncle, Irving Ravetch.

My aunt didn't seem to understand. She asked Roger to take his blood pressure. Not once—twice. Twice the needle circled all the way down to zero. He shook his head, and she let out a single wail.

My cousin led her out of the room. My brother took my mother away.

I reached over and tried to close that open, clouded left eye. Irv was right. His eyelid persisted in staying open, even when it could no longer see.

NINE

GOODBYE TO THE CLOSET

My aunt did not believe in funerals. She considered religion and ritual alike to be barbaric. She thought that the talks people gave at memorial services brought out the superficial, the trite, and the insincere. She refused to allow one to be held for my uncle, just as she had with her mother. She had no need to see him buried, and since she didn't, she assumed no one else did either. She said that once he left his body, she no longer had any interest in its fate. She simply dispatched Josh to deal with the details, and that was that.

It fell to my brother to drive her from the hospital back to the canyon that afternoon. In the car she said to him, "Michael spoke very firmly and very forcefully today, and I listened to him. I'm glad that I did."

She never said anything like this to me, then or later. But it didn't matter. What mattered was that she had found it in herself to let my uncle go while he could still go with some degree of dignity.

At home she opened her phone book and made two calls. "Well, that's about it, I guess," she said to my brother, who then brought her to our house for dinner. She was quiet and spent, yet sufficiently herself to be able to eat and to comment on the arrangement of pottery in my mother's cupboard.

She went home that evening in the company of her longtime housekeeper, Maria. The following morning, I walked over to the maison after breakfast, and there I witnessed the life force that was Harriet

Frank Ravetch gearing itself up for the next chapter with a resilience that was as impressive as it was astonishing.

There had been a number of scenarios, or hypotheses, over the years as to what would happen after my uncle died.

My uncle would die, one went, and she would soon follow—they'd be like their heroes the Durants, going within two weeks of each other. My uncle would die, went another, and she would choose to take her own life out of desperation and grief and a fundamental inability to be on her own in the world. My uncle would die, went still another, and she would, at the very least, implode as she had after her mother's death, succumb to a period of such hysteria and prolonged blackness that everyone feared she would never function in the world again and might have to be *put away* somewhere, looked after by hired hands (because by who else?) to the end of her days . . .

Instead that life force of hers, that life force that she was, asserted itself in ways that were quite unexpected.

My uncle died—and my aunt underwent an almost instantaneous hardening; something inside her toughened up or closed down. Was it age? Rage? Pragmatism? A gritty survivor instinct? Perhaps it was the simple fact that my uncle was no longer there to help put her back together if she allowed herself to fall apart, so therefore she could no longer allow herself to fall apart. I watched with amazement as, after losing her husband of sixty-five years, my aunt cried only twice, the day she and I spoke in the hospital waiting room, and again later that afternoon just after the moment itself, when my uncle took his last breath, and she let out a wail. After that day, where her sorrow went was, like so much about my aunt, a mystery.

What came up instead was language, floods and floods of it that began that very next morning.

This marriage was the perfect expression of marriage, you must know that. You all could learn from me. From your uncle. A lot, oh yes you could. You especially, Michael. Take it from me, from us. Love, it must be like his was—pure. It must follow the pleasure principle. Your uncle and I, we never had a moment of conflict. Irving always met all my needs, his mission in life was to make me happy. He and I were a marriage of true minds. The physical, you know, is not enough—all that goes away anyway—but thinking alike, living alike, loving alike: that is the thing. The only thing that matters.

In the end we made love in words and with our eyes. Do you know what I mean by that?

Our love was the most beautiful thing ever. Every thought he had was for me. He was the one who guided our marriage, who made it fun, happy, giving. We were supreme life partners.

How can there be such a gift as love—you live it so fully all your life, and then it gets snatched away. Nothing could be more cruel. Nothing.

There was a certain beauty in the hermetical way my aunt spoke and thought. In a way, a certain way, I suppose I was envious. I could never imagine feeling anything quite that pure or uncomplicated about my own marriage, but that was probably because I could not imagine omitting from its measure so much of the actuality of life. Or, more plainly, telling and believing such myths. It was simply not how I was made.

My aunt was a very different creature. She took comfort in— more than that, she lived by—absolutes; I think they made her feel in control. This latest absolute was a variation on the hierarchies she used to organize her worldview: Proust over Zola, Woolf over Stein, De Sica over Fellini, period over *mo-derne*, she and my grandmother above even Sido and Colette, her marriage to my uncle above every other, in the history of mankind, forever.

——— ———

I was not the only member of the audience that next morning on Skyline. My aunt had already summoned my cousin Lisa to the maison. Lisa was Dee Dee's sister, the younger daughter of Aunt Trudy and Uncle Pete, who had died two years before. Between her and my aunt there was, inevitably, a long and fraught story. Several years earlier my cousin had fallen into some financial difficulty, and my aunt had bought her a house in nearby Studio City. This had been a transformative event for my cousin and her family, in particular because it made it possible for her young son to attend a good nearby school, yet most regrettably my aunt missed the opportunity, once again, to be pure, or even neutral, in an act of kindness. She never for a moment let Lisa forget that she had been the recipient of her largesse, calling on her, or her husband, day and night when she needed help around the house or had an errand to run and wanted company or was in one of her blue moods or was agitated during one or another of my uncle's health scares. By the time Irving grew seriously ill, all this was very old history, and their relationship had been through many permutations, but I must say I was quite unprepared for the fierceness with which my aunt infused the morning's conversation.

We were sitting in the living room, on the pair of settees by the fireplace. There was no trolley at this visit. No tea, no cookies, simply my aunt facing my cousin across the low coffee table and with blazing eyes, saying, "As you know, Lisa, I am incapable of living on my own."

Even when Irving was still alive, my aunt had been saying this to anyone who would listen. She had never lived alone as a young woman, she explained, and she and my uncle had only very rarely been parted in their six-plus decades of marriage; but where the idea originated that she was *incapable* of being on her own I cannot say. Nevertheless it was considered fact, or her fact, which essentially amounted to the same thing.

If Dee Dee looked like Hank, Lisa bore a resemblance—a striking resemblance—to Huffy, our shared grandmother. She looked more like her than Hank did, by far. Watching her sweep her mane of curly hair around to one side of her head as she listened to my aunt was almost like watching my grandmother, risen from the dead, listening to her daughter.

"There is something I want you to do," Hank continued. "I want you to drive out to Cheviot Hills and pick up your mother. I want you to help her pack a bag, enough for a week, two weeks, and I want you to bring her here so that she can see if she likes living with me."

My cousin nodded, but she did not speak.

"Your mother and I lived together as girls, you know. Twice. When we were married, it was just after the war and there was a shortage of apartments in town, so we continued, both of us young couples, to live with Mamma on Tigertail. And after that, we both moved out to a building on Veteran, Irvy and I were upstairs and Pete and your mother were down. It was a very larky time for all of us."

Again my cousin nodded.

"We have known each other all our lives. We have kicked up our heels and traveled together, and with great joy too."

Hank paused, then went on: "We have spent oh-so-many Saturdays antiquing together. We have both lost our husbands, and we are both, of course, going to be grieving terribly for years and years to come. Your mother will have company here, and care here, delicious food, and, if I say so myself, beautiful surroundings. She won't be so lonely, and she and I will fight our sadness and make as decent a life as we can for ourselves together." She paused. "All I'm suggesting is that we experiment. We can consider this a trial. If she feels it's not a fit, all she has to say is, 'Hank, this isn't for me.' And she'll be free to go. No questions asked. The only thing *you* have to do is collect her. Today."

Finally my cousin spoke. "Hank, you do know that Mom loves her house, just as you love yours."

"It's just a place," Hank said. "Four walls and a few sticks of furniture. Lovely sticks, it's true—I should know because the majority of them have come from me. But nevertheless they are material goods. I'm speaking about something much more profound, Lisa."

"She and my father lived there for more than half a century. With her bad eyes and her failing memory, she knows her way around. She has her routines, her friends."

"Your job will be to convince her. It's as simple as that."

"I can *speak* to her," my cousin said. "*You* can speak to her. But it's going to be her decision."

My aunt leaned forward and planted both her hands on her knees. This was always a somewhat alarming posture: the hands on the knees, the torso leaning forward, the whites of the eyes beginning to flash . . .

"Darling," she said sternly, "I saved your *ass*. The house? Your new life up here? Surely I don't need to remind you of any of that."

"No," my cousin said. "You don't."

"Now it's time for you to do something for me."

——— ———

Trudy was there in time for soup and *Jeopardy*. She spent the night in my uncle's bed, and the next day my aunt took her out to lunch and antiquing. Already. They made the rounds of the shops in Studio City, and they came back to the maison for tea. This time the trolley was wheeled in and fitted out in even more splendor than usual, sandwiches *and* pastries *and* fruit *and* tea *and* sherry, in the best eighteenth-century glasses too, and decanted into a bottle that refracted the setting sun into a kaleidoscope of rainbow hues that played across the living room walls. There was something exaggerated about the lavishness with which the tea trolley had been put together. It was like my aunt was romancing—seducing—my other aunt.

I had returned that afternoon, and I observed Hank in all-out campaign mode, cooing over Trudy and talking about the fun they would try to have—despite, of course, the black holes in their hearts that would remain open forevermore—and how they would put on old-timey movies on rainy afternoons and have lunch at the club whenever they didn't feel like being domestic and how they would do everything they could think of to cheer themselves up, because life was precious and the point of life, after all, was to squeeze every last drop out of it for as long as one could.

All through this whirlwind of charming and caressing and convincing, Aunt Trudy, who, like her mother before her, had begun to lose a certain crispness of mind, merely delivered an opaque Buddha-esque smile, complacently eating her cookies and sipping her sherry, as if her installment in the maison were already a fait accompli, which in the end it turned out to be.

Before long my aunt was calling Trudy her roomie, and as time went on and Trudy became more and more befogged, Hank took to saying things like *It's my job to remember her life for her now*; and *I know what my roomie would enjoy, she'd like the grilled fish, sauce on the side, and extra sugar for her salad dressing* s'il vous plaît; and *It's not only her mind, it's her heart. She's grieving for her darling husband the way I'm grieving for mine. Grief has a way of consuming all that's left of you, truly it does, but nevertheless, my dears, we must make what effort we can, because take it from me, old age is hell, so it's essential to follow the pleasure principle—in fact, it's fundamental.*

All this was in the future—the near future. In the moment, my aunt's desperation was so achingly palpable to me that I could not bring myself to ask her the one thing I wanted to ask her before I left for New York, which was to wait to deal with my uncle's closet until I returned to Los Angeles on the following weekend for my niece's bat mitzvah or at some later date when I was next in town.

It was only because I knew my aunt's rhythms that it occurred to me even to ask such a question so soon. I wasn't interested in having anything material from the closet, though I did very much want to see the room, to see it and smell it and remember it as it had been while my uncle had lived and maybe also, yes, to be part of its undoing so that I could make sure it was undone properly—because who, other than my uncle, knew (and cared for, indeed loved) that special room as well as I did?

———— ————

I returned to New York early the next morning. It was a kind of folly to fly across the country for three days, only to return again at the end of the week, but my daughter kept asking where I was and when she would see me, and I myself was tired, bone tired, after all those days spent sitting by my uncle's bedside, or his deathbed as it turned out to be. I needed a break, however brief.

On the plane I thought about my aunt's relationship to death and loss and to the physical traces people leave behind and how this, like so much, was particular to how she was made. I thought about how when her father died she scarcely mentioned his name again and once told me that she could count her memories of the man on one hand (I heard this then and forever after with great incredulity, since she was nearly thirty at the time). I thought about how her mother, by contrast, became her lifelong lodestar after her death and was invoked regularly for her sagacity and insights, and how my aunt cherished every last thing that had belonged to her, including most prominently the diary Huffy had written over the course of her life and addressed to her children and grandchildren, but which my aunt maintained was written for her exclusively and for that reason—even though I had asked to read it, as my grandmother promised me I one day would—refused to show it to anyone else, my father included, and most of all me. I thought about how, after Huffy died, she would not enter The Apartment because it brought her mother back too painfully and yet how, on the very day Sylvia died, she had no trouble letting herself into that same apartment and dismantling it and throwing away Sylvia's possessions since they meant nothing to her. I thought about her brother Pete, Trudy's husband, whose funeral she chose not to attend either because she did not believe in funerals or because perhaps she didn't care so much for him or, at that moment, for his wife and children or (as she maintained later, when not having attended wasn't so convenient for her) because she had a sick husband to look after at the time. I thought, too, about her friends, both the excommunicated, who once they were broken with were never mentioned again and might as well have been dead, and the few who stuck it out until they actually did die but were, equally, never mentioned afterward, either with sadness or joy or nostalgia or any hint that they made any mark on the formidable human being born Harriet Louise Goldstein, later renamed Harriet Frank, Jr., or Harriet Frank Ravetch, Hank, Auntie Hankie, Tantie, my terrifyingly unterrifying now-widowed aunt.

I thought of all this and I began to have a queer feeling in my stomach. It evoked the pains I used to have when I was growing up. It started on the airplane, increased in the cab on the way from the airport to the city, and continued after I returned home. And so, after I had hugged my daughter and my wife, I picked up the telephone to check on my aunt, and then I asked her what I had hesitated to ask when I was still in Los Angeles.

I did not mean to be offensive by bringing this up so soon after Irving had died, I said, but would it be possible for her to wait before she did anything with his closet? It would mean so much to me, I added, to be able to be there and participate.

At the other end of the line there was scarcely a hesitation. "Oh, my dear, that's all been taken care of already."

The telephone seemed to grow suddenly ice cold in my hand.

"Already—when?"

"This morning. Today. I had Maria and her husband come and dispose of everything."

My uncle was still not yet even buried.

"Everything?"

"Everything."

"Shalom's tefillin?"

"No, not those. Your mother asked for those."

"The photographs."

"No. Merona has those also now."

"The portrait of you?"

"That dreadful daub?" she snorted. "His clothes. His things."

"But *why?*"

"That should be obvious," she said. "I needed the space for Trudy."

"In that enormous house there's no other place, no other closet?"

"It's her closet now. She's moving in for good—have you not heard?"

I tracked down Maria at the end of the day. It was not the most comfortable phone call I've ever made. She did not want to get into trouble with my aunt, she said, or with me. She was not going to get into any trouble, I told her. I just wanted to know what happened to my uncle's possessions; just *know*. Her husband took a few jackets, she said, and as for the rest, they had taken everything down to the thrift shop on Ventura Boulevard. "The one your aunt likes to go junking in. You know the one, yes?"

I knew the one, yes.

I put the phone down with so much force that it skidded across my desk and fell off the edge onto the floor. Unbelievable—and yet, of course, entirely believable. All too.

Irving was buried the next morning. Steve called me from the graveyard, pretending with that dark humor of his to greet various of our relatives and members of my aunt and uncle's social circle, past and present, living and dead—actually more past than present and more dead than living. In truth, he and Josh were the only two people to watch Irving's coffin being lowered into the ground.

Two days later I was back in Los Angeles. On the Monday after my niece's bat mitzvah I made time to peel away and drive down to

Ventura Boulevard in Studio City, where just down the road from Du-par's, for years the site of that sacrosanct Coffee Hour, there had recently opened a Jewish Council Thrift Shop, where, as my aunt had aged, she had begun, as Maria said, to go junking. It was a long way from the markets of London and Paris, but she amused herself by managing to discover the odd presentable bibelot; she did after all have The Eye.

I sat in the car for a few minutes, alternately thinking, *This is insane* and *Even if I find just one familiar sweater...* and *Irving would be amused* and *Irving would be incensed* and *I don't know what Irving would think, actually, but I'm going in.*

I went in.

The place was vast—rack upon rack, a sea of old clothes. It didn't smell dirty or foul, exactly, but pungently of old fibers and dust and dry-cleaning plastic and a trace of sweat and I don't know what else. Time. The past. The dead. The lingering sweat-spiked afterlife of the dead. If forgetting had a smell, this was what it would be like: one man's, one woman's, individual scent, which presents itself in all its specificity and plants itself deep in memory when you borrow a scarf on a cold day or hang up a coat or come in for a kiss, combined into a medley of aromas that was almost toxic in its unindividuated profusion.

I went through one rack, then another. Then another. The scope of it was daunting; there was simply too much stuff, even for determined, sleuthing me. My skin began to itch from touching all that dry wool. I decided to forget about the sweaters, the shirts, the trousers, the shoes, and all the rest. I decided to focus on just one thing: the belt. Buck Ravetch, custom-tooled on a movie set in Arizona in 1967: how hard could that be to find? In three days, who would have plucked that strip of dry old leather out of the dozens, the hundreds, that hung on the racks in front of me?

Someone, apparently. If the belt had even made it here, and not been tossed for the very particularity that brought me in search of it. I reached the last hook on the last rack, and then I gave up.

——— ———

Before I left town I went to see my aunt, now my aunt*s*, at the maison. The tea trolley was up and humming. The sandwiches were profuse, and cut on the angle, of course; there were cookies, nuts, tiny chocolates in paper wrappers. It was fall. My aunt had put up her seasonal decorations, the pumpkins and the branches of silk leaves, the pottery pilgrims and the Indian corn and the lady apples. How I had loved those lady apples when I was a child. They were little jewels to me: the wrong size, but the right taste. The essence of apple, green with a blush of red: how did she find them, how did she know such things even existed, how did she guess they would look so perfect in that footed dish, how did she intuit that we would prize them as much as she did? Artful at the beginning, artful at the end—that was my aunt.

We visited but had nothing to say. Nothing *left* to say. My uncle's name came up, then floated off, weightless. The tea kept being poured, the sherry offered and declined.

At one point I excused myself. I went to the bathroom—my uncle's—and turned on the water in the faucet. Then I slipped across the hall.

His closet door was closed. I opened it and stepped inside.

The room was stripped. Only the leather-bound manuscripts were in place. All the rest, the clothes, the shoes, the memorabilia, the photographs, even the portrait of my aunt, was gone, tossed, donated, or in the case of the portrait, I imagined, moved elsewhere.

In place of my uncle's prolific wardrobe there were a few jackets and a leopard-print dress hanging to one side. And on his drawers there were now labels:

Panties
Bras
Undershirts
Socks
Sweaters (pullover)
Sweaters (cardigan)
Handkerchiefs

These signs were written in oversize clear letters in my cousin Lisa's hand and taped to the middle of each drawer, presumably to help my forgetful aunt Trudy dress in the morning. Next to each sign was a small bright paper flower. *Make beauty at all times!*

If I had learned that six-step sigh from my uncle, this would have been the moment to produce it. Instead I let out my own single sigh and took one last look at the room. It was just a room now. A room with empty shelves, nearly empty hanging space, and a dusty brown floor.

A square room of about twelve by fourteen feet, with four walls that needed painting, no windows, and a single door.

A room in a house on a hill in a canyon in a city where I no longer lived.

I backed out of the room and closed the door behind me.

Hey, Mike, that's my closet door you just bumped into.

Wait a minute. Look at that. It's open.

It's a special room, this closet. My own special room.

The only one in the whole house that will belong to me, probably.

Want to come in and see? Do you, Mike?

Sure, I do, Irv. Just show me the way.

TEN

FALL AND DECLINE

My mother went down at eleven o'clock on a Wednesday morning. She refused to refer to it as a fall. Falls were what happened to unsteady, infirm, fading older people, and she was none of these—yet. Instead, she maintained, she skipped a step. She was coming down the stairs on her way to her weekly poker game and noticed a light on in the bathroom, which had just been repainted; she was distracted, lost her footing, and went flying. She called out for my father, who was too deaf to hear, and for Hilda, her housekeeper, who was out of hearing distance, and then she hoisted herself up, stuck a bag of ice into her pants, and proceeded with her day.

A third of the way into the game, when it came time for her to go to the bathroom, she took one step, heard a crack, and sat down again. Being the mother of a physician, as well as a highly alert human being of eighty, she had made an instantaneous diagnosis: right hip fractured, partial or full replacement, a week in the hospital, outpatient rehab if she could manage it at home, a round-the-clock team of those nice Filipino ladies for the first week, down to day shifts for ten days or so after.

What to do next, though, presented a dilemma. Her fellow card players, most of them her contemporaries, were not much help. Everyone agreed that she ought to be looked at, probably by a professional in the emergency room, and so she phoned an ambulance—herself.

Before she was hoisted onto the gurney, the poker players asked her to be so kind as to cash in her chips, since she had been losing that afternoon, *bien sûr*. As she was wheeled away she heard the sound of cards being back-shuffled. These were the kinds of details it delighted Merona to impart—after the fact.

——— ——

Seeing my brother Steve's telephone number register on the phone during midweek daylight hours was usually as bad a sign as seeing the name of the school nurse appear in that same location.

I picked up on the first ring. "What's wrong?"

"Aren't you going to say hello?"

"Okay. Hello *and* what's wrong?"

"Well, I'm here with Mom in the ER at Cedars . . ."

Cedars—again. Our home away from home, it was mapped out in my dreams, a recurring vortex we were compelled to visit at regular if unpredictable intervals. I knew the number for the general operator by heart. I knew which wings had the most comfortable chairs. I could visualize the prints on certain floors: Motherwell next to Ruscha next to Johns . . .

Even as my brother was still filling me in on the details, I had brought Expedia up on my computer screen and was looking at flights to Los Angeles. In the end I decided to wait until the morning, to see whether the X-ray confirmed my mother's self-diagnosis. It did.

She was on the floor with the Ruschas, a series of prints that appropriated images of the globe. Was that tantalizing by design? You are the patient, confined to that big gloomy complex and you go for a stroll in the halls—providing you are able to go for a stroll in the halls—and there you are confronted with a lithograph of the continents and the oceans in crisp shades of blue, the wide unreachable world that you will see again, if you are able to see it again, at some point in the far remote future.

"Stupid, stupid, stupid," my mother said when I walked into her room. "Stupid, stupid, stupid."

She was still in the angry, tough phase. There would be a number of gradations of moods and complications over the next week as we saw her through the partial hip replacement (she had been lucky on that front), the physical therapy that followed, and the rebalancing of her own personal pharmacopeia, which was a little sobering to hear detailed when the nurses gave their report at the change of shift.

As I put on my sharpest Nurse Ratched demeanor and urged her to get out of bed and baby-step her way along those Cedars corridors, an epigraph to a Maxine Kumin poem, "Looking Back in My Eighty-First Year"—the age my mother turned the day she had her surgery—kept running laps in my brain. Kumin had borrowed these lines from Hilma Wolitzer:

> How did we get to be old ladies—
> my grandmother's job—when we
> were the long-leggèd girls?

My mother was not of long-leggèd construction—that was my aunt's build—but the sentiment still obtained: it was not quite clear how the baby of the family had become an octogenarian who sailed distractedly over a step and landed *here*.

——— ———

I had attended enough surgeries to know that the third day is usually the hardest. The first day the parent is pumped full of drugs and, brimming over with post-surgical adrenaline, is all aflutter with woozy humor and a considerable amount of sloppy (if also sometimes quite valuable) secret-sharing. On the second day the adrenaline carries her to about lunchtime. By that evening there is a dip, usually followed by a dreadful insomniac night. The next day is when things can go afoul, as they did with my mother, whose heart decided to throw off an alarming arrhythmia when I slipped out for a break.

"Stupid, stupid, stupid," she went back to saying when I returned and found her transferred to a monitored floor.

Some slow-moving and rather unpleasant hours followed, but by mid-afternoon my mother was on her way to being back to herself again. She had gotten out of bed, she'd done a bit of that baby-stepping. She was beginning to dictate answers to her dozens of emails when at about three o'clock Steve phoned. This time I answered with a simple hello.

"Aren't you going to say what's wrong?"

"Why would I say what's wrong when I am in the room with what's wrong?"

"Oh, really?" He emitted a devilish laugh.

"I just spoke to Dad five minutes ago," I said.

"It's not Dad." He paused dramatically; we were in generation three, after all, of drama queens—and kings, and princes. "You don't even want to guess who was brought into the ER last night?"

He couldn't see me shake my head, but he could sense it, I suppose.

"Tantie."

This was how he and I privately referred to our aunt.

"Tantie who has never been sick a day in her life?"

"The very same. You see, it appears that she has been double-dipping the narcotics . . ."

As I listened to my brother I felt my head swinging back and forth with incredulity. I knew that for the past several weeks our aunt had been complaining of a bad lower back, its cause (despite multiple doctors' visits and an MRI) an utter mystery. I knew that she had decided, seemingly out of nowhere, that she could no longer walk, and had ordered herself a wheelchair, from which she continued to command daily life at the maison. I did not know, though my brother now informed me, that she had been prescribed some potent painkillers by the very same doctor who, at my uncle's deathbed, told me that he believed he was treating not merely a mortally ill man in considerable physical distress but his wife as well, and that he believed he was justified in helping my aunt by doing everything he could to prolong the life of my uncle, even if it caused my uncle pain. Now, it appeared, his philosophy had undergone a shift. Now he seemed to be all about *alleviating* pain, since he had put my aunt on some very serious drugs, which she had then given herself permission to double or possibly triple—it was unclear—the way she used to triple the butter in her brownies (*more is more!*), or take an extra caffeine pill when she was feeling sluggish, or in the good old days, before Derwin had become our family doctor and put the kibosh on this sort of thing, she would take half a "dex" as a pick-me-up. The result of this most recent upward adjustment in her medicaments meant that she had become angry and violent and other; differently, even scarily, other; so other, in fact, that her housekeeper and my cousin Josh, who since my uncle's death had emerged as her all-season majordomo, had decided she needed to be taken to the hospital for assessment, or detox, or both.

It was next to impossible to hear the word *detox* used in conjunction with my aunt, almost as impossible as it was to picture this particular long-legged girl confined to a hospital bed at Cedars. Other than the day she was born, she had not once spent a single night in the hospital as a patient in ninety years.

I don't do illness was, after all, one of her favorite refrains.

It went with *I don't believe in tired.*

And *There's plenty of time to sleep in the grave.*

Or in a more savage mood, *I don't get cancer; I give cancer!*

I asked my brother what room she was in, and he told me.

"That's on the south wing," I said. "I can see her window from here."

"Whose window?" my mother asked from across the room.

"You won't believe this," I said after I got off the phone.

My mother had another dip that afternoon, so it took me several hours to make it to my aunt's room. When finally I arrived, the door to number 4804 was firmly closed, the only one thus positioned on the entire floor. I approached and knocked.

A voice I recognized as belonging to Maria told me to come in. I hesitated for just a moment, allowed a breath to wash over my lungs, then opened the door.

What I saw caused me to come to a standstill. Lying crookedly on her side, like a statue toppled off its base, was my still formidable (still in my mind formidable) ninety-year-old aunt. She was wearing a hospital-issue gown and yellow anti-skid socks, and she was hooked up to both an IV and a catheter. The catheter, Maria told me, was a consequence of the bladder infection she had kicked up in the past few days that might have been further monkeying with her mind; the IV was helping to "clean out" her system from the misjudged cocktail of drugs that had been building up in it. But surprising as it was to find her toppled, gowned, and fitted out with these unaccustomed hospital accoutrements, far more shocking—heart-twistingly shocking—was her appearance.

She was transformed. She was stunning. Radiantly, and I mean that in the purest sense, luminously, exquisitely beautiful. Her pallor, her entire palette, shimmered—it was as if Matisse, her cherished Matisse, that sorcerer of light, had climbed into her body and painted her from the inside out: an odalisque in extreme old age. Lying there on that hospital bed, she glowed. She had abandoned the chestnut-colored hairpiece that she had begun wearing in the late 1970s, after her hair had begun to thin demonstrably; what little remained had turned, in privacy and concealment, a soft shining silver. She did not have on a lick of makeup, and the skin that her elaborate maquillage had been covering (and, no doubt, also protecting) for a lifetime was nearly unwrinkled, pale, and almost translucent. She had removed all her jewelry too, so there was just my aunt, just her very own flesh and hair and skin, lying nestled on a plain white pillow. She looked like a little-girl version of herself; she looked like someone had come along and cracked and peeled away her shell, like an egg, to reveal the true and actual Hank underneath.

And for the first time in nearly a century she was docile. In the sweetest voice I had ever heard her emit, she said, "Why, how good of you to come, dear."

Maria said, "Do you know who this is, Mrs. Ravetch?"

"Of course I do. It's Michael, and he's come to see me all the way from New York."

"And do you remember why you are in the hospital, Mrs. Ravetch?"

"I have had a—problem. Obviously you don't come to a hospital if you don't have a problem."

A "problem"? From customarily the most precise of speakers?

To me she said, "I have had severe memory loss, as you can see."

"I saw you less than a month ago," I said. "I don't know how that's possible, really."

"My dear, I tell you it is. All of a sudden I am not . . . right." She clutched her pillow for comfort, the way a child might.

"But what are the doctors saying?" I asked. "Have you had physical therapy?"

"Darling, I cannot get out of bed."

"Why can't you get out of bed?"

"Because I cannot walk."

"Why can't you walk? What happened?"

"I wish I could tell you."

"But what are they going to do for you?"

"So many questions, darling. Too many questions . . ."

Maria had been shaking her head behind my aunt. Now she spoke over my aunt, as one might speak over any old old-lady patient. She said that the doctors were perplexed. They had done two MRIs of her back, and nothing showed up. Physical therapy had been ordered, but Mrs. Ravetch, she said, refused to participate—she merely sent the girls away. The only thing they had done since she came into the hospital was diagnose and treat the bladder infection and wait for all the "other" drugs to leave her system. She was not eating. She was barely drinking water. To get her up out of bed to sit in a chair took a nurse *and* an orderly . . .

"But this is impossible," I said. "Where's her doctor?"

"Diving in the Caribbean."

"Is there no plan, then?"

She opened her palms to the heavens.

I could not quite believe what I was hearing . . . or seeing. I stood there absorbing this vision of my aunt, drinking her in. It was so unreal. *She* was so unreal. But not moving? Not fighting or thinking clearly? What happened to *quick-quick* and *there's plenty of time to sleep in the grave* and all the rest?

A nurse appeared with a fresh bag of fluids. As she attached it to the IV pole, I asked her if it was advisable for my aunt to be spending so much time in bed.

"It most certainly is not," the nurse said, "but Mrs. Ravetch is very determined."

"She's famous for that," I said.

I approached the bed and touched her on the foot. Her foot was icy. I said, "Auntie Hankie, did you hear what the nurse just said? Lying in a bed is not good for you. Actually it's quite bad for you. You do know that?"

"Who made you a doctor, Michael?" she said, coming into sudden sharp focus. "The last time I checked it was your brother who was awarded the medical degree, not you."

It was almost a relief—almost—to hear her sounding more like her usual self.

"You won't even *try*?"

"I won't even try, no."

"But this cannot be," I pleaded. "You cannot simply lie here in this bed and *give up*."

"Says who?"

The next morning my mother was up patrolling the halls, albeit with those baby steps. She had made friends with her physical therapists, two sharp young women whose active senses of humor were a good fit for her. By the second session they were sending selfies around to their respective social and family circles. I did not, until then, even know what a selfie was.

"You are such a dinosaur," said my mother, wielding her stylus with a flourish.

After her pals left, my mother leaned in toward me and whispered, "Promise me you will *not* tell them you are acquainted with the *other* patient. *The one downstairs.* I don't want them to know we're related."

"There's nothing I can do if they're assigned to her case," I said.

"They won't be. She's on the looney wing, isn't she?"

"I don't think that's what they call it, Mother," I said.

"Well, I do," my mother said. "It's taken ninety years, but finally she's where she belongs." She tapped her head with two fingers. "Can you imagine if someone treated that woman for what is *actually* wrong with her?"

She thought for a moment, then continued: "I don't know if you know this, but just after they made *The Reivers* together, Mark Rydell suggested to them that they consider going into psychoanalysis. Both of them. He told them he thought it would make them deeper writers. They didn't speak to him for years afterward."

" 'There will be no psychiatrists in this family!' " I said, quoting my aunt.

"The Mighty Franks? Your grandmother had it wrong. The Mighty *Crazy* Franks is who they are, and your aunt is their mascot."

When I returned to my aunt's room a couple of hours later, the door was again closed. Again I knocked, and again Maria told me to come in.

Only there was just Maria, no Hank. When I looked at her inquiringly, she said, "They've taken her to surgery."

"For what?"

"She has a broken hip."

"A broken *what*?"

Because my aunt had been complaining about her back, Maria said, no one thought to examine her hip; but when a different physical therapist came by, he noticed that one of Mrs. Ravetch's legs was slightly shorter than the other and decided to order another MRI. This time they concentrated on her hip, and they found a fracture. Several weeks earlier, Maria went on to explain, my aunt had been having a fight with my cousin Lisa. "You know how your aunt can be," Maria said. "*Muy fuerte.*" During this fight, Hank apparently sat down abruptly. And very angrily. "It must have happened then," said Maria.

One of my aunt's vituperations had caused her to fracture her hip? Really? And the right hip? The same one as my mother's? Of course it figured that, in this family, with all its doublings—brother and sister marrying sister and brother, the two grandmothers living together, the practically related girls across the street, and all the rest—there couldn't be just one fall; there had to be a pair. Or a fall and a not-fall.

A fall and an abrupt, angry landing in a chair that resulted in the same type of fracture to the same hip. The same fracture, the same hip, the same surgery, the same hospital—and both happening at virtually the same time. After all, all the best (or in this case, all the worst) things come in pairs.

My mother was home within a week, set up with her Filipino aides, as she predicted, and pushing hard, very hard, to put herself back together again. She had some pretty grueling days and nights on Greenvalley Road—nights especially. Sometimes the pain and the drugs that eased it kept her awake and wandering down some very complicated mental byways. "Perspective does not come to us while we are living life," she said to me during one episode. "Only afterward."

Another time she said, "Your father and I let you down. I ask myself all the time why you aren't angrier with us—why we didn't realize earlier on what was going on with your aunt and uncle."

"It wasn't all that clear early on," I said. "And I was a headstrong child. For a long time I wanted what they had to offer me. I wanted it desperately. Hank was like a drug, I wanted more and more of her back then."

"Yes, but you were a child. We should have known better. Done more."

"You tried. The Punishment. The therapist. And when things became more extreme, you took my side, always. You and Dad both did."

"It wasn't good enough," she said. "I wasn't who I am today. It took me a long time, too long, to find my voice. Now that I have, no one's around, or sane enough, to listen to what I have to say."

"I am," I said.

"And you're probably writing it all down too," she added with an ambiguous sigh.

My aunt stayed on in the hospital. She refused to do physical therapy. She refused to try to walk. She refused, half the time, even to move from the bed to the chair.

I visited her every day, and every day we had a version of the same conversation. I'd spoken with my brother the doctor, I told her, beefing up my qualifications on the authority front, and he said she had to get up, or else she might never walk again. I had the identical conversation with her physical therapist, the nurses, and the attending physician assigned to her case. They all agreed. Every day, every hour, she spent in bed would only make it more difficult, perhaps even impossible, for her to walk again.

She was intractable. "I will not get up," she said. "That is simply all there is to it."

"What happened to the pleasure principle?" I asked.

"It's no longer pleasurable for me to be on my feet."

"But what kind of pleasure can you have from a wheelchair . . . especially when there's no medical reason why you have to be in one?"

"Plenty. You'll see." She gestured at Maria. "I have my day staff, my night staff. I have Josh. Why, he could not be more my son if I gave birth to him myself. He would breathe for me if he could." She allowed a pause to hang there for a moment, as if to emphasize how spectacularly Josh had succeeded where I had fallen so miserably short.

"The one person I no longer have," she added, "is your cousin Lisa, who did this to me. I will never speak to that girl again as long as I live. In fact, I have instructed Josh to make an appointment with my lawyer."

I emitted a long, weary sigh. "You know, if you used some of this determination to get out of bed, you might be a lot farther along than you are."

"But what's wrong with you? Are you deaf? Have you not heard what I've been saying? I can no longer walk. I no longer will. *C'est fini!*"

It was like an anxiety dream sprung into three dimensions. I thought about how hard my aunt had been on her older brother, Pete, who when he reached his mid-eighties began to embrace old age, as she put it, as if he'd been waiting for it all his life. *Reprehensible and lily-livered*, she had said at the time. *Giving in to diminished capacities is nothing to be proud of. Old age has to be fought off at every turn. Every turn! Do you hear me?*

"You *can* walk, you know," I said. "You choose not to."

"Fine, I choose not to, then."

"I don't understand why you're giving up," I said, hearing my voice rise in pitch. How could it be that this giant had fallen? And so rapidly, and so far? It surprised me how much I still cared.

"I recognize my limitations," she said with an oddly diabolical smile.

"You? Limited?"

"Even I am allowed to get old, Michael."

——— ———

Unlike my uncle, my aunt received a get-out-of-jail card from Cedars. After bouncing her upstairs to rehab for ten days, they sent her home with a flotilla of medical equipment. Since she refused to tamper with the aesthetics of the maison by installing grab bars or a ramp for the wheelchair she now regularly used, she quite literally had to lean on that staff of hers to navigate the world.

At first she showed some signs of wanting to come back to herself. She finally agreed to let the physical therapist visit. She worked up to taking fifty, eighty, one hundred steps a day. Her caretakers, Maria and an alternating shift of women who now spent the night at the maison, counted them up and noted them down in a little leather notebook. Afterward they reported them the way, at the other end of life, you report a baby's first steps.

For a while, a good while, she remained fixated on what had happened to her; it almost seemed to fuel her drive. "Lisa nearly killed me, you realize," she said over and over. "You have to wonder what that girl was thinking." Alas, it was not so difficult to imagine, since regrettably the "roomie" arrangement at the maison had played out pretty much as most of us predicted it would, though with the added complication that it wasn't only Trudy who was trapped there but Lisa as well, since whenever my aunt felt the impulse she summoned Lisa up the hill, sometimes reasonably to watch over her mother but often, too often, to help out with decorating projects or to listen to our aunt's litany of disgruntlements or merely to appear, *quick-quick*, to fill out the ever-emptier (but always beautifully set) lunch or dinner table with a warm body. By the end my cousin had to plead to take her mother out on her own, or to her old house, or to *her* house, even just for a night or a visit or a meal. "I will not allow Trudy to leave," Hank at one point announced. "It's too dangerous for her to go anywhere without me or the staff. These vagabondages of hers imperil her and worry me to death. They are finished."

The frustration built and built; there were words; there was the fight, the not-fall, the broken hip; then came the drugs, the detox, and the surgery. The irony—the tragic irony—was that the prison Hank made for Trudy became at the same time a prison she made for herself, because as Trudy's mind shut down more and more, Hank became more and more trapped with her absent sister-in-law. *It's like living with a stick of wood,* she grumbled. *She no longer speaks, she no longer responds. And I'm all that she's got left. Her daughters, those ingrates, she's lucky if they check in once a week. I have to tell her about her husband, our friendship, the past. I'm her memory now.*

Inevitably all this became less pertinent after Hank returned from the hospital. "I told the girls they will have to take care of their mother until I'm back on my feet," my aunt announced wearily, surveying the empty bed next to hers. "At that point we will reassess."

Only she did not get back on her feet, at least not for very long, and she never did reassess. Now when I called, the number of steps she was taking started moving in the opposite direction—all the way to zero.

When I saw her on my next visit to town, I fell back into that old pressuring, incredulous stance. "You do know there is no reason for you not to be walking."

"Yes, there is. I'm afraid of falling."

"Your body is atrophying. Are you just going to *lie* here for no medical reason?"

"Yes, Michael, that is exactly what I'm going to do."

"And your doctor? What does he say?"

"I pay him a substantial amount of money every year to listen to me," she said, not quite logically and yet, given my aunt, perfectly logically at the same time.

"You really could try harder. I know you have it in you. This is all just so crazy . . ."

She even had the blinds in her bedroom pulled low. The figures in the toile-patterned wallpaper, the shepherds and shepherdesses, the children with their hoops, the dogs and the goats and the birds, went about their gambols and their frolics in a light made all the more lugubrious by the suggestion of a strong midday Southern California sun that slipped in through the interstices between window shade and wall. The old Hank would have had the blinds up, and light and air pouring in. The silvered mirrors would be washed and the crystal prisms on the chandeliers sparkling. There would be flowers—energy—puttering—hope. Or if not hope at least determination and drive; and tenacity. Tenacity always.

"You know, Michael," she said after a long pause, in an unusually faraway voice. "You don't need to have such a hard outside shell all the time. Inside you are a very soft person actually."

I looked over at the figure lying in the hospital bed, the purified, whitened, weakened woman from whose mouth these words were just spoken. I looked at her, and I felt a gradual and unexpected tightening in my chest. For a moment I found it difficult to breathe. In a flash I saw that for years, for decades, I had had to put up, or put on, a carapace in my aunt's company; it had been the only way I had found to speak to her, to deal with her volatility, the only way I could remain in safe-distanced contact with her; and yet it was no longer working so well and, what's more, it was no longer relevant; and, worse still, I no longer liked myself for being the sort of person who put on that carapace. I was hectoring her to get up, to recover, to be herself, to remember that there would be plenty of time to sleep in the grave (and all too soon at that), but what I truly meant was, Please don't die. Not like this. Not while the story is still so unresolved; not yet.

"I'm just trying to help," I said softly.

"I don't require that kind of help, thank you very much," she said.

——— ———

As my aunt underwent her inexorable decline, the maison followed, as houses will.

The house had always been a reflection of her state of mind, in the same way a canvas is to a painter's. At the height of her angriest and most unstable period, around the time of the incident in Paris, Hank had gone through a red phase: red fabric, red leather, red chinoiserie, red lacquer, red jackets on red-faced English gentlemen posed on red cushions in grand red-walled English (or sometimes French) country houses: a fiery palette for a fiery, fired-up interlude that lasted nearly a decade. Next, in the years just before and during my uncle's final illness, came the brown period. The painted Venetian furniture was sent to auction or given away, and good (to my eye, soulless) brown English furniture took its place. Tables were skirted in brown velvet; curtains, cushions, and upholstery followed. After brown came that Death Barge black: black velvet, black fabric, black paint on the terra-cotta pots outside; even the statuary was darkened with inky paint that the rain, when it fell, began to wash away, so that the Cupids and the Psyches and the Roman emperor busts and all the rest seemed to be weeping from up on their (blackened) plinths. Then, after my uncle died and Trudy moved in, everything started turning gold. Suddenly the bronzes were replaced by vermeil and ormolu and gilding and brass and even, late in the game, plain old gold paint; my aunt would steady the can while Maria climbed up a ladder to daub it onto the buttons, shoe buckles, and earrings in the eighteenth-century portraits. *Midas has nothing on me!* she would say, standing back, pleased—more than that, exalted.

It was heartbreaking—almost heartbreaking—to find The Great Eye beginning to dim, but there was more, and worse, ahead. After her return from the hospital, when she was increasingly exiled, self-exiled, to her wheelchair, my aunt would on good days have Maria load her into the car and take her down to "the village"—Studio City—where she would make the rounds of the nearby junk shops or antique malls, favoring in particular the thrift shop to which she had dispatched my uncle's clothes the day after he died. *You'd be surprised what treasures you can find down there. Those nice Jewish ladies don't have a clue about what comes through their door!* Slowly her dish closet, that onetime Aladdin's cave of gems and treasures, began to fill up with the most incomprehensible kitsch: bad cut glass and cheap ceramic cherubs and the dreariest, most depressing little bibelots that, in her prime, my aunt would have stuck her nose up at. Now, instead, they were grouped in mushrooming clusters and pronounced *fetching* or *charming* or *amusant*—*especially if you are setting that sort of table.* But what sort of table was that, exactly? The table of a blind woman, a mad-woman, the un- or anti-Hank? Everything was wrong-side up and in-side out, the ur—Mighty Frank had crumpled, both woman and house had lost their tooth, old age wasn't burning and raving at the close of day but junking its way to oblivion. *It's all so n.g.,* I wanted to scream, *all of it n.g., n. fucking g.!*

I didn't scream, though; I shook my head at the mercilessness of time. My aunt used to say it herself: *Old age is hell.* Though I don't think she ever believed she would be the kind of old person who had that kind of old age. *Initially it's patch, patch, patch, and then all of a sudden you don't even know what you're patching anymore.* But it was worse than that: she didn't know she was getting the patches all wrong, from buying the cheap cherubs to dismissing the physical therapists to lying there passively waiting for what—for death? Nine decades of fierce embrace of life, a juicy, often angry attack on life, of reading and writing and making beauty (*make beauty at all times, make beauty at all costs!*) and giving (and taking) and loving and hating, too much hating, and talking and criticizing and vituperating (too much vituperating) and now you are simply holding on because the body and the soul—the will—are programmed to hold on, because the sun continues to come up over the maison and night is not ready to receive you, because your caregivers spoon-feed you meals you don't taste, or even want to taste, anymore, because Ensure ensures that you will be less and less (and less) yourself as the days draw on.

When I visited Skyline now I no longer felt that engulfing fa-tigue. Instead I wandered through a house that had already taken its place in memory, or in my dreams. Sometimes I felt I had wandered out onto a stage or a movie set at a pause in the drama, when the key players had stepped away. As on a set I could hear distant puttering—Maria in the kitchen—a phone ringing—the gardener blowing leaves outside—the television (formerly derided, now playing all day long as though in the house of any standard-issue old lady)—a snatch of murmured or sharp conversation emanating from the hospital bed or possibly somewhere else. But it was difficult in these moments to know whether the voices were real or speaking to me from my imagination or from the past, or the soon-to-be past, meaning the soon-to-be future. Time circled through those once-enchanted rooms the way dust circled through the canyon when a Santa Ana came over the mountains, and it brought on the same uneasy physical sensation, a feeling of disquiet that put a clamminess under the arms and between the toes, and a knot would form in my stomach, a variation on the old familiar knots of times gone by.

Often I wondered, What if this is my last visit, my last look? What if Josh, who *could not be more my son if I gave birth to him myself*, having been placed in complete, unmonitored control of the current Hank's post-Hank affairs, decreed after her death that the maison were to undergo a kind of lockdown? Was there something I wanted? There was nothing I wanted. Not from the house. Not any longer, I told myself, and believed in my heart, even from her. Why did I keep returning, then? Because this was the story I was born into, because with every return, every visit, I might just possibly grasp a bit more, with a bit more clarity or precision, the lives that had unfolded within these walls and the people who lived there and had once held so much power over me, over so many of us, and because, I suppose, the little boy who still lived on in me, and will, doubtless, still be living in me when I am patched and prone and my own version of de-toothed and de-wigged, still hoped for one last thing, one last——I don't know what; one last insight that would *explain*. As if it ever happens like that in real life or would be convincing if it did.

——— ———

My aunt had bad days and good days, better days and worse days. She held on and she let go, in an alternating rhythm that made no sense at all. As long as she could sit upright, she guided her staff to rearrange the *objets* on the bookshelves. After a visit from Ruby, she said, "Dear darling Ruby and that lovely wife of his, I really should see more of them." When my brother Danny made a rare appearance, she sat up with him in the library and said, "Now remind me, where is it exactly that you fit into the family?"

Sometimes when I called she told me that she had had another fall; Maria got on the phone afterward to explain that she had simply lost track of when the original fall—which was not even exactly a fall—had happened.

Once when I called to check in on her she said, out of the blue, "I love you, darling." I had not heard those words from her in years, decades. Forever. I doubted I would ever hear them again.

I visited Los Angeles at regular intervals. Everything there was just so persistent, so intact. At night, when I tucked my daughter into bed in my former bedroom, the only one belonging to us three sons to have been left untouched since we moved out of Greenvalley Road, I often looked around and wondered why, after all these decades, the shelves were still packed with fading books by Colette and Virginia Woolf and Henry James and my great-grandmother's brittle, little-read complete Balzac; why my bedroom walls were still hung with eighteenth-century engravings of Greek temples and Roman ruins. Even that pencil box, whose broken lid had long ago disappeared, was still in the desk drawer, filled with colored pencils that, a generation later, my daughter put to occasional use. It was almost as if the house itself insisted on holding on to the material evidence just as my memory insisted on holding on to experience, allowing it to accrue until I was ready to come find it and make sense, or try to make sense, of it all.

I kept going back and back and *back*. I went back even in my dreams, where I railed at my aunt and uncle, who—as only in a dream—listened patiently or acknowledged that there was another version, another truth. In life, apart from that one moment at my uncle's death, nothing like that ever happened. Certainly nothing significant ever shifted in my aunt. It was entirely up to me to reach an understanding of the experience we had all lived together. I could have absented myself, as Danny did, or retreated to a neutral distance, as Steve did, but that was not how I was made. I was made to return, to keep sifting and seeking, to see what it was like to introduce my own child into this world, so that she would come to know it and so that she would come to know me, one day.

In the afternoon I often walked with my daughter from Greenvalley to the maison. When I did, I always paused at the top of the hill a few feet from the place where the old gray asphalt of Crest View met the darker, newer pavement of Skyline, because a view opened up there in which our house on Greenvalley Road was cupped in a fold of lush hillside, in the way that a toy house might be cupped in a furry Brobdingnagian hand. I stared at it for long unbroken stretches, mesmerized by this dramatic change in proportion, by the peace and solidity with which our black-and-white Cape Cod sat just so in its bend of the canyon, by the neatness of the roof and the wingspan of the now-enormous Japanese elm whose lacy branches spread protectively over the whole of our backyard. From above, everything about the house looked compact, intentional, safe; contained and protected. The garden. The driveway where we used to play basketball. The jewel-like kumquats Sylvia loved to eat, still proliferating after all these years.

When I looked left from the junction of the two roads, I could just barely see over the rooflines and identify the tall dark mansard roof that rose up above my aunt and uncle's front door. Skyline was two blocks away from Greenvalley but a world, a universe, apart.

My parents and my surrogate parents, my parents and their siblings: each pair represented two different worldviews, two different paths through experience that had intermittently been aligned but more often were set against each other, toggling, or torquing, between the reasonable and the dramatic, the ordinary and the magical, the largely sane and the largely less (at times far less) than sane, since long before I was born. When I stood at the top of the hill, midway between these two houses, these two worlds, it was as if I were standing on my own personal equator. On one side, life—reality—spiraled in one direction; on the other, the opposite. From both axes the gravitational pull was powerful. The hard part had always been finding a way to stand in upright balance between them. Only it had not been hard so much as impossible.

•

My aunt brightened, often quite remarkably, when my daughter appeared at her door. Maria wheeled Hank into the living room and parked her at a right angle next to the settees flanking the fireplace. Hank called for the tea trolley, where the tiny cucumber-and-cream-cheese sandwiches were decrusted and cut on the diagonal (Maria had been well tutored) and the chocolate eggs still abounded, even though the cookies came from Gelson's instead of the long-vanished Weby's.

"Why have just one, darling?" my aunt said as she slid the eggs closer to the eight-year-old. "More is more."

"I think one is enough at this hour," I said. "After all those cookies."

"Don't spoil her pleasure now, Michael!"

"Yeah, Papa, don't spoil my pleasure!"

Another egg disappeared. My daughter looked around the room. "You have a lot of statues of that soldier with his hand on his stomach."

"Napoleon, you mean."

"His hand is on his stomach because it aches," I said, "from eating too many sweets."

"Nonsense," my aunt said sharply. "He suffered from an ulcer. You would, too, Michael, if you were conquering the whole of Europe." She looked around the living room. "I *do* have lots of Napoleons, it's true. Not—mind you—because he was a dictator but because he freed the Jews from the ghetto and wrote such beautiful love letters to Joséphine."

"Joséphine?"

"His empress."

On the low table between the two settees was a lacquer tray filled with miniature leather-bound books. The eight-year-old leaned forward to look more closely. "They're like dolls' books," she said.

"The complete works of William Shakespeare in miniature," said my aunt. "Every word an expression of genius. He changed the way we think about human nature—the way we think about the world. Would you allow me to make you a present of one?"

She said this in the exact same voice with which she had offered me my first treasures.

"Yes, please," said my daughter, with the same excitement I had shown, accepting them.

"Take any one you choose. Take two. You know, of course, that all the best things come in pairs."

The eight-year-old picked out two books as invited, releasing a shower of dust onto the surface of the table.

I felt suddenly lightheaded. I was there, in that room, with my child, and I was there in that room *as* a child. What had happened to the intervening years—the decades? They seemed, at that moment, to have no more form, or weight, than the dust that had shed from those tiny books.

Bent over in her wheelchair, my aunt watched my daughter closely as she turned the pages of the book in her hand.

"You realize that you're old enough now to begin learning Shakespeare by heart," Hank said, "just the way your father did when he was your age. Shall I teach you some?"

Was it some kind of test from the fates? Was I supposed to say aloud to my child, *It really is all right to say no*? Was I supposed to think, *This is where it all begins*? Where what begins? My aunt was approaching ninety. Her world had shrunk to the size of a postage stamp. She was more alone, and more powerless, than she had ever been.

"Oh, yes, please."

Down went the teacup. "I see you've selected *Twelfth Night*. An excellent choice. 'If music be the food of love, play on.' "

" 'If music be the food of love, play on.' "

"That's right. Now: 'Give me excess of it, that, surfeiting—' "

"What's 'surfeiting'?"

"Too much," I interrupted, doing my best not to gesture at the tea trolley, the room, my aunt, our lives—all of it.

" 'Give me excess of it, that, surfeiting,' " my aunt repeated, " 'the appetite may sicken, and so die.' "

Hank's fogged eyes brought up some residual shine as she continued, " 'That strain again. It had a dying fall; O, it came o'er my ear like the sweet sound that breathes upon a bank of violets, stealing and giving odor—' " She stopped abruptly. "Dammit, I forget the rest."

I hesitated, but the words were there. She had taught them to me herself. " 'Enough, no more. 'Tis not so sweet now as it was before.' "

With wide eyes the eight-year-old looked first at her great-aunt, then at me. "How long will it take *me* to be able to do that?" she asked.

"With a brain like yours?" said my aunt. "Minutes—seconds. It'll be quick-quick, I promise."

I sank back in the settee. Actually, I thought, it'll be more like a lifetime.

Acknowledgments

The author owes the very deepest gratitude to three of the most astute, demanding, and stalwart readers imaginable, Andrea Chapin, Lindsey Crittenden, and Steven Frank; to the tenacious and insightful Sally Wofford-Girand, assisted by Shaun Dolan, at Union Literary; and to the unparalleled Ileene Smith and her impeccable team at FSG, who are altogether the mightiest of publishers.

Profound alphabetical thanks in addition to Barrie Berg, the late Wendy Berg, Sarah Boxer, Harry Cooper, Camuggi Frank, Daniel Frank, Julie Frank, Marty and Merona Frank, Sophie Frank, Alice Gordon, Jane Varkell and the late Paul Varkell, and the late Dino Zanini.

And, of course, to Jo Anne Schlesinger and Lucia Frank, without whom there would be no new life and therefore no possible way to have written a book about the old one.